EFFECTIVE BUSINESS COMMUNICATION

Effective Business Communication

M.V. Rodriques

Chh. Shahu Central Institute of Business Education and Research
Kolhapur

CONCEPT PUBLISHING COMPANY, NEW DELHI 110059

ISBN 81-7022-421-7

First Published 1992
13th Reprint 2003

Published and Printed by
Ashok Kumar Mittal
Concept Publishing Company
A/15-16, Commercial Block, Mohan Garden,
NEW DELHI-110059

Phones : 5351460, 5351794
Fax : 091-11-5357103
Email : publishing@conceptpub.com

TO

VISHENT

PREFACE

The primary purpose of this book is to discuss the principles and practice of business communication and to impart to the Readers knowledge of putting these principles into use creatively, functionally and effectively in the direction of problem-solving and decision-making. The book should prove helpful both as a textbook for classes and a manual for business communication.

The term 'communication' means many things to many people. Accordingly, this book has attempted to cover as many aspects of communication as possible. It covers the major aspects of verbal and non-verbal communication as they dominate the human interactions in all the business situations. Humanity in the present times is so interdependent that an individual can do very little alone *sans* effective communication.

Any individual who is interested in fine-tuning his communication skills and honing his communication tools, certainly needs specialised knowledge for that purpose. This book springs from this need.

The book offers the reader the standards for evaluating effectiveness of interactive communication that takes place through different channels and media used to serve a variety of communicative purposes in business situations. The book presents business communication both as an art as well as a science.

My students, those in the classroom and those working as executives in business houses, have earned my gratitude in special and valuable way – it is their frequent call to bring a comprehensive book on the subject of Business English and Communication that this book has seen the light of the day. I extend my warm and sincere thanks to Dr. A.D. Shinde, Director, Chhatrapati Shahu Central Institute of Business Education and Research, Kolhapur; Dr. T.A. Shiware, ex-Dean, Faculty of Commerce, Shivaji University; Dr. D.K. Patil, Principal, Night College, Ichalkaranji; Mrs. Lilian M.

Rodriques; Prin. Dr. P.S. Rao, CSCIBER, Kolhapur, for their help, co-operation and worthwhile suggestions. I am also grateful to Concept Publishing Company for its investment of resources in this book.

Kolhapur M.V. RODRIQUES

CONTENTS

SECTION II

SECTION I

A. An Introduction to Communication
- (1) Communication through Arbitrary Symbols
- (2) Human Interactions through Communication
- (3) Communication Technology and Media
- (4) Communication in Managerial Activities

B. Definitions
- (1) Some Definitions of Communication
- (2) Appraisal
- (3) Definition of Communication

C. The Process of Communication
- (1) Some Models of Communication
- (2) Communication Situation
- (3) Model of Communication
- (4) Components of Communication Cycle
- (5) The Process of Communication

D. The Significance of Communication
- (1) Healthy Organisational Environment
- (2) Management-Employee Relations
- (3) The External and Internal Communication Network
- (4) Functionalisation
- (5) Complexity of Business Activities
- (6) Trade Unions : Labour Problems
- (7) Multinationals and Language Problem
- (8) Competition
- (9) Participation and Delegation

1

MEANING AND PROCESS OF COMMUNICATION

AN INTRODUCTION TO COMMUNICATION

Communication Through Arbitrary Symbols

The civilisation is reflected in three priceless possessions of mankind, the first is the human ability to think, the other is his innate capacity to communicate and the third is his specie's specific competence to acquire and use the arbitrary symbol systems of language. The manifold gifts of civilisation and all the branches of human knowledge have their origin from this ability to think in abstract and to communicate the abstract thoughts through arbitrary symbols of the languages. Above all the other media of communication, language is the most significant because the human knowledge and relationships are gathered, stored and imparted through it. The process of communication permits us to use and reuse the experiences of others in present as well as in future. We can draw the experience and knowledge from the past into the present and make it ready for reuse in future with the help of the symbols of communication which stand for some abstract idea.

Human Interactions Through Communication

Communication is the means by which people relate to one another. The society in general or an organisation of any type cannot exist without the relations that are built and strengthened by communication. Throughout our lives, we are involved in communication situations. When we talk and work with our colleagues, friends, subordinates, superiors, experts, teachers, students, family members and with the people in all walks of life;

when we read and/or write the books, pamphlets, periodicals, special journals, reports, letters, memos, newspapers, etc,; when we listen to or deliver speeches; when we listen to the radio or watch the TV and films; when we buy or sell the products or services; when we manage our business and when we are involved in any other activity, we are invariably involved in communication situation.

Communication Technology and Media

Human behaviour is dominated by communication in all aspects of life to such an extent that we can aptly call him as a communicating creature. He has applied advanced science and technology for the tremendous development of communication system. With the help of dramatic inventions like printing press, telephone, telegraph, radar, telephoto, radio, television and many other devices, we have made our modern communication instantaneous and effective. The advanced technology of mass and telecommunication has attracted the attention of the experts and specialists in many fields. The artists, poets, writers, artisans, architects, etc., are exposed to different subjects of interest by this technology and it helps them to conceive new creative thoughts and ideas. The technology, skills of using media and some concepts of communication are useful to psychologists in order to investigate certain problems of human behaviour and therapy. As the social and political order can remain constant or change by the effective use of communication media, the political and social scientists are also interested in it. The political as well as social traditions, myths, customs, styles of living, morals, etc., are passed from one generation to another or they are changed or destroyed with the help of communication media. The success of any commercial man depends upon his reception and transmission of information regarding the market, production, rival business houses, transport, raw material, government laws, insurance, banking, labour, innovations in modern technology, etc. Computers play a vital role in receiving, storing, translating, analysing and imparting the information for the mathematicians, chemists, physicists, engineers, etc.

Communication in Managerial Activities

In a business organisation, the employees come to know what their co-workers are doing by communication. The managers give orders, instructions, warnings and advices to the subordinates and receive information and suggestions from the departmental heads, supervisors, and workers. Communication is always instrumental in the management of business organisation because the orders are issued, the advice is sought and given, the decisions are conveyed by the functional authorities to the concerned people, the instructions are given by the supervisors to the operators and a number of other activities such as planning, directing, coordinating, organising, controlling, etc., are carried out by maintaining communication.

> Communication is a required skill at every level of organisational functioning for organisations of all types. The effectiveness with which a person will be able to perform in almost any organisation, whether social, governmental or commercial, will depend in large measure upon the ability to communicate effectively.
>
> *Wofford, Gerloff*, Cummins in 'Organisational Communication : The Keystone to Managerial Effectiveness'.

The lack of communication invariably results in the collapse of the business organisation. When people do not communicate their needs, thoughts and feelings to each other, the cooperation and mutual understanding becomes impossible. Thus, a hardening of the information arteries results in impaired efficiency of the organisation.

The scholars who define communication give stress on the transmission and reception of information. The concept of communication is broad enough to mean almost anything to almost anybody. As it is the binding agent of all social systems and sub-systems, it is understood and used in different ways by the people in different walks of life. Let us consider some definitions of communication.

DEFINITIONS

(1) Some Definitions of Communication.
(2) Appraisal.
(3) Definition of Communication.

Some Definitions of Communication

(i) Communication is the process of transmitting feelings, attitudes, facts, beliefs and ideas between living beings.

—*Birvenu*

(ii) Communication is any means by which thought is transferred from one person to another.

– Chappell and Read, in: *A Textbook of Business Communication*

(iii) Communication is an exchange of facts, ideas, opinions or emotions by two or more person.

– William Newman and Charles Summer, in: *The Process of Management*

(iv) Communication is process for conducting the attention of another person for the purpose of replicating memories.

– F.A. Cartier and K.A. Harwood, in: *The Journal of Communication,* Nov., 1953

(v) Communication is a process which involves the transmission and accurate replication of ideas ensured by feedback for the purpose of eliciting actions which will accomplish organisational goals.

– William Scot, in: *Organisational Theory*

(vi) Communication is the process by which information is transmitted between individuals and/or organisations so that an understanding response results.

– Peter Little in: *Oral and Written Communication*

(vii) Communication is a continuing and thinking process dealing with the transmission and interchange with understanding of ideas, facts and courses of action.

– George R. Terry, in: *Principles of Management*

(viii) Communication is the broad field of human interchanges of facts and not the technologies of telephone, telegraph, radio and the like.

– Charles Redfield

(ix) Communication is the sum of all the things one person does when he wants to create understanding in the mind of another. It is a bridge of meaning. It involves a systematic and continuous process of telling, listening and understanding.

– Louis Allen

(x) Communication is composite of information given and received of a learning experience in which certain attitudes, knowledge and skills change, carrying with them alterations of behaviour; of a listening effort by all involved; of systematic fresh examination of issues by the communicator himself; and of a sensitive interaction of points of view leading to a higher level of shared understanding and common intention.

– Ordway Tead

in his "Lecture of the School of Commerce, Accounts and Finance", New York, delivered on 11th February 1959.

(xi) Communication is the exchange of meanings between individuals through a common system of symbols.

– I.A. Richards

(xii) Communication is the process of passing information and understanding from one person to another.

– Keith Davis, in:
Human Relations at Work

(xiii) Communication is the process of meaningful interactions among persons in an organisation resulting in meanings being perceived and understanding effected among such persons.

– Rustom S. Davar, in:
The Management Process

Appraisal

Most of the above definitions have dwelt on some common

characteristics of communication. Birvenu's definition appears to be simple and straightforward but it does not mention anything about feedback which is a part and parcel of the communication cycle. He has given more emphasis on the transmission of ideas, feelings, attitudes, facts and beliefs, but he is not clear about the reception, understanding and response. On the other hand, Louis Allen and Ordway Tead have given more stress on listening and understanding of the message by the receiver. Chappell and Read think that the message transmitted by the communicator consists only 'thoughts', but on the other hand, Birvenu, Charles Redfield, William Newman and Charles Summers have stated that the feelings of a person, his attitudes towards different person, objects and things, his beliefs and ideas are also transmitted along with the facts and figures. Peter Little, William Scott, George R. Terry and Louis Allen have given weightage to the communicator, the message and the transmission; but unlike Birvenu, they have also given equal importance to the receiver, his understanding of the message and his response to the communicator's message. Peter Little has pointed out that the aim of communication between individuals and/or organisations is to get the understanding response. His emphasis on 'transmission of information' means the transmission of news, knowledge, attitudes or 'the frame of mind' of the communicator. Chappel and Read have neither accounted for the transmission of feelings and attitudes of the communicator nor for the feedback from the receiver but William Newman and Charles Summer have said that communication is an 'exchange' of facts, ideas, opinions or emotions by two or more persons. The word 'exchange' in this definition denotes that there is a feedback to the massage transmitted by the communicator.

The definition given by F.A.Cartier and K.A.Harwood differ from the definitions given by Birvenu, Peter Little, Chappell and Read and Newman and Summers. Cartier and Harwood have used the concept of 'replicating memories' they say that the purpose of communication is to replicate memories. When the message is received by the receiver, he perceives and interprets it in the light of his past experience. Therefore, the same message can be interpreted differently by the two receivers. In order to fulfil the purpose of replicating memories, the communicator has to direct or influence the attention of the receiver to refer to his past experience. He has to bear in his mind the fact that the message is perceived and understood by the receiver in his own way. The words that carry the meaning are important but the sense in which they are perceived and understood is of real significance in communication. For example, when the word 'childhood' is uttered, it may bring pleasant memories to one receiver whose childhood days were happy but may depress another person whose childhood was passed in misery and hardships. This definition does not explain the nature and transmission of message, the role of the communicator and the need of feedback. Cartier and Harwood have given dominance to the receiver and have underestimated the role of the communicator. The term 'replication' also appears in the definition given by William Scott. He states that the process of communication involves 'the transmission and accurate replication of ideas'. According to Cartier and Harwood, the purpose of communication is to 'replicate memories' whereas William Scott has said that the purpose of communication is to elicit 'actions'. To him, all the actions elicited by the accurate replication of ideas are directed towards the accomplishment of the organisational goals. Rustom S. Daver and Keith Davis have defined communication in the context of the interactions that take place among the persons in the organisations. Charles Redfield, in his definition, points out that a good deal of misunderstanding prevails about the nature and function of communication. In our everyday life, we use the word 'communication' for a variety of meanings. We generally use it for a letter, newspaper, radio broadcast, TV programmes, periodicals, telephone, telegrams, etc. Redfield says communication is the broad field of human interchange of facts and opinions and not the technologies of telephone, telegraph, radio and the like. He gives more importance to the purpose, spirit, objectives and the substance of communication than to the technology, which is applied to fulfil the purpose. No other definition of communication, except the one given by I.A. Richards refers to the 'common system of symbols'. Which is used for encoding the message. I.A. Richard's definition of communication is very broad and general in nature. It includes almost all kinds of human and animal communication systems.

To explain his definition, he says:

> Communication takes place when one mind so acts upon its environment that another mind is influenced and in that other mind, an experience occurs which is like the experience in the first mind, and is caused in part by the experience.

Having considered the merits and demerits of the above definitions, we are now in a position to define the concept of communication in the following words:

Definition of Communication

> Communication can be defined as an exchange and exact replication of thoughts, feelings, facts, beliefs and ideas between and among the individuals through a common system of symbols to cause some actions or change in behaviour.

THE PROCESS OF COMMUNICATION

(1) Some Models of Communication,
(2) Communication Situation,
(3) The Model of Communication,
(4) Components of Communication Cycle, and
(5) The Process of Communication.

Some Models of Communication

(i)

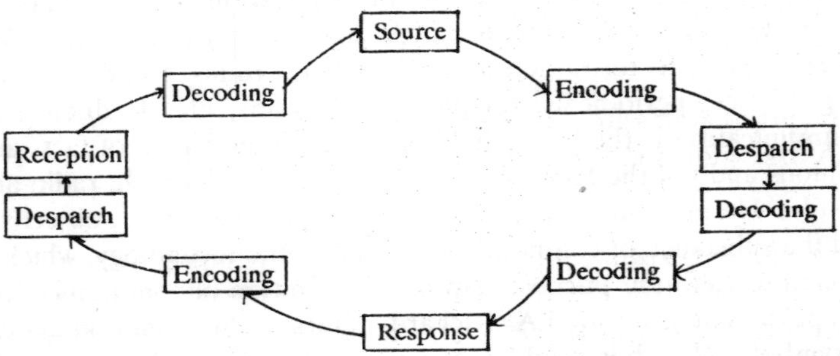

— Rajendra Pal & J.S. Korlahalli, in:
Essentials of Business Communication

(ii)

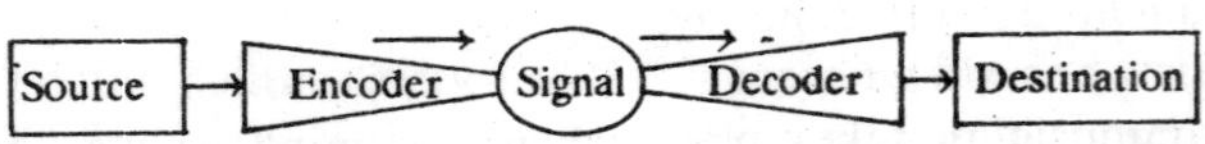

— Wilbur Schramm, in:
How Communication Works

(iii) 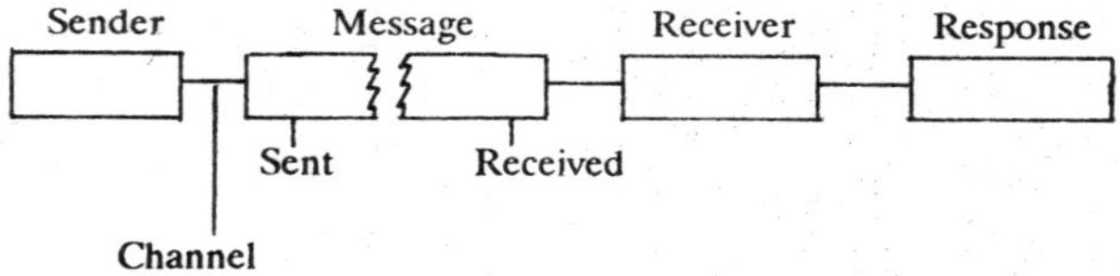

Semantic Gap

— R.C. Sharma and Krishna Mohan, in:
Business Correspondence & Report Writing

(iv) 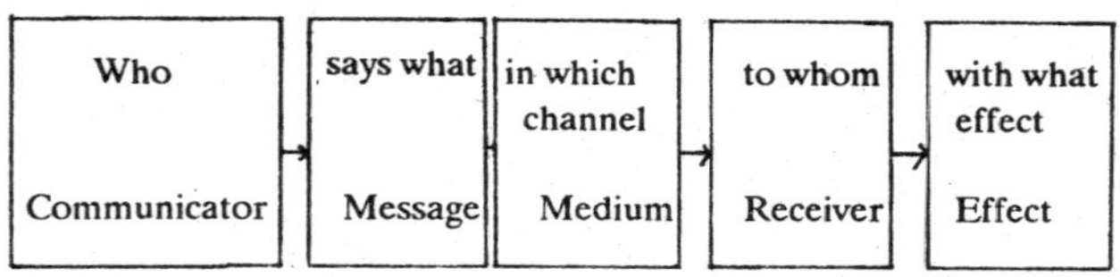

— H.D. Lasswell, in:
The Structure and Function of Communication in Society

(v) 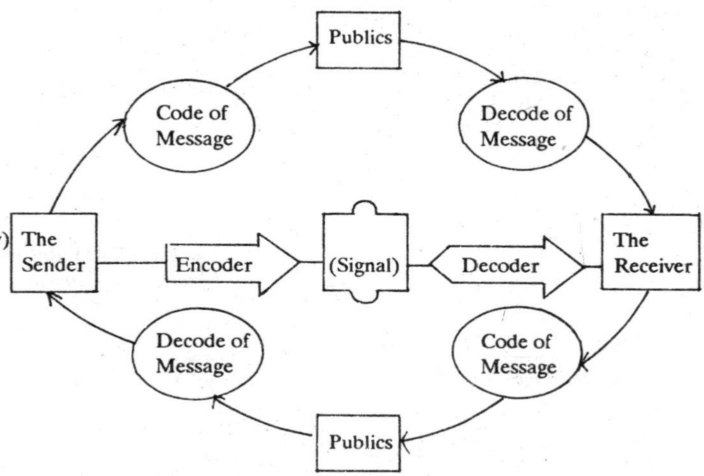

— Rhoda Doctor and Aspi Doctor in:
Principles and Practice of Business Communication

(vi) A

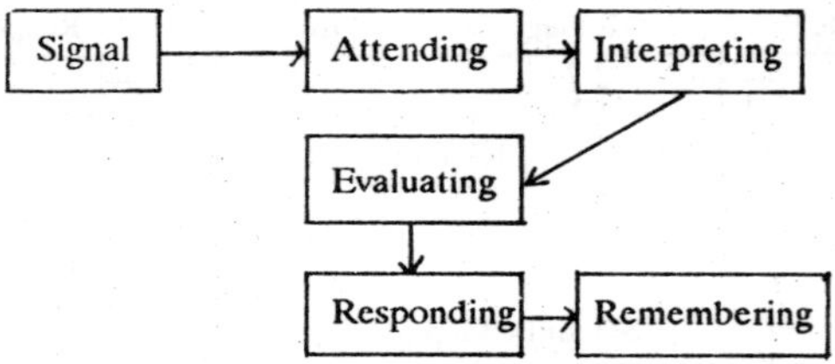

B

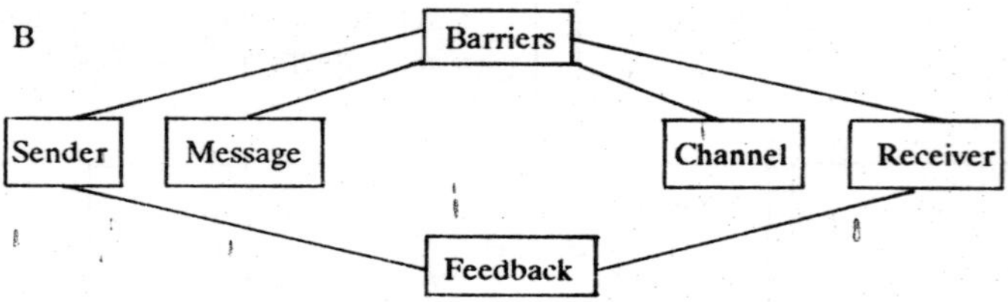

— David A. Thomas & Maridel Fryer, in:
Business Communication Today

(vii)

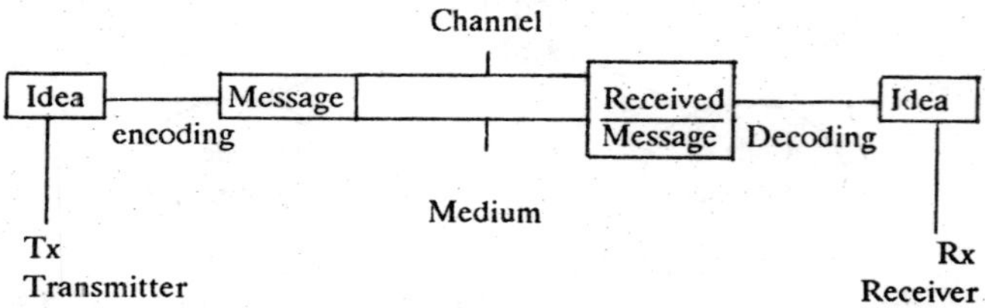

— U.S. Rai and S.M. Rai, in:
Business Communication

(viii)

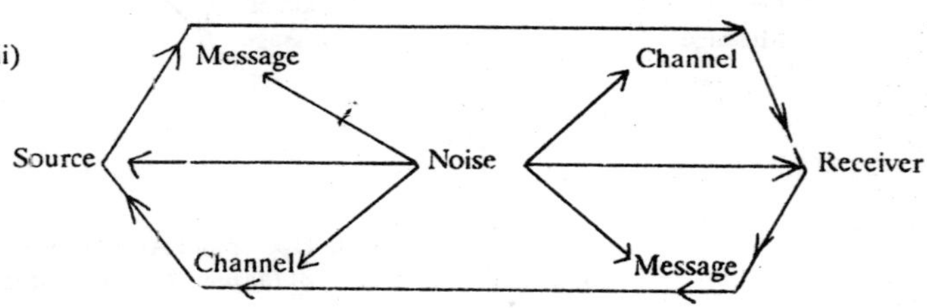

— Robert A. Vogel & William D. Brooks, in:
Business Communication

(ix) 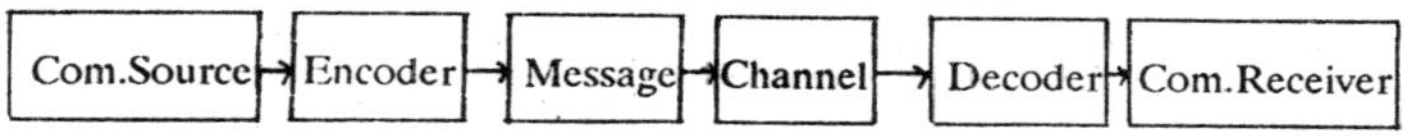

— Jerry Wofford, Edwin Gerloff and Rober Cummins, in: *Organisational Communication*

(x) 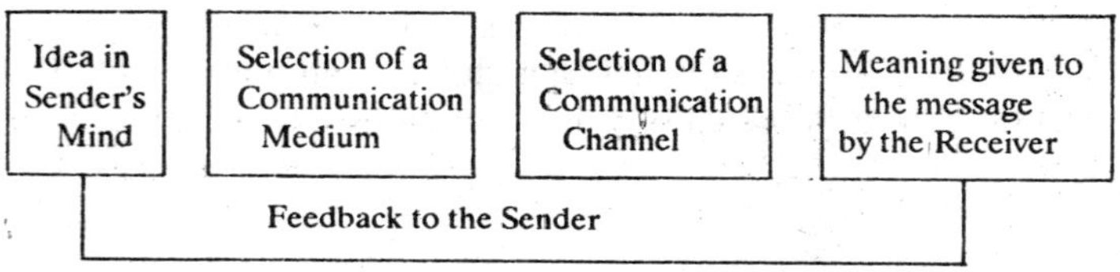

— Herbert G. Hicks and C. Ray Gullet, in: *Modern Business Management*

Communication Situation

The models given above obviously show that the process of communication can be interpreted in various ways. But all the factors given below are invariably essential.

(i) There are both the parties, the communicator and the receiver.
(ii) The communicator has an idea or experience to share with the receiver.
(iii) The communicator feels the need of transmitting his ideas.
(iv) There is a suitable medium and channel of communication for transmission and reception of the massage.
(v) Both the parties have common language or symbol system.
(vi) Both the parties have purpose to communicate the message.
(vii) Both the parties cooperate with each other by attending each other's message.
(viii) The communicator expects response from the receiver while transmitting the message.
(ix) The receiver understands the message encoded in the signals and gives feedback.
(x) Both the parties are conversant and skilled in the art of

communication and know how to use the communication media and communication channels.

Some Examples

The communication situation exists when all the components of the communication model, i.e. the communicator, receiver, origin of idea, encoding, decoding, semantic selection, transmission, reception and feedback are present. Though 'noise' is an unavoidable factor in all communication situations, it is not an essential requisite for it. If any one of the above factors, except noise, is missing, the communication situation does not exist. For example, when someone talks to himself loudly, there are three factors – the communicator, the origin of idea and encoding; but the remaining six factors are not present. The absence of these factors does not allow the cycle of communication to get completed. When a lunatic lover conceives some idea and wants to impart it to his beloved, he encodes it by putting it into figurative language. He expresses his thoughts and feelings orally and his beloved receives the message as she listens to what he says. This brings the message through the six steps. But the encoded message is in highly figurative language, which is not understood by the beloved. The figurative code language is not common to both the parties involved in the process. The receiver is unable to decode the signals. She cannot understand the message and the young man cannot get the feedback from her. As the message is not understood by the receiver, the communication situation does not exist. The purpose behind transmitting information is also an essential factor for the communication situation. The purpose behind transmitting information can be to change the opinion, to persuade, to issue some order, to request, to suggest, to warn, to motivate, etc. If the communicator has not any of such purpose in his mind, he will not communicate any message. The communication situation exists only when there is willingness in the mind of the communicator to bring about some change in the behaviour of the receiver.

The Model of Communication

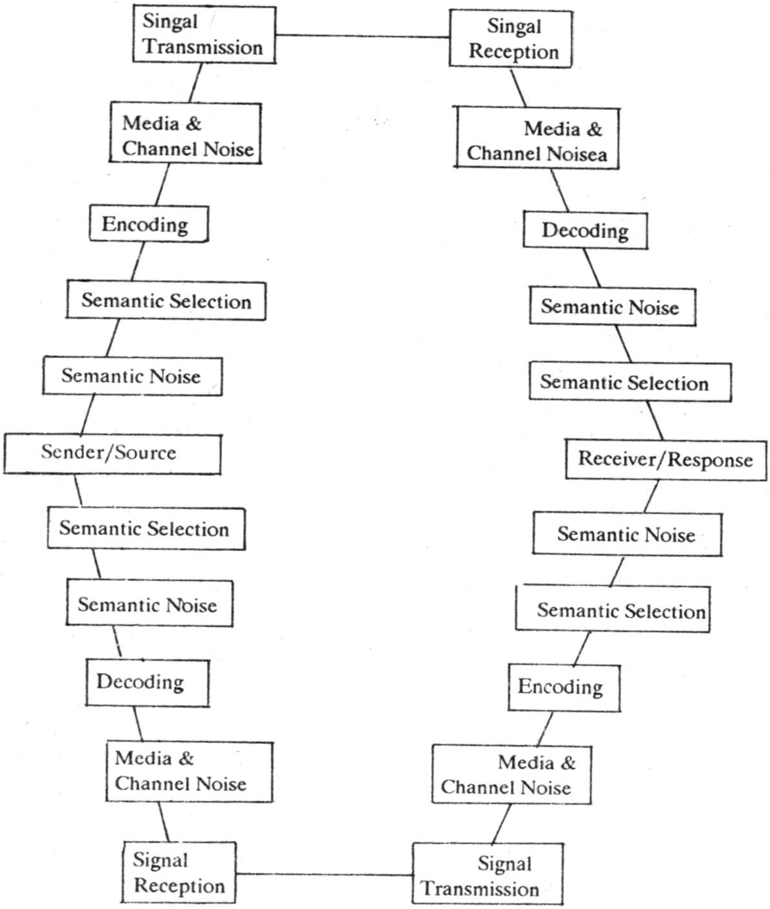

Components of Communication Cycle

(i) *The Sender*: The sender is the communicator who encodes and transmits the message. He is also called as the encoder or the transmitter. The idea or impulse is generated in his mind.

(ii) *The Receiver*: The receiver is the decoder of the message. He receives the message, decodes it and sends the feedback to the communicator.

(iii) *Encoding*: Encoding means to translate the meaning into arbitrary symbol system which is common to both the communicator and the receiver.

(iv) *Decoding*: Decoding means to translate the arbitrary symbol system into meaning which is common to both the communicator and the receiver.

(v) *Semantic Noise*: Semantic noise is any interference with the identification and transmission of the intended meaning in the mind of the communicator and the receiver.

(vi) *Semantic Selection*: Semantic selection means definite realisation of a particular idea and its meaning.

(vii) *Signal Transmission*: Signal transmission means transmitting the encoded message by the communicator.

(viii) *Signal Reception*: Signal reception means receiving the encoded message from the communicator

(ix) *Media and Channel Noise*: Media and Channel-noise refer to any interference that may occur in the medium or channel of communication through which the message is transmitted.

(x) Feedback is the receiver's response to the communicator's message.

The Process of Communication

The idea or impulse in the mind of the communicator is the source of communication process. The communicator transmits the message to the receiver in order to get the response. The ides of the message in the mind of a communicator must be clear. If the communicator himself is not clear or certain about the message, he has to transmit, his message will lack clarity and completeness. This lack of clarity and completeness is a kind of semantic noise. The receiver is likely to receive a wrong message if the communicator does not overcome the semantic noise. The semantic noise in the process of communication can be defined as any interference with the transmission or reception of the intended meaning by the communicator. While receiving the message, the semantic noise occurs when the receiver's interpretation of the message is likely to be at variance with the intended meaning in the mind of the communicator.

The semantic selection for the communicator means selecting the exact meaning without any ambiguity for encoding the message. For the receiver, semantic selection means selecting the appropriate meaning of the encoded message. For the receiver, semantic selection is possible only after decoding the message whereas for the communicator, it takes place before encoding the message. The study of the receiver and planning of the message are helpful activities to the communicator in his semantic selection. In case of the receiver, the meaning derived from the symbol system, depends on his knowledge of the communicator, clarity of the encoded message and adequate knowledge of the media. The semantic selection will become a difficult task for the receiver if the communicator uses improper vocabulary and writing style.

Encoding means to prepare the message by converting the ideas into the code signals which are mutually understood by both the parties. The code signals are composed of a systematic arrangement of arbitrary symbols. After semantic selection, the communicator encodes his ideas for transmitting meaning to the receiver. The communicator or the sender of the message is also called as an encoder because he encodes his ideas and impulses for transmitting them to the receiver. The translation of the perceptions into code signals is a formal expression of the message. The code signals or the symbol systems stand for an object or idea perceived by the communicator. Language consists of systematic structures of arbitrary sound symbols. When we write something, we use the letters which stand for the consonants, vovels and dipthongs. Different arrangements of systematic sound structures stand for different ideas and objects. For example, the letters e-a-r stand for the organ of hearing and a different arrangement of the same letters, like e-r-a stands for a period in history. All the language communities adopt such arbitrary and conventional symbol systems for the transmission of meaning. The encoded signals have their arbitrary pre-arranged meanings. The arbitrarily accepted meaning has conventional usage in that language community.

The set of symbols used by the encoder is a type of code or language which must be arranged in a systematic structure so that the message does not get distorted. The morphemes or the words are the symbols of language. These symbols are organised into correct structural patterns to avoid defects in the encoding process. Sometimes, the correct composition of symbols with accepted structural patterns appear to convey more than one meaning due to the conventional attribution of the various shades of meanings to the symbols used in the encoded message. The symbols must be selected carefully and arranged properly to avoid the ambiguities.

The encoded message has two sides, the message perceived by the encoder and the message perceived by the decoder. As the sources of information are of infinite variety, the form and content of the message is encoded with a variety of systems and sub-systems. This enables different people to understand different meanings of the same encoded message at different times and situations.

Before encoding the message, the encoder must consider the multiple meanings of a symbol. Then he can select a particular meaning which is conventionally attributed to the symbol. Proper semantic selection is essential for the accurate replication of ideas on the mind of the receiver. Still there remains uncertainty about the exact perception of the message by the decoder, because of the multiple denotative and connotative meanings of the symbols used for encoding the contents of information.

Human perceptual mechanism is responsible for drawing different meanings from the conventional symbols and their systems of organisation. Every individual has his own 'personal' perceptual lens. The experience of the same situation by two individuals bring quite different reactions. Research concerning variability of human perceptual mechanism concludes that individual needs are important determinants of his perceptions. The experience, education, training intelligence and emotional set of two individuals are responsible for the perception of entirely different meanings of the same message.

Any of the verbal or non-verbal media of Communication like face-to-face conversation, hand-gestures, eye-contact, touch, postures, letters, newspapers, memos, telegrams, telephone, books, periodicals, films, radio, television, etc., are used for the transmission of signals. These and innumerable other media are used to establish the channels of contact between the encoder and the decoder. There is an infinite variety of communication media and the communicator has to select any one or more of them. He has to select the most suitable medium available to him for his set purpose and may even change it and take over another medium which is more effective when the situation changes. The correct choice of the medium which is suitable for the related encoding and decoding system can help to enhance the effectiveness of the communication process. In the selected media, there can be several other barriers to effective communication, like defects in the devices used for communication, variety of interfering sounds, smudged typewritten copies, illegible handwriting, etc. The channel noise refers to misunderstanding caused by the defects in the hierarchical pattern of the organisation. When the lines of upward and downward communication are very long, the message which passes through many levels of authority is likely to be delayed and distorted. In the selected channel, there can be a number of other barriers to communication, like loss of information, exaggeration, making understatements or overstatements, under-communication, or over-communication, awe of authority, emotional states of mind, personal attitudes and opinions, closed-mindedness, inattentiveness, bypassing the authority,etc.

THE SIGNIFICANCE OF COMMUNICATION IN BUSINESS ORGANISATION

Healthy Organisational Environment

A fact that all people are different is supported by science too. When they form a group or an organisation, they manage to do it by communication. The organisations are the social systems formed on the basis of mutual interest. The mutual interests are safeguarded by various activities of planning by the management. They must skillfully apply the communication systems to keep the healthy organisational environment. It must be remembered that the activities of the management and the employees in any business organisation are governed by social as well as psychological laws. If the management has to keep the healthy organisational environment and healthy relations with the individuals from outside, other business houses, government authorities, etc., it must use the communication channels and media effectively. Sociologically, organisations are social systems in which people have their individual as well as social roles and status.

Management-Employee Relations

A genuine interest in other people, their groups and organisations is required for strong and stable personal relations and for the success of business activities of the businessman who is genuinely interested in others, shares their hopes, aspirations, successes and disappointments. The following questions asked by Wolf, Keyser and Aumer throw light on the importance of effective communication in achieving business goal:

> Unless you admit the importance of others to yourself and of yourself to others, how can you succeed as a human being or as a business person? And unless you use words and actions to establish and sustain beneficial human relations, how can you reap the profits of goodwill?.

As organisations need people and people also need organisations, people can use organisation and organisation can use people to reach their objectives by communicating properly with each other. When the objectives of the organisation are made clear to the employees, the workers are motivated to work in that direction. It should be made clear that the organisation can not survive, it its objctives are not reached; and if the organisation does not survive, there would be no chances of employment opportunities in it. The employees and the management should develop the link of communication for better mutual understanding and encourage each other to achieve their self-interests.

The External and Internal Communication Network

Every businessman finds it necessary to maintain both the internal and external communication. The communication between the management and the workers is an internal communication. The management must be well-informed about the internal activities of the organisation. They require the information about the efficiency, qualifications, capabilities and the training of the workers and also about the production, marketing and sales capacity of the organisation. The progress and profitability of the organisation depends upon how well the management and the employees are informed about these matters and what steps are taken by them in order to improve the situation. When the management is informed about some faults related to job assignments, exact designation of the officers and their decision-making, the responsibilities of the employee, etc., the management will make necessary changes and the business can thrive after the relevant changes are made.

The dynamics of the internal system influence the activities of the external system. Communication about the product studies and market analyses flow smoothly between persons of equal status, between friends and between persons who support and encourage one another, conflicts growing out of the internal system of the group can binder the communication regarding external activities. The manager must give attention to both the internal and the external group systems.

– Jerry Walford, Edwin Goerloff and Robert Cummins, in: *Organisational Communication*

The effective internal network of communication is essential today because of the large size of the business houses. They have their branches and sub-branches which are further divided into functional departments. Some business organisations are spread over the different places in the country. These divisions and branches maintain a link with the management of the central organisation. The appointments, designations, relationships, responsibilities, functionalisation, objectives and all the activities and duties determined by the division of work are communicated and assigned to the branches by the central management of the organisation. The branch manager who is appointed by the board of directors accepts the responsibilities and assignments which are assigned by the parent body. Through him, the centre gets reports about the various activities of the branch. He has to accept the directives of centre which are given by centre after receiving the reports. He acts as the delegate of the board of directors and has to clarify the objectives and directives of the organisation to his subordinates. In some of the multinational corporations, the directors and the managers spend their ninety per cent time in maintaining communication links.

Functionalisation

The division of work into different kinds of duties can be called functionalisation. For example, the difference between an office supervisor and an operator's assembly or machine shop supervisor is a functional one. This order of functionalisation. This idea of functionalisation is found in most of the business organisations today. Functionalisation naturally leads to specialisation. The most salient feature of this age is specialisation. There are specialists who acquire a vast knowledge and experience in their limited subject. This specialised knowledge, training and experience will be useless if it is not communicated. The accountants, engineers, scientists and the experts of many kinds must be able to communicate their knowledge to the management and the employees. The Company may get benefit by the advise, suggestions and information provided by these experts.

The Complexity of Business Activities

Though specialisation has brought great benefits to the business organisations, it has rendered modern business activities into an extremely complex phenomenon. As the specialisation is most fundamental to modern civilisation, the industrial society cannot exist without it. In an organisation, planning, finance, accounts, purchase, production, advertising, marketing, stores, sales, labour-welfare, cultural activities, adjustments of complaints and claims and a number of other activities are handled by the people who have developed unique skills and knowledge in their fields. As these functions are assigned to different departments, they have to coordinate among themselves by communicating with one another horizontally. They must communicate with the management to which they are responsible for carrying out their duties. The functionalised group within the organisation is more complex and difficult to coordinate than the original group of workers which is not divided into different kinds of duties. The managers and the supervisors must be well versed in communication skills in order to bring coordination among the functionalised group. The productivity gains of the specialisation can be achieved only if the harmonious human relationship and coordination of departmental activities are well maintained.

Trade Unions: Labour Problems

The businessmen are mostly after productivity gains and other economic and technical benefits. Sometimes, this tendency of the businessmen comes in conflict with the problems which are primarily human. The employees are now more conscious of their rights than before. They are organised into trade unions which continuously demand for rights of the employees, better working conditions and dignity of the labour. The progressive employers are convinced that there ought to be some ways of effective communication between the management and the workers to develop better employees satisfaction and a sense of security. If the insecurity and frustration of employees is successfully dispelled by the management, the employees feel motivated for better working. In order to satisfy the security needs of employees, a number of companies have started welfare programmes based on custodial model of organisation which is popularly known as paternalism by which employees depend on the organisation for their security and welfare. As the success of the custodial approach depends on the economic resources of the organisation, the management must be able to communicate with the employees regarding the financial state of the organisation and should motivate them for better work in order to make the organisation financially strong enough to support its employees.

Multinationals and the Language Problem

Modern business relationships have spread worldwide and the communication links play a significant role in establishing and strengthening such relationships. Multinational business can help the economic as well as social development, therefore, it can also be regarded as a social institution. When a business expands beyond national boundaries, it is also a step into different legal, political, social, economic and educational environments. With the expansion of business, the communication links are also lengthened because of which the control of the multiple business activities becomes more difficult. It is hard enough to run a multinational business in one language. When there are number of other language in a country and the overall languages are used as a medium of communication, the management faces the compounded difficulties. The complexity of the business increase to the maximum. Under these circumstances, the management has to put its communication skills to their limits.

Competition

Businessmen seek to obtain profit from the sale of their goods and services and the consumers seek the satisfaction of their wants by buying them in the market. In a free market economy, production is for profit and consumption is for the satisfaction of wants. Both the producers and the consumers naturally try to promote their own interests. This system works fairly when free competition is present in the market place. The products of common consumption are available in the market in many brands and the buyers are free to buy any of them. As the decision to buy depends on their own initiative, they cannot be forced to buy a particular product or service. The similar products with different branding from different companies cannot enjoy equal demand from the buyers. A businessman who wants to survive in this world of free competition, should know his competitors, the quality and the prices of their products, the discounts, terms and conditions of sale, the policies of advertising, government laws, etc. If they are not able to communicate better in this respect, their sale will not be satisfactory. A good salesman is efficient communicator who can attract the customer, induce him to buy his goods and services. The demand requirement for an absolutely perfect and fair competition, production and marketing, is an idealistic concept. We can approach closer to perfection but can never reach it. When people are very much aware of the products available in the market, their brands, qualities and prices, there can be keen competition. A businessman who knows the market situation properly by keeping communication links alive, can bring about certain changes in his advertising policies, he might find some way to minimise the cost of the product or he might just change the wrapper and give some discount, or he might offer attractive terms to the buyers. All these and other measures at his disposal can be effective if he has the qualities of a good salesman; and salesmanship depends on his art and skills of communication.

Participation and Delegation

Participation, cooperation and team-work of the management and employees can yield best results because of their common commitment to goals that encourage better performance. Participative managers communicate with their employees. They ask for the opinions, views, suggestions and recommendations of the employees in the decision-making process so that they work together as a team. But the benefits of participation in decision-making process may not be substantial if the superiors neglect the delegation of authority. Dr.R.S. Daver says, "The term 'delegation' is generally used to mean the granting of rights and approval to others to function within the prescribed limits". The delegation of authority trains and develops the efficiency of the subordinates and reduces the manager's burden of performing the duties of routine nature. The delegation of authority can be communicated in oral or written from, but it is always better to use the written form in order to avoid the conflict and confusion.

In participatory management, the manager retains the ultimate responsibility of his unit, but he shares the operating responsibility with the employees who actually perform the work. This gives a sense of involvement and satisfaction to the employees who work with high morale to achieve the objectives of the organisation as the manager seeks participation of the employees in policy matters and decision-making.

Exercises

(1) What is the meaning of the word 'communication'? Attempt a definition of communication.

(2) Give any three definitions of communication and comment upon them.

(3) Explain the process of communication.

(4) What is 'communication cycle'? What are the essential elements of this cycle?

(5) What is meant by 'business communication'? Write a note on the significance of business communication.

(6) What is the role of language in human communication? How are the language symbols useful in communication?

(7) Write the explanatory notes on 'encoding' and 'decoding'.

(8) What is the significance of feedback in communication? What role does it play in the cycle of communication?

(9) 'Communication is a two-way process'. Explain.

(10) What is 'communication situation'? What are the essential components of communication situation?

A. Information
   (1) Significance of Information
   (2) Types of Information
      (a) Internal Information
      (b) External Information
   (3) How to Obtain Information

B. Order
   (1) What is an Order?
   (2) Types of Orders
      (a) Written Orders
      (b) Oral Orders
   (3) How to Issue the Orders

C. Advice
   (1) Meaning and Importance
   (2) Counselling
   (3) Advice and Communication Channels
   (4) Advice in Managerial Activities
   (5) Advice and Professionalism
   (6) Essentials of Effective Advice

D. Suggestions
   (1) Importance of Constructive Suggestions
   (2) Suggestion and Other Forms of Communication
   (3) Suggestion Schemes

E. Motivation
   (1) Meaning and Importance of Motivation
   (2) Essentials of Effective Motivation
      (a) Clarity of Purpose, Objectives and Procedures
      (b) Participation
      (c) Employer-Employee Relation
      (d) Primary and Secondary Needs

F. Persuation
   (1) Meaning and Importance of Persuasion
   (2) Essentials of Effective Persuasion
      (a) Understanding the Needs and Interests of the Receiver
      (b) Using Gentle Touch at Subtle Suggestions
      (c) Preparing the Receiver to be Open-minded
      (d) Selecting the Appealing Arguments
      (e) Presenting the Message
      (f) Motivating the Receiver to Act

G. Warning
   (1) Meaning and Importance of Warning
   (2) How to Issue the Warning

H. Education
- (1) Meaning and Significance of Education
- (2) Education and Training for the
  - (a) Management
  - (b) Employees
  - (c) Outside Public

I. Raising Morale
- (1) Meaning and Importance of High Morale
- (2) How to Keep the Morale High

2

OBJECTIVES OF COMMUNICATIONS

INFORMATION

Significance of Information

The prediction of future activities related to the organisation, the planning of administrative actions, accurate decision-making process and number of other business activities are dependent on the reception of accurate, concise and complete information.

> He that judges without informing himself to the utmost that he is capable, cannot acquit himself of judging amiss.
>
> – Locke, *Human Understanding*, Bk.II, Ch. XXI.

The manager of every business organisation always need various kinds of information for planning, controlling and organising his activities. He requires information about the present and future trends in business, political changes, government control, social, economic, geographic and climatic conditions, and cultural background. He requires information about the purchase, production and sale of the Company. He requires information about the availability of raw material, machinery, labour, electricity, water, marketing and transport facilities, etc. He has to gather information about the efficiencies and weaknesses of his every staff member. He must know their habits and tendencies. He must be well informed about their technical knowledge, professional skills and educational qualifications. He requires information regarding the legal matters, government rules and regulations of licences, permits and taxation, etc. Finally, he requires the information about the rival companies and competitors in the market. He must know their production capacity, the quality prices of their products, their relative merits and demerits, their performance in past and present, and their predictable activities in the future. The employees also are to be informed about the policies, customs and objectives of the organisation.

Types of Information

The Internal Information

> Managers in organisation use information to analyse and solve problems. They depend on information. People used to think of information much as they thought of air; it was everywhere, it was free, and people took it for granted. The environmentalist began making the public aware that air is not free — atleast not clean air. And managers, likewise, are becoming aware that information, is not free either. Just as people must manage the things that influence the quality of the air they breathe, managers must manage the things that influence the quality of their information.
>
> – John A. Pearce-II & Richard B. Robinson (Jr.), in *Management.*

(i) *The information on the Policies, Objectives, Customs and Programmes of the Organisation*

Every business organisation decides its basic policies. These policies are followed in farming and executing the plans of the organisation. The employees must be well-informed about these policies. They should also be informed about the objectives of the organisation and the expectations of the employers. It is found that the well-informed employees work better than those uninformed employees in the same organisation. It is also found that the workers who are informed about the objectives and expectations of their employers, are motivated to do better work and to achieve those objectives. This information also raises their morale and gives them job satisfaction.

(ii) *Information on the Nature and Procedure of Job*

The management must keep files that give clear and complete

information about the employee, his designation, his responsibilities, his powers, his area of jurisdiction, his limitations, etc. The same information must be clearly imparted to every employee. He must know the nature of the particular job assigned to him and also the procedure in which that work is expected to be done.

(iii) *Information on the Designation, Status and Decision-making Powers of the Authorities and Officers*

If the employees and the management are not well-informed about the designation, status and decision-making powers of the officers and the authorities, it may lead to confusion, clashes, conflicts, misunderstandings and other complications. For smooth and satisfactory functioning of the organisation, it is necessary to inform both the superiors and the subordinates about their designations, status and decision-making powers. This information should be communicated in written form so that the employees get clear idea about the powers, authorities and responsibilities.

(iv) *Information on the Availability of Raw Materials, Skilled Labours and otner Essentialities*

The management requires information about the availability of the raw materials, machinery, its spare parts, etc. A productive unit requires raw material from which a finished product is made. It may also require the machinery and its spare parts. The management must gather information about the quality, variety, prices, packing, transportation and delivery of these goods. They have to get information about the different brands available in the market and their comparative suitability to the requirements of the unit. The unit cannot work without the workers. Therefore, the management has to gather the information about the availability of the workers with their professional knowledge, skills and experience.

External Information

Almost every business unit requires external information on following aspects:

(i) *Information about the Terms of Credit*

A business organisation requires capital which is the backbone of every business. The management must know the means of raising capital resources. They can acquire the capital from the bank loans, capital issues, mortgages from finance corporations, etc., but they have to get the information about the terms and conditions on which they can secure the capital resources.

(ii) *Information about the Market Environment*

The management needs information about how the product made in their Company is received by the consumers in the market. They must know how the competing products of other Companies stand in comparison with the product made in their own manufacturing unit. They must know the demands of the consumers and trends in the market. A product which has tremendous demand in the country, may not sell well in another country because of the difference in their cultural and environmental backgrounds. Therefore, a company must get information about such differences.

(iii) *Information about the Government Rules and Policies*

The Constitutional laws, rules and regulations regarding licence, permits, taxation, turnover and expansion of the business must be known to the business organiser. The political environment, the stability or the changes in government bodies affect the business policies regarding importation, exportation, licences, exchange-control, trade-duties, taxes, etc. Government can even put control over prices of various commodities. In case of certain types of industries, licence is made compulsory. Government also puts limitations over the sizes and expansions of certain industries. Therefore, it is essential for every businessman to be well informed about the political changes, government policies, constitutional laws, rules and regulations.

(iv) *Information about the Effective Advertising*

The management requires information about effective and suitable ways of promoting sale through the advertising media. He must know the needs of market and the way in which such needs can be satisfied. He must know the customers' choice which depends upon the psychological variables of the customers' personalities. There are price-cognitive people who always think about the comparative prices. There are habit-determined customers who always remain loyal to their favourite brand. Thus, there are people who are motivated to purchase the commodities with different incentives. The psychological variable which determines the customers' choice of commodity is his own personality. Before preparing the advertisement, the advertiser must be informed about choice and personality of the prospective customer.

(v) *Information about the Sociological Factors*

All the human organisations are social organisations and business organisation is not an exception to it. As the products of the Company are made for the society, the manager must get information of the various aspects of the society. The manufacturers of cars, refrigerators, television, radios and even those who manufacture the commodities of daily use, must know the standard of living of the people and their economic capability. He has to know the difference between the marketing demands of the urban population and that of the rural population. The literacy rate of the society also affects the business enterprises in various ways. The management should be informed about these sociological factors which affect the commercial activities.

(vi) *Information about Science and Technology*

The face of the commercial world puts on new appearances with the technical and scientific innovations. These innovations are applied in the business and industries in order to increase the productivity and to facilitate smooth functioning of the organisational mechanism. The latest scientific inventions and discoveries have changed the structure of most of the industries and have added new dimensions to them. The recent technological innovations in electronics and computers have brought economy in the investment of money, labour and time required for manufacturing a variety of products.

How to Obtain Information?

1. The Libraries:
   - Research Reports,
   - Annual Reports,
   - Statistical Reports,
   - Pamphlets,
   - Journals,
   - Reference Books.

2. Interviews,
3. Questionnaires,
4. Trade Fairs and Exhibitions,
5. Office Files,
6. Personal Observations,
7. Mass Media:
   - Newspapers and Periodicals,
   - Radio,
   - Television,
   - Cinema.

8. Meetings:
   - Committees,
   - Conferences,
   - Seminars,
   - Workshops.

The internal as well as external information can be available from the number of sources. But before accepting it, the receiver must verify the reliability, accuracy and completeness of it. A businessman can get the information about the particular industry from the libraries. For example, a sugar industrialist can find a number of research reports, statistical reports, pamphlets, journals and reference books devoted to the particular subject of sugarcane industries. It is also possible for him to gather information by interviewing the experts and experienced people in that field. When it is difficult to approach a large number of people, it is better not to take personal interviews. He can send questionnaires to a number of people by post. He can expect better replies from maximum people if he prepares the questionnaires carefully. Nowadays, trade fairs and exhibition are organised in most of the countries of the world. These trade fairs and exhibitions are arranged on one theme, i.e. electronic products, books, paintings, defence products, etc. It is possible to get much information related to the particular theme or subject from such trade fairs and exhibition centres. But the chances are rare to get an opportunity to visit the trade fair which is organised on the 'expected' themes.

It is possible to get a lot of information regarding the internal functioning of a business unit from the office files, if they are maintained and kept neatly. The past performance of the organisation regarding its purchase, production, sales, etc., can be understood from the information given in the files. The office files may also give the statistical data of the financial and labour resources of the organisation. Though files may give some information about the employees and their performance, it is better to assess their honesty, loyalty, efficiency, reliability and sincerity by personal observation. Actually, it takes more time and patience to draw conclusions about the personality of an employee by personal observation, but the information gathered through it is more reliable than the old files.

The mass media of communication like newspapers, journals, radio, television, cinema, have brought about information explosion. Some programmes on the television and radio may not provide the essential information required by the people in different walks of life. But they may find some other programmes on TV and radio, which may be relevant to their field of specialisation. The same can be said about the journals. There are magazines meant for the topics of general public interests and there are some periodicals that are devoted to specialisation.

Business managers are spending more of their time in attending the meetings of the committees, conferences, seminars and workshops than at any time in the past. They can get internal as well as external information from these sources. Some large business enterprises and multinational corporations convene the conferences and seminars of the experts on a particular theme or subject. Those who participate in such meetings of the committees, conferences, seminars and workshops get an opportunity to know the latest research and developments in their files. When the experts and other people get together to exchange their views, they actually share each other's knowledge and experience.

ORDER

What is an Order?

An order communicates the directives of the management to the subordinates in the organisation in an authoritative manner. These directives are issued in order to achieve the goals of the organisation. The subordinates are directed to modify, start or stop an activity as per the order given by the superior in an oral or written form.

Types of Orders

Written Orders

The written orders are given when the directives are very important and specific. The written orders are issued in the following cases:

1. The receiver of the directive is situated far away.
2. The work is of repetitive nature.
3. It is necessary to keep the record of the orders issued.
4. The directives are to be given in specific forms.
5. The order is of a highly important and responsible nature.

Oral Orders

The oral orders are given when there is face-to-face communication between the communicator and the receiver. While giving order orally, the communicator can make use of his facial expressions, gestures and variations in the pitch of his voice. But the oral orders cannot be always recorded to take follow-up actions in the future. They are less specific as compared to the written orders. The oral orders are effective and more convenient when the action is required to be taken immediately. Secondly, when it is not necessary to keep record of the orders which are concerned with the ordinary works in the unit, the oral orders are suitable and effective.

How to Issue the Orders?

As the orders are the directives to the subordinates only, they are to be issued only by the superiors to the subordinates and secondly, they are to be issued only for the sake of internal communication in an organisation. The superiors should issue the order which is absolutely clear and complete in every sense. It should be given in a simple language. If the order is given without considering the competence of the receiver, it is likely to confuse him. If the directives given in the order consist incomplete information, the receiver will be baffled and confused, and he will not be able to follow the exact course of action. The communicator should consider the capability of the receiver to carry out the order. The receiver's knowledge of how to do a particular work and when to do it is also necessary to be considered. The communicator must ensure that the execution of the order is possible and there are no difficulties in it. If he feels that there may arise some difficulty in the way of executing the order issued by him, he should specifically point them out to the receiver and should also guide him as to how those difficulties can be overcome.

The order must be given in such a tone and language that it does not provoke resentment in the mind of the receiver. If the order is given in a friendly way, there is every likelihood that it will be carried out nicely, smoothly and effectively. It is also necessary to specify the objectives and the intentions behind the order. Anyway, the receiver must receiver the order in a right spirit for its satisfactory accomplishment. For that purpose, the order must be issued in courteous, friendly and firm tone. The commanding, harsh and bitter tone cannot stimulate the willing acceptance of the order. When the order is carried out, the communicator should confirm whether it is carried out correctly and satisfactorily. He should appreciate the work of the employee who has executed the order satisfactorily. If he finds something wrong with its execution, he should assess the work of the employee without using harsh and critical language and tone. He should remove the difficulties that come in the way of the execution of the orders; or, he may adopt a new course of action and issue fresh orders.

ADVICE

Meaning and Importance

Advice is an important objective of communication. To give advice means to give an opinion about what to do, how to do, when to do and where to do a particular course of action. As the advice involves personal opinions of the advisor, it is likely to be subjective. It cannot be always factual or objective like the information. Its purpose is to bring about a change in the behaviour and opinion of the receiver. When the advice does not depend upon the facts and realities, it may be disastrous to the receiver. If it completely depends upon the beliefs, judgement and opinions of the non-expert and unexperienced person, it may not prove helpful to the receiver's needs.

Counselling

Counselling is a form of advice which is offered by a man of greater skill and knowledge in some subject. It is almost professional, and in business organisation, it offers solutions to the different domestic and personal and on-the-job problems of the employees. The employees, who are disturbed and upset by some domestic matter or health problems, cannot work efficiently in the work-unit. They certainly require counselling and sympathy of the superiors, experts, doctors, social workers and psychologists, which may bring back their normal mental and physical health.

Advice and Communication Channels

Advice usually follows the channel of downward of horizontal communication. When the advice flows down from the manager to the employees, it is downward advice. When an expert in his field of specialisation advices the manager, the flow is horizontal. A supervisor of spinning department who advices the supervisor of the weaving department he is engaged in horizontal communication.

In business organisations, advice always flows from the supervisor to the subordinates. Usually, the supervisory staff which is experienced and skilled in the working and policy matters of the company are the authorised people in giving advice. But, advice never flows from the juniors to their superiors.

Advice in Managerial Activities

Advice plays an important role in the managerial activities. The managers have to seek expert advice frequently in order to optimise human, material and financial contributions to achieve the goals of the organisation. The business houses with limited experience in business management have to refer to the people outside the organisation to get advice for planning, analysing and controlling the present and future activities of the business house. An ongoing new business venture can be successfully established with the assistance and advice of the experts. In this age of specialisation, the business activities have become so complicated that even the owners and managers of the well-established firms find them difficult to be managed without expert advice.

Advice and Professionalism

The experts are usually the learned, experienced and research-oriented persons in their areas of specialisation. Even a most competent businessman finds himself incapable of acquiring the specialised knowledge in various branches of trade and commerce. Therefore, he has to find out the sources of advice available in the private sector. There are typical sources of expert advice and counselling in the private sector like tax-consulting firms, management consulting firms, accounting firms, finance consulting firms, etc. The businessmen have also to obtain advice from the independent consultants or experts in the field of marketing, advertising, engineering, etc. The professionally managed organisations always run on the advice of the professional experts. These experts can be the employees of the organisation or they can be outsiders.

Essentials of Effective Advice

(i) The recipient should identify the key people having reliability credibility, sound knowledge and experience. These people are able to serve the company not only as the 'advisers' but also as the 'sponsors' or 'facilitators' of the new ideas.
(ii) While preparing advice, the adviser should consider the competence or the understanding capacity of the receiver.
(iii) The adviser should explain the ideas clearly, completely and correctly.
(iv) While explaining the ideas, the adviser should have a lot of patience, especially when the receiver does not understand the ideas quickly.
(v) Advice should be given in such a tone that the receiver might

feel that the adviser is keenly interested in the upliftment and welfare of the receiver.

(vi) Advice should not create a feeling of inferiority in the receiver. The adviser should not talk with the air of superiority.

(vii) While imparting advice, the adviser must be genuinely motivated to help the receiver in achieving his betterment and welfare.

(viii) The adviser should seek feedback from the receiver.

SUGGESTIONS

Importance of Constructive Suggestions

The employees in any organisation are actually engaged in operative functions. The procedure and operation of any work is better known in those who are always in touch with it. The employees, especially the lower staff, come across many procedural or operative difficulties. They may also conceive a new idea which may bring smoothness and effectiveness in their work and thereby the productivity may increase. If such ideas are properly attended and applied by the management, it may bring good fortunes to the organisation. Therefore, it is not necessary for any business management to presume that the creative ideas can be conceived only by the higher-ups and the employers. It must be remembered that the employees too are capable of contributing new and useful ideas to the organisation. The idea or suggestions put forth by an employee is a kind of proposal which the management may accept or reject. It clearly indicates the authority of the receiver to evaluate, assess, appreciate or criticise the ideas. The communicator is not in the position to put compulsion on the receiver to accept and implement his ideas.

Suggestions and Other Forms of Communication

Suggestion is a subtle form of communication because it gives a feeling of importance to the receiver. He may attend to the suggestions, he may form his own opinions about it or may reject it as being impractical, imaginary, utopian.

The advice comes from the expert who is superior in knowledge and experience to the receiver. The adviser is supposed to communicate in an authentic manner. But suggestions, on the other hand, is a mild form of communication in which the communicator gives the hints of some facts and figures to the receiver without an air of authenticity. He is always aware that the receiver is in a position to decide whether or not to adopt the course of action which would be suggested by him. When advice, order or recommendations are communicated, the receiver is conscious of his inferiority to some extent but when suggestion is put forward, he does not feel inferior to the communicator. He knows that he can turn down the proposal and even assesses it merits and utility to the organisation.

Suggestion Schemes

The suggestion schemes implemented by a number of business houses have proved that they help to foster better understanding between the workers and the management. When the superiors accept the suggestions of the subordinates, the morale of employees is raised. The communicator feels confident and satisfied when the suggested course of action is adopted by the receiver. In order to encourage the employees to offer useful and positive suggestions, the suggestion boxes can be located at some convenient places in the work-units of the organisation. If the suggestions dropped by the employees in these suggestion- boxes are daily examined and the positive suggestions are rewarded, the employees are still more motivated to think constructively for the organisation.

MOTIVATION

Meaning and Importance of Motivation

Motivation is an inner force that channelises our activities towards the objectives. It is possible for any manager to motivate the workers in his organisation for better work if he communicates skillfully with them. It is obvious that higher wages can motivate the workers for better and effective work, but there are some other factors also, which may motivate the workers and create interest in them for whatever work they do. The communicator who motivates the receiver, keeps himself in the background. The receiver is not ordered to follow any course of action. The motivated workers work hard on their own without being asked to do so. They work willingly, eagerly and effectively without any supervision of the superiors. They do not require to be supervised because they perform their duties and carry out their work to completion as if it were their own.

> Motivating is a complex process. It involves external rewards such as wages and salaries, recognition and promotion. It also includes internal rewards such as satisfaction with a job well done and challenge of a job to be done. A manager must provide the right "mix" of satisfactions, if the individual is to be motivated in the desired direction.
>
> – Herbert G. Hicks & C. Ray Gullett in, *Modern Business Management*

There is no doubt that monetary incentives are the most effective forces of motivation, but 'money' is not the only motive behind the efficient and sincere work. When the supervisor puts trust in the subordinates, the latter only naturally tries to prove worthy of the trust. If the workers get job satisfaction, social recognition, status of prestige and sense of belonging to the organisation, he is certainly motivated for better work for the development and the welfare of the organisation. But it cannot be denied that different people are motivated to different extents by different forces of motivation which depend on their psychological, physical and social needs.

Essentials of Effective Motivation

Clarity of the Purpose, Objectives and Procedures

It is essential to set specific objectives before the workers. They must understand the purpose behind their work as well as the objectives they are to achieve, so that they may work hard to reach them. It is natural that they get job satisfaction when they complete their work successfully. The workers must be well informed about the plans and policies of the organisation and how they are to be brought into actual practice. If the management does not clarify their plans, policies, procedures and the objectives to the employees, it will be difficult for them to motivate the workers and to expect quantitative work from them. The employees must be informed about the background, history, efficiency, utility, contributions, benefits and targets of the organisation. This information can be imparted to them with the help of house-journals, seminars, training programmes and face-to-face talks. The information should be presented in such a way that the employees must feel a sense of pride for being the employees of a good business organisation.

Participation

When workers are invited by the management to participate in the decision-making process, they experience a sense of belonging to the organisation and it motivates them to work better. It is found that the successful business organisations which encourage their employees to offer their suggestions for the improvement of the working procedure and overall development of the organisation were successful because they could thereby motivate the employees. These employees cooperate with the plans of the management when the management earns their confidence by inviting them to participate in the decision-making process. The employees are motivated when the management appreciates and accepts the suggestions given by them.

The Employer-Employee Relations

There must be mutual understanding between the employer and employees and also between the supervisory staff and the junior staff. They must come together in an informal atmosphere and discuss their views and opinions. There should not be resentment, confrontation and lack of understanding between them. The supervisors must behave in such a way that they should be able to earn the respect and trust of the subordinates without forcing for it. The sincerity, capability, loyalty, honesty, competence, hardwork and simplicity of the supervisors can set an example before the employees. It can easily motivate them to work harder and better.

The Primary and Secondary Needs

It must be remembered that almost all the conscious activities of the workers are caused by either primary or secondary needs which motivate them to take action in order to fulfil them. There are certain human activities which occur without motivation. The growth of nails and hair does not require any motivation, nor does a mean require motivation to fall asleep. But almost all the organisational activities are egged on by motivation. The employees are motivated to take actions that satisfy their needs and wants. Generally, the needs are classified in two groups — (a) primary needs, and (b) secondary needs. The primary needs, which arise from basic human requirements include water, food, air, sex, sleep, cloth and shelter. The secondary needs include self-esteem, self-assertion, safety, security, belonging, social involvement, status, love, care, affection, self-recognition, self-actualisation, etc. The management must identify and activate the motives of the employees towards the performance of their duties.

PERSUATION

> Business today consists in persuading crowds.
>
> – Gerard Stanley, Lec, in *Crowds*

Meaning and Importance of Persuasion

Persuasion is an important objective of business communication. A businessman always tries to persuade the receiver to accept his point of view and opinions. He makes an effort to bring desirable change in the attitudes, beliefs, feelings and thoughts of the receiver. He uses all his tact and skill to persuade the prospective buyer to buy the goods and services from him. The management and supervisory staff have to persuade the workers for better and hard work. Sometimes, the subordinates have to persuade the superiors to take some course of action in favour of them. Nobody likes to mend his views and actions, if he is forced to do so by compulsion or repression. It is natural that force, compulsion and repression bring resentment and anger of the receiver. Therefore, it is better not to impose our views on the others.

The Essentials of Effective Persuasion

Understanding the Needs and Interests of the Receiver

Before organising a message for persuasive communication through oral or written media, the communicator must try to understand the needs, requirements and interests of the receiver. The communicator must confirm that the course of action which he is going to suggest the receiver is in the favour of him. The receiver should not feel that the suggested alternative is based on the selfish motives of the communicator.

Using Gentle Touch of Subtle Suggestions

It is not necessary to overwhelm the receiver with your arguments or to impose yourself on him. It is natural that the managers as well as the workers resist the proposed change if it is against their views and beliefs. The communicator should not consider it easy to find a way of putting an end to this resistance. People know that a change is likely to be either a success or a problem of failure. The communicator can minimise the resistance by skillfully showing how it can be a success. It is the gentle touch of the subtle suggestions rather than the dry and rough arguments that is more likely to persuade the receiver. For this purpose, it is essential to know how to channelise the receiver's thinking so that he accepts the views or the suggested actions easily and naturally.

Preparing the Receiver to be Open-minded

The closed-minded and headstrong persons are very difficult to be persuaded because they are either deeply prejudiced or self-opinionated persons. When they are not flexible enough to adjust their views with the views of the others, it becomes even more difficult to persuade them. It is essential to make tactful appeal to them so that they develop adaptibility and open-mindedness. It means the receiver must be prepared to accept the message. If your ideas run contrary to the views and beliefs of the receiver, it is better to start with the points which are agreeable to the receiver. When the receiver is prepared to open his mind and accept some of your ideas, you can gradually convince him the other points.

Selecting the Appealing Arguments

It is always better to avoid the topics which are strongly disliked by the receiver and which are likely to bring his resentment. Such topics are risky in the sense that a mere mention of them might suddenly snap the communication link between the communicator and the receiver. You must know what he likes and what he dislikes. It is always better to look at the issue from his angle. Therefore, select the argument which might strongly appeal him and mould them in such a way that he readily accepts them.

Presenting the Message

Having prepared both the receiver and the message, the next step is to present the message in a proper way. The persuasion is likely to be effective and successful if the ideas are put forth step-by-step in a forceful but courteous manner. The arguments must be organised carefully so that the easy and pleasant ideas come before the relatively difficult and unpleasant ones.

Motivating the Receiver to Act

The communicator is successful in persuading the receiver when the later is convinced that the proposed suggestions bring him gains and no losses. The rewards, gains, security, and the fulfilment of primary and secondary needs are the motivating factors for prompting the action. It must be remembered that the receiver of the message can be prompted to act on the basis of the motivating factors in the message.

WARNING

Meaning and Importance of Warning

Warning is a forceful means of communication by which we inform a person of unfavourable and unpleasant consequences in future. In an organisation, warning is given by the superiors to the subordinates either in oral or in written form. It is expected by every management that the employees should abide the rules, regulations, norms and customs of the organisation.

I know the past and thence I will essay to glean
A warning for the future, so that man
May profit by his error and derive
Experience from his folly.

– Shelly, *Queen Mab*, III.

But it is likely that some of the employees under certain circumstances are unable to abide the prescribed norms. Sometimes, they are guilty of arrogance, defianace, irregularity, negligence, pilfering, etc. in such cases, it becomes necessary for any management to warn the employees and correct them. It can be issued to an individual employee or to the group of subordinates. It demands an urgent and immediate improvement in the behaviour of the employees. The effectiveness of warning as a means of communication depends upon its occasional and discreet usage.

How to Issue the Warning

(a) A warning can be given in the form of notices which inform some possible danger or inconveniences in the future.

(b) Often warnings are given in the form of reprimand which invites resentment of the receiver. Though it is a part of disciplinary action taken by the management, it is likely to build tension in the management-employee relationship. Therefore, it must be administerted discreetly and only after a careful study of the charges levelled against the employee. The superior must analyse the charges objectively and should not put the colour of his prejudices in the warning.

(c) The receiver of the warning must be given an opportunity to explain himself and his inability in abiding the rules and norms. The superior should try to understand the circumstances in which the subordinate could not have followed the rules.

(d) Reprimand should never be administered while the communicator has lost his temper. It must be given clearly and in a matter of fact style. The superior might lose the balance of his mind when some subordinate violates the norms and discipline. The reprimand, in such circumstances, is likely to be administered in harsh and bitter words. The sarcastic style of warning may defeat the very purpose of it.

(e) A warning can also be administered horizontally by an advisor or a friend. They inform the receiver about the possible danger or loss in the future. The purpose behind such warning is to save the receiver from the unpleasant consequences. The aim of it is the betterment of the receiver. Such warnings are to be given in clear words and firm style so that the receiver understands the significance of it.

EDUCATION

Let him who is taught the word share in all good things with him who teaches.

– The *Holy Bible*. Galatians 6:6.

Meaning and Significance of Education

Education is a process of instructing a learner in knowledge. It bridges a gap between the knowledge and the learner. Educational communication takes places when the members of learning and teaching groups come together in order to teach or learn something about a given subject. In business, the new recruits as well as the existing managerial and subordinate staff requires development of their knowledge, skills and abilities. The lack of higher or university education is a serious barrier to the success in managerial functions and similarly, the lack of adequate training and orientation to the junior staff can lead to inefficient operational functioning of the functionalised departments.

The demand for multi-professional employees is increasing nowadays, and it has resulted in the need for education and training of the employees to acquire high level skills. The nature of jobs changes as the technology changes. The developing technology has developed the requirements of the more professional scientific and educated white-collar employees in the business organisations. The steady advancement of technology has created the work which is more intellectual and less manual. It emphasises mind more than hands. Therefore, it is essential to widen the knowledge and to improve the skills of the workers through the education and training. The objective of education is to be achieved at three levels.

(a) Management,

(b) The Employees,
(c) The Outside Public.

The Management Education

There is a high demand for multi-professional managers who are educated in some technical speciality in addition to management, so that they can manage technical work more easily and efficiently. The intellectual work of the employees requires an altogether different quality of motivation than manual work. The managers must be trained to know this difference. For example, a manual worker can be easily persuaded by the use of authority or by the threat of penalty for the spadework. But the manager must acquire sophisticated skills and means of motivation to motivate an intellectual employee to write a creative composition. As the senior managers are to be educated and trained in the latest technological advances in their particular fields, the juniors and assistants in the organisation are also required to be trained because they have to succeed their seniors in future. They can be trained through the formal education in staff training colleges with the help of lectures, seminars, books, etc., and also through informal education in which they are given an opportunity to work actually under the direct supervision and guidance of the senior-members of the management.

The Employees

The employees also require the education and training regarding the latest innovations in the field of business, science and technology. Now, the labourers to not believe that the machinery threatened their jobs. They are ready to accept the technology regardless of its consequences. The moving technology has allowed a very few jobs to remain static. It does not abolish jobs for all time, but certainly it creates different kinds of jobs for the employees, which requires different skills. It is not possible for any business firm today to terminate the employees on the pretext of their outdated skills. The only alternative available to the management is to arrange retraining programmes for the employees. The retraining programmes are also known as the re-orientation courses in which the employees are educated through lectures, discussions, demonstrations, case-studies, study-tours, house journals, magazines and books.

The Outside Public

It is through advertising and other means of publicity that the business units try to educate the outside public regarding their new products in the market. The business organisations can communicate with the outside public in this respect through the devices of mass media. They can arrange an informative talk on radio. On television, they can arrange the informative talk with the visual demonstrations. They can also select the media of newspapers and journals for pictorial advertisements or the informative articles on the utility and speciality of different brands, their substitutes, concessions, discounts and comparative prices of their products in the market.

RAISING MORALE

Meaning and Importance of High Morale

When the morale of the employees is raised high, their courage, confidence and efficiency of performance is also raised high. The morale of the employees can be described as their attitude towards their organisation and their job.

To keep the morale of the employees at the high level is one of the important objectives of internal communication system. When the morale of the employees is raised high, their courage, confidence and efficiency of performance is also raised high. The unity, sense of togetherness and teamwork of the employees are the factors of high morale which are essential for the success or any business organisation. The self-confidence of an employee as well as his trust and confidence in the management of the organisation are dependent on the morale of that employee. The healthy relationships among the people in an organisation, the smooth functioning of all the departments, effective co-ordination, mutual understanding and discipline are all the outcomes of good morale, if there is a lack of discipline and confidence in the organisation, it is usually due to low morale. In such organisations, the good works and achievements of the employees are not appreciated or rewarded by the management. The relationship between the supervisory staff and subordinates and among the subordinates themselves are marred by jealousy and suspicion. Every worker thinks about his personal gains rather than about the gains of his organisation. They do their jobs unwillingly, therefore, they cannot derive any satisfaction or pleasure from it. Low morale requires immediate attention, diagnosis cure which depends on the alertness of the top management and their awareness of the need of effective communication network.

How to Keep Morale High?

(a) Every worker must have a sense of belonging to the organisation. He must be initiated by the management to pass his suggestions regarding some of the decisions to be taken by the management. When his suggestions are considered by the management, he feels involved in the decision-making process. He feels proud for working in that organisation because of his sense of belonging to the organisation. He devotes himself to the work of the organisation as if it is his own work.

(b) The management must pay attention to the performance of every worker irrespective of his designation and status in the organisation, so that the worker may feel that his contributions to the organisation are important. Therefore, the management should never forget that the performance of every employee deserves attention of the higher-ups.

(c) It is found that the undesirable checks and restraints from the supervisory staff are responsible in lowering the morale of the employees. Therefore, the superiors should put restraint on their abuses of authority to such an extent that it does not come in the way of the worker's freedom to do his work as per his individual efficiencies and likings.

(d) The management must assign the work which is suitable to the physical capabilities and intellectual competence of the worker. An employee with good intellect and sound academic background should not be assigned with the heavy manual work or the repetitive mechanical work that does not require creative thinking and skill. An employee should not feel his work as too easy or too difficult to accompiish.

(e) The employees must be well-paid for their jobs. The monetary incentives should be available to them. Low morale is usually found in the organisations where the employees get inadequate salary.

(f) The management must take care that the employees do not

feel boredom, tedium and monotony of the work. The atmosphere in the premises of the organisation must be pleasant, fresh and healthy.

(g) The employees must feel free to discuss with their superiors regarding the issues affecting their work, and also the issues affecting their domestic life. The employer must earn the trust and confidence of the employees. The supervisors must try to earn the faith and respect from the workers. They must display their own efficiency before demanding good work from the workers.

(h) The supervisors must not issue the directives with sarcasm, ridicule and harsh language. On the other hand, they must give a fair hearing to the grievances and the suggestions of the employees before issuing the order.

(i) The management must appreciate and reward the good work and achievements of the employees.

(j) The management should use the official channels to contradict the false rumours, if any.

The morale of the employees can be studied by maintaining a steady flow of communication between the employees and the management. The management must use the devices like meetings, conferences, seminars and talks in order to draw the information through various channels. Sometimes, the replies of the specially prepared questionnaires are also used to collect the information regarding the morale of the employees.

Exercises

(1) Discuss the objectives of Business communication.

(2) Why does a business organisation require information from external sources? What are the sources of this information?

(3) Briefly discuss the importance of internal information in business organisation. What are the sources of internal information?

(4) What precautions should be taken while accepting information from various sources? What precautions should be taken while imparting information?

(5) Briefly discuss the importance of advice in business organisation. Explain the difference between advice and counselling. How can an advice be made effective?
(6) What are the ways of classifying orders?
(7) What are the characteristics of an effective order? What are the steps in order-giving operation?
(8) Explain the difference between order and instruction.
(9) What is the importance of suggestions as an objective of business communication? Write a brief note on the suggestion schemes.
(10) Discuss the importance of the art of persuasion in business communication, especially, in presenting proposals and in sales.
(11) What are the important steps in the art of persuasion?
(12) "Because persuasion deals with people's minds and with human interaction, very little about it is absolute". — Discuss.
(13) What is the importance of education for the management, the employees and the outside public?
(14) What precautions should be taken while issuing warnings to the subordinates? Explain the difference between warning and reprimand.
(15) "Interpersonal conflict often arise in business when co-workers do not share similar motives. The single factor that can lead to resolving the conflict is the ability of each person to communicate effectively with the other". — Discuss.
(16) How can we use motivation to activate and direct the behaviour of employees towards organisational goals?
(17) What are essentials of effective motivation?
(18) Explain the meaning of 'high moral' and 'low morale'. What factors are responsible for lowering the morale of the employees? How can the morale of the employees be raised?
(19) Write short-note on the following:

(i) Information for planning
(ii) Warning and Advice
(iii) Preparing order-receiver
(iv) Reliability of information
(v) Suggestions boxes
(vi) Environmental Information
(vii) Counselling

A. What are the Channels of Communication?

B. Downward Channel of Communication
   (1) What is Downward Communication?
   (2) Media of Downward Communication
   (3) Redundancy of Message
   (4) Objectives of Downward Communication
   (5) Essentials of Effective Downward Communication
   (6) Limitations of Downward Communications

C. Upward Channels of Communication
   (1) What is an Upward Channel of Communication?
   (2) Methods and Policies of Upward Communication
   (3) Problems of Upward Communication
   (4) Effective Upward Communication

D. Horizontal Channel of Communication
   (1) What is Horizontal Channel of Communication?
   (2) Methods of Effective Horizontal Communication

E. Grapevine
   (1) What is a Grapevine?
   (2) Importance of Grapevine
   (3) Limitations of Grapevine
   (4) How to use the Grapevine?

F. Consensus
   (1) What is Consensus?
   (2) Significance of Consensus
   (3) Limitations of Consensus

3

THE CHANNELS OF COMMUNICATION

In all your ways acknowledge Him,
and He shall direct your paths

– The *Holy Bible*, Proverbs 3:6

WHAT ARE THE CHANNELS OF COMMUNICATION?

The Channels of communication are the formal and informal ways of communicating with other people. Every business organisation has to maintain the internal as well as external communication. The internal communication is concerned with the transmission and reception of information, orders, suggestions, warnings, etc. within the organisation, whereas the external communication is concerned with the transmission and reception of messages with the banks, government offices, insurance agencies, customers, exports, other business houses, etc. For both the internal and external communication, the company has to build up its communication systems. The organisational setting and the hierarchy of offices, authorities, clerks, operators, etc. form a context for all kinds of communication that takes place in the organisation. In other words, we can say that the patterns of communication depend on the structure of the organisation. If one has to understand and manage the 'How' of communication, he has to understand the informal and formal communication systems.

A communication channel runs along with the hierarchical line of authority in the organisational pattern which is designed with the view of carrying our organisational activities. In business organisations, usually the policy matters are decided by the Board of Directors and information regarding it is transmitted to the Managing Director, who is supposed to execute the policy decisions. He issues the directives to the assistant departmental managers. The supervisors receive instructions from the assistant managers. In their turn, the supervisors pass the relevant instructions to their subordinate clerks or to the operators who are actually concerned with the operational function. When the information is communicated through the hierarchical lines of authority, it is called as 'formal communication'. The formal communication puts obligation on all those who communicate internally to follow the prescribed channels and not to by-pass the authority. For example, a supervisor is not expected to communicate directly with the Managing Director. He must impart the message to the departmental manager who will pass it on to the Managing Director. These lines of authority are actually the channels of communication, which generally follow the upward, downward and horizontal directions. These line must be kept as short as possible so that the original message does not get distorted. The communication channels can be divided under the following sub-heads:

1. Downward Channel,
2. Upward Channel,
3. Horizontal Channel,
4. Grapevine,
5. Consensus.

Downward Channel of Communication

What is Downward Communication?

Downward communication is a supervisory communication, which is initiated by the upper management. It flows downward through the hierarchy of command. The effective downward communication is crucial to the success of the organisation. The management or the supervisory staff has to communicate with the subordinates in order to organise, coordinate, and direct the operational aspects of the organisation. It is a very suitable channel to the organisation in which the 'chain of command' is arranged in the ranks that are distinctly one below the other.

Media of Downward Communication

The downward flow of communication is dominated by oral media. It is convenient for a departmental head to give oral instructions and orders to the supervisor. Instead of issuing lengthy written instructions, the Managing Director usually convenes a meeting of the departmental managers in order to impart the essential directives or to gather their suggestions on various issues. Yet, the management may use both oral and written media for downward communication. There are various alternatives of communication media at the disposal of every management. Some typical alternative devices of communication media which are effective for downward communication are letters, circulars, memos, company journals, video and audio recordings, telephone calls, meetings, face-to-face conversations, speeches to the employees and the posters.

Redundancy of Message

It is found that using a combination of media tends to give best results because it increases the effectiveness of communication. When the same message is sent through more than one media, it creates redundancy. Redundancy is helpful in receiving and memorising the message. The busy people in the organisation require more message redundancy in order to act on the directions they receive from their superiors. On the other hand, the law of diminishing returns is also applicable to the organisation in which the employees are overburdened with the overflowing downward communication. The increasing number of phone calls, memos, letters and meetings may make each employee much businer but as it requires adequate time to attend each of these messages, the employee will not be able to give proper justice to the every piece of work in his hand. Therefore, the management must remember the proverb "More is better, up to a point".

The Objectives of Downward Communication

The superiors communicate with their subordinates with the objective that the employees may do their work with accuracy, neatness, sincerity, steadiness, thoroughness, honesty and punctuality. They give specific directives or instructions to the employees that clarify the ways and procedures of job performance. They expect that the employees should maintain the standards of work quality. The employee is instructed with the view that he does not commit mistakes in his operative or supervisory works. the downward communication is also required to check, assess and appreciate the performance of the employees.

The employees are also required to be well informed regarding the policies, procedures, rules and regulations of the organisation and these are communicated through the downward channel. Frequently, some workers are found uncooperative and antagonistic. They may have little willingness to work and little interest in the associates. They may usually help the others, but grudgingly. They may be tolerant, but not friendly with their colleagues. In case of such employees, the downward channel is used to instruct them. Some times, the superiors have to warn or reprimand the workers for their undesirable behaviour. Sometimes, the managements use the downward channel to motivate the employees for better productivity by imparting propaganda messages. If a worker's comprehension of work details is inadequate, the supervisors use this channel to educate him and to assist him for the improvement of work.

Essentials of Effective Downward Communication

(i) The superior or the communicator must have a clear and complete idea of the message.

(ii) The communicator must be well informed about the policy decisions taken by the management in the past.

(iii) The communicator must know the past performance and achievements of the organisation.

(iv) The communicator should have a clear idea of the aims and objectives of the organisation.

(v) Adequate volume and substance of the information must be well-organised before its transmission.

(vi) The substance of the message to be imparted must be prepared by keeping in view the competence and understanding ability of the subordinates.

(vii) The message must be channelised at adequate time.

(viii) There should neither be over-communication nor under-communication.

(ix) The information must pass through the hierarchical structures of the organisation. There should not be by-passing of any authority.

(x) The lines of communication should be shortened in order to minimise the possibility of distortion.

(xi) The language in downward communication must be simple.

(xii) The subordinate employees must be conditioned to expect that most of the important messages regarding their work come to them from their immediate superior.

Limitations of Downward Communications

It is essential to take care that the message is reliably transmitted through each level of the downward authority. However, there are certain difficulties that come in the may of achieving exact reproduction of the message from the source.

Delay

A message has to pass through a number of levels which involve the time limitations. When the line of downward communication is long, it takes much time to reach the message at its destination.

Message Abbreviation

At each level, at least some part of the message is likely to be lost because of the lack of understanding or by shoddy handling. It also occures that the participant abbreviates the message because he does not want to spend much time in transmitting all the contents of the message. The abbreviation of message has always an adverse effect on its fidelity.

Message Distortion

The downward communication has to go through some filter points, therefore, the chances for distortion are more. The more filtering points assure more distortion of the message. Slanting, interpreting, condensing and twisting are the possible ways to distort the message. The fidelity and authenticity of the message is affected both in quantity and quality by the successive judgements of the several members in the chain of communication.

Message Overload

A real danger of message overload is found in the business

organisations which generate a very high volume of messages and impose them on the employees. It is like an electric circuit in a house which operates normally with the appropriate amperage demand. When the amperage demand overloads the circuit, a fuse blows. When the superiors overcommunicate with the subordinates, the balance of handling the messages is disturbed. The major cause of message overload is the increasing complexity of business life.

Incomplete Information

If an employee does not receive enough information to do the job, the possible outcomes are dysfunctional. The incomplete information or the lack of sufficient instructions to the subordinates result in errors and unsatisfactory performance. The management then has to use up the additional time for correcting the errors and also for assessing them.

UPWARD CHANNEL OF COMMUNICATION

What is an Upward Channel of Communication?

The behavioural scientists have shown the relationship between the communication and performance. The findings related with it have a tremendous effect on the managerial practices today. The business managements have become concerned more than ever before about what is going on at several levels below them. They have employed some fairly new techniques like open-door policy, suggestion-schemes, etc., and they are still anxious to know any new or revolutionary method to get information from the lower ranks. It is generally found that the superiors are better communication-senders because they are better talkers and writers than their subordinates. The subordinates are generally more cautious and less confident than their superiors when they are to pass some information through upward channel of communication.

The two-way flow of communication in any business organisation is supported by efficient and effective upward communication. The management can keep itself in touch with the needs, requirements, difficulties and grievances of the employees when it receives messages from the employees. The management is also helped to make sound decisions on the basis of the sufficient information secured from the subordinates. In order to improve the productivity, it is not necessary to put pressure on the employees or try to motivate the employees towards more loyalty and hardwork by merely putting articles in the company magazines. But, on the other hand, it is necessary for the management to develop the procedure for encouraging upward communication to receive the information regarding production, quality-control, absenteeism, inventory control, profits, costs, new schemes and programmes, inventions, advertising, sales, complaints, research, etc., and constructive suggestions regarding various other matters that promote the welfare of the organisation, etc. When the management receives information and suggestions from the subordinates regarding the matters given above and many other, it is able to issue the fresh directives to the employees regarding their works and procedures. The management can also get an idea of how the subordinates receive the directives and how the directives are followed. When the management realises the problems, difficulties and grievances of the employees, they can try to find out the solutions. The upward communication gives an opportunity to an employee to express his frustrations of the work situation and helps him to relieve the pressures of the pent-up emotions, which are associated with their daily problems. Finally, it must be noted that the employees' sense of participation in the enterprise is enhanced by the upward communication.

Methods and Policies of Upward Communication

Meetings

The meetings with the employees are found to be very useful in building upward communication. The higher-ups are to encourage the employees to talk about their constructive suggestions, job problems and needs. They are also to be also encouraged to express their views on whether the managerial practices help the job performance or interfere with it. The meetings enable the management to ascertain the worth of their directives imparted to the workers.

Counselling

> As a bamboo conduit makes a round jet of water/
> so taking counsel together rounds men to one mind.
>
> – Malay Proverb.

The workers can be encouraged to seek the counsel of their superiors. When an employee comes to his superior with his personal or official problems and difficulties which adversely affect his working in the organisation, the superior has to earn the trust and confidence of the employee by encouraging him to talk freely and by taking firm steps to solve his problems. The managers get valuable information by the method of counselling, if they can successfully encourage the employees to talk freely about themselves and also about the organisation.

An Open-Door Policy

The purpose of open door policy is to remove the blocks in the way of upward communication. The employees are encouraged to walk into the manager's cabin without any hesitation for having a problem and without being afraid that they would invite disfavour of their manager. Though the open-door policy has good purpose, it is very difficult to implement because of the socio-psychological barriers that come between the managers and the employees.

Correspondence

The employees are encouraged to write letters. First the management sends enquiry letters to the employees and the replies are encouraged. This is a direct and personal way for the employees to transmit the information to the management.

Participation in Social Gatherings and Group Events

Some casual events provide opportunities for arranging social gatherings in different departments of the firm. The informal atmosphere during the sport events, picnics and parties offer spontaneous information from the employees to the firm.

Reports

The management may ask the subordinates to present the reports. The reports are the basic tools used by the management in decision-making. In the large business organisations, where a large number of employees are engaged in different activities, the reports from the subordinates are extremely important and indispensable for the success of managerial functions. As the senior managers cannot keep a personal watch over all the business activities, he requires reports about the progress of the work done by the employees.

Suggestion Boxes

The employees are encouraged to drop their suggestions and new ideas in the suggestion boxes. The managements which are aware of the fact that the small problems and complaints of the employees that go unnoticed have way of mushrooming into major problems, encourage the employees to drop their complaints also in the suggestion boxes. These suggestions or complaints boxes are placed at some convenient places in the firm. These boxes are opened at regular internals. The management is supposed to reward the positive and constructive suggestions.

Problems of Upward Communication

Positive Encouragement

The upward communication goes to minimum if the management does not positively encourage it. What goes unrewarded does not thrive in the organisation. Lack of rewards for employee feedback stands as a problem in upward communication. The management must take positive action to initiate the employees to communicate upward. Simply waiting for the employees to come in with some information is of no use.

Concealing Unfavourable Facts

The employees tend to conceal their difficulties and the on-the-job problems from their superiors. Especially, they conceal the ignorance and inability from the boss. They feel the risk in imparting unfavourable information to the boss because of the belief that the surest way to get ahead is to agree with the boss.

Delay, Distortion and Filtering

Usually, the upward communication is subject to delay, distortion and filtering, especially when the lines of communication are long. Each level in the hierarchy is reluctant to take a problem to the higher authority, because in so doing, he is afraid that he may lose the favour of his superior. At each level, an effort is made to solve the problem. All this results in delay, distortion and filtering.

Bypassing and Suspicion

> Suspicion on one side breeds suspicion on
> the other and new weapons beget counterweapons.
>
> – John F. Kennedy.

Some workers become so bold in the process of upward communication that they by-pass their immediate-superior authority, which results in the bypassed authority's getting suspicious about the intentions of the subordinate.

Poor Listening

Poor listening skills of the superior often discourage the speaker to communicate his message-listening. Listening does not mean just hearing a message. It requires careful attention and exact decoding of the signals received from the speaker. If the superior goes on shuffling the papers while listening to his subordinate, he pays divided attention to the speaker's message. This divided attention is usually interpreted as his lack of interest in the message. The superior's divided attention can adversely affect the superior-subordinate relationship. Poor listening skills of the superior does not allow him to attend and interpret the message accurately. If the superior does not develop his listening skills, it will surely minimise the opportunity for both the superior and subordinate to benefit from the upward communication.

Communicating Criticism

The subordinates carefully screen or filter the information before transmitting it to the high status persons. It is very difficult for any subordinate to communicate criticisms on the superiors and management policies.

Effective Upward Communication

(1) The lines of communication should be kept as short as possible to avoid the distortion by filtering, screening and editing.

(ii) To find out how the employees feel about their jobs, it is always convenient to conduct the employee attitude surveys.

(iii) There should be a formal system to handle the suggestion objectively and seriously.

(iv) Positive efforts must be taken by the superiors to eliminate the fear and awe of the authority from the minds of the workers.

(v) Constructive suggestions for the improvement of the organisation must be suitably rewarded. If the information transmitted by the employees is ignored, they will quickly abandon this channel. Therefore, the upward communication must be reinforced and rewarded with adequate attention.

(vi) The management must ensure the workers that they feel genuinely concerned for the problems and grievances of the subordinates.

(vii) It is essential to build a corporate atmosphere of trust. There must be mutual trust in the relationship between the superiors and the subordinates. If the workers think that they are going to be rewarded with punishment for their feedback, they will never provide it.

HORIZONTAL CHANNEL OF COMMUNICATION

What is Horizontal Channel of Communication

The complexity of todays business organisations has made 'horizontal communication' a vital subject for management studies. It takes place between and among the people who belong to the same level of the hierarchy. We have now realised that the survival of any modern business organisation depends on the degree of specialisation achieved by it. Because of this specialisation existing in the business organisations today, each unit of the same organisation is differentiated from others. The horizontal channel of communication is the primary method of coordinating inter-dependent units and departments. To keep the organisation running efficiently, it is essential to coordinate or integrate all its diverse units. For example, if the sales manager has to give exact date of delivery to the customer, he must get certain information from the head of the stores and packing department as well as from the head of the department of transportation. Horizontal or lateral communication, if effectively used, socialises people into the system and gives them a sense of belonging to the organisation.

Although many business organisations generally consider horizontal communication to be unproductive, it is, in fact, most productive form of communication because almost all of the employees exchange information regarding different aspects of the company with their follow-employees through horizontal channel. Secondly, it is possible for them to judge their performance by comparing it with the performance of other employees in the organisation. But the autocratic organisations tend to discourage the horizontal communication. Such managements are afraid that the employees may get friendly and their union may pose some problems to the Company. They believe only in the downward communication which is dominated by the directives, orders and warnings. They should realise the role of horizontal communication in preventing the inter-departmental conflicts which may arise due to slanting, misconceptions, distortion of message, misunderstanding or by lack of understanding. In order to facilitate the process of problem solving and to promote friendly and cooperative spirit among the employees of the organisation, the horizontal channel must be used effectively.

Methods of Effective Horizontal Communication

Telephone and Face-to-Face Communication

The telephone conversations and face-to-face conversations are the primary means of horizontal communication which facilitate the coordinating activities of the organisation. Today, thousands of rupees are spent by the modern business houses on telephone services. The telephonic communication cannot be as effective as the face-to-face communication because people cannot use facial expressions and gestures in telephone conversations. But it is possible to make it effective through modulations of voice.

Meetings

The meetings of the employees belonging to different departments is a means of achieving horizontal communication. It can bring about the organisational integration. The activities and discussions in the meeting can be well-directed if the purpose of meeting is specific and the agenda is strictly followed. The meetings help to heighten the team-spirit and assure the necessary information flow by encouraging two-way communication. The horizontal communication can also be channelised by meeting of the standing committees which are designed to integrate the inter-dependent departments. As the employees are associated with the decision-making process of the committee, their relationships are improved. The useful knowledge and experience of the employees is mutually shared by them. If a committee consists of departmental heads, if promotes coordination, the spirit of understanding and cooperation.

Written Media

The letters and memos are also used for horizontal communication. (An entire chapter deals with this subject later in the text).

GRAPEVINE

> In the old days of barbarism, the people fought with hatchets.
> Civilised men buried the hatches and now fight with gossip
> – Edgar Watson Howe, in *Country Town Sayings*.

What is Grapevine

Grapevine is an informal communication network which ignores formal channels of communication and spreads rumours and gossips at all levels of the organisation. Although every business-organisation has its formal channels of communication, the informal channel of communication called grapevine also operates in it. It can be easily found that a large portion of the communication in almost every business house is not formal or pre-planned. The employees communicate through informal channel as they do their jobs. It is neither pre-planned nor deliberately motivated by the management. It is neither written nor documented or recorded. Therefore, it refers to any communication that takes place outside the prescribed and pre-planned channels of formal communication. It is not set with the lines of organisational hierarchy. As it has no set rules and regulations, it is not confined to a particular direction. It just spreads like grapevine.

Importance of Grapevine

Though the structure of the grapevine is not so well defined, as that of the formal channels, it should not be taken for its weakness. The messages flowing through grapevine have greater speed than that of the messages flowing through the formal channels. The grapevine may carry equally vital message through it for the achievement and success of the organisation. It is not correct to underestimate the grapevine by saying that the vital messages pass only through the authorised, formal channels. On the other hand, though the formal channels are systematic, pre-planned and documented, it is authority-laden. It can never be as speedy and spontaneous as the grapevine. The employees communicate through grapevine, not because they are compelled to communicate but because they earnestly want to communicate with their associates.

The method of formal written communication is slow and expensive method of information transmission. The grapevine, on the other hand, is non-expensive and most-rapid oral method of transmitting the information to the maximum number of the communication receivers. Being a multi-directional channel, grapevine is a convenient means to cross the hierarchical boundaries. The grapevine is not restricted to any particular line of hierarchy or to the vertical and the horizontal directions. It can flow wherever the participants wish it to flow, therefore, the manager can use the properly cultivated grapevine in dealing with the problems that require crossing the boundaries between the departments.

Grapevine originates from the psychological need of the employees to talk about their jobs and their associates as the subjects of their main interest. The absence of grapevine surely creates the dull, sick and unfriendly atmosphere in the organisation. Grapevine is also described as the barometer of public opinion in the organisation. If the manager is sensitive to it, he can gather information about the ideas, opinions, attitudes and interests of the employees.

The grapevine gives an opportunity to the employees to let off the suppressed air of anxiety, worries and frustration. When they talk about their associates, they get emotional relief. The fact that the employees talk about their associates or that they have the interest in their associates is a proof of the high morale. Thus, the grapevine not only promotes unity, integrity and solidarity of the organisation but it also helps to raise the morale of the employees.

Limitations of Grapevine

1. The grapevine may carry some degree of error in it.
2. The baseless, imaginary and non-factual messages may prove harmful to the organisation.
3. Often the grapevine is fed with self-serving information by the employees. They add to the facts rather than simply report.
4. The grapevine often carries incomplete information which leads to misunderstanding of the receiver.
5. The communicator does not take the responsibility of the message.
6. Sometimes the grapevine spreads the message so swiftly that it causes damage to the organisation.

How to use the Grapevine

The management can use grapevine to supplement the formal channels of communication. Though it carries some degree of error and distortion, efforts can be made to correct it. Ignoring the grapevine is nothing but to ignore a valuable source of communication. The management can eliminate its negative consequences and, at the same time, it can nourish its positive benefits. The managers have to learn to manage and control it.

(i) The management can open up all the channels of organisational communication to present the facts positively before the employees and thereby can fight the negative messages with the positive weapons of facts and figures.
(ii) Better job design and better quality of worklife can easily bring the grapevine under the control of the management.
(iii) It also prevents the boredom, idleness and suspicions among the employees.
(iv) The negative consequences of the grapevine can be easily eliminated if the management is successful in creating trust-relationship with the employees.
(v) The rumours flourish beyond limits when the employees are

not well informed by the management regarding the policies, objectives and the work procedures of the organisation. The inadequate access to information and the feeling of insecurity are the reasons behind the negative outcomes of the grapevines. The managers must give their employees an adequate access to information and the feeling of security.

(vi) The rumours spread when the situations are unpredictable, unstructured, unplanned and are beyond the control of a person or the persons who are involved in them. Therefore, the best way to manage and control it is to provide accurate and substantial information of the situations to the employees.

The managers should pick up the false rumours and dispel them by providing correct information.

(vii) Before taking any decision or action, the managers must consider its possible effects on the informal groups and systems in the organisation.

viii. The management can use the grapevine as a barometer of the public opinions in the organisation or to feel the pulse of the employees in a particular situation. This will surely help them to take right policy decisions.

(ix) In the formal activities of the organisation, the management should avoid threatening the informal groups which are responsible in spreading the grapevine effectively.

(x) The management should find out the people in the informal groups who are more active on grapevine. These people should be accurately and adequately informed so that the false rumours causing excitement and insecurity do not spread among the employees.

(xi) The management should remember that the workplace community is maintained not only by the work itself but also by the informal human relationships. Therefore, the manager should honestly try to integrate their interests with those of the informal groups.

CONSENSUS

But in every matter, the consensus of opinion among all nations is to be regarded as the law of nature.

– Cicero

What is Consensus

The concept of consensus has become quite familiar and desirable means of informal communication not only in the political fields but also in the commercial spheres as well. It is a common agreement of opinion on a given problem among the majority of people in a group or community. The board meeting of commercial organisations take certain decisions through consensus. Sometimes, merely a copy of resolution is circulated among the members of a particular group to get their approval. When the decisions are taken unanimously, the unity and informity of the group is recognised. It projects a good image of the business house and the status of the organisation is raised. It also suggests high morale of the management to the employees, customers, shareholders and other people. Consensus does not mean that there exists no opposite views among the members of the group. Of course, perfect unanimity should not be expected because it cannot exist. As consensus does not imply perfect unanimity, it implies that the majority of people express a particular view which is accepted as the consensus by all the members including those who actually oppose it. The dissent of the opposition is sacrificed in the interests of the harmony among the members or in the larger interests of the organisation.

The consensus is sought through consultation. The problem is presented before the board meeting by the chief of the management in the form of the proposal or resolution. The problem is analysed and some additional information regarding it is also collected. The chief listens to the divergent views and opinions of the members. He tries to discuss the issue with every individual member. As last, he is confirmed about the solution which is most likely to be accepted by the majority.

Significance of Consensus

(i) The consensus communication projects a good image of the management.

(ii) The essential image of the management presented through consensus strengthens the confidence of the employees in their superiors.

(iii) There can be little or no chance for conflict among the employees because the instructions issued by the directors never conflict with each other.

(iv) The consensus is always based on the attitude of mutual respect which enables the members to accept and support the views of each other.

(v) The decisions of consensus are promptly accepted by the members because they are derived after mutual consultations.

(vi) The process of consensus ultimately leads to an unquestioning acceptance of the authority of the chief.

(vii) The trust of the members in their chief helps to avoid the splits and conflicts between the majority and the opposition.

Limitations of Consensus

(i) While the superiors receptively listen to the ideas of the subordinates, the latter sometimes undermine the authority of the superiors.

(ii) The dissents are never encouraged. The views and opinions of the minority opposition are not attended.

(iii) A member of the group can be forced to accept the view which he does not hold.

(iv) A member who is accustomed to being consulted may misunderstand the chief if the latter fails to consult him on some occasions.

Exercises

1. Explain the need of external and internal communication in business organisations.
2. What is meant by 'channel of communication'? How does it run along with hierarchical line of authority?
3. What is downward communication? What are the main objectives of downward communication? What are the limitations of downward communication? What are the written and oral means of downward communication?
4. What are the essentials of effective downward communication? Why should the lines of downward communication be kept as short as possible?
5. Describe the importance of upward communication in business organisation. Why is upward communication considered very useful and very difficult?

6. What are the methods of upward communication? How can we increase the effectiveness of upward communication?
7. What are the merits and short-comings of Horizontal communication?
8. What is the significance of informal communication in the business organisations?
9. What are the characteristics of Grapevine? How does it operate in business organisation?
10. What is the significance of Grapevine in business communication? What are its demerits?
11. How can the Grapevine be used for the benefit of the business organisation?
12. What is the significance of consensus process in business communication?
13. Why does a business organisation need multiple channels of communication?
14. Write a detailed note on vertical or two-way communication
15. Write short-notes on the following:

    (i) Open-door policy
    (ii) Lines of communication
    (iii) Informal channel of communication
    (iv) Three dimensions of communication
    (v) Diagonal or Lateral communication.

A. Oral Media
   (1) Meaning and Importance of Oral Media
   (2) Effective Oral Communication
   (3) Advantages of Oral Communication
   (4) Disadvantages of Oral Communication

B. Written Media
   (1) Increasing Specialisation and the Need of Written Media
   (2) The Art of Written Communication
   (3) Advantages of Written Media
   (4) Limitations of Written Media

C. Non-Verbal Media
   (1) Meaning and Importance of Non-verbal Media
   (2) Kinesic Media
   (3) Proxemics
   (4) Chronemics
   (5) Paralanguage
   (6) Artefacts

4

MEDIA OF COMMUNICATION

ORAL MEDIA

> Stop lying to each other; tell the truth, for we are parts of each other and when we lie to each other, we are hurting ourselves.
>
> – The *Holy Bible*, Ephesians 5:25

Meaning and Importance of Oral Media

Our spoken words have greater power than that of the sword taken out of the scabbard. The speeches given by Voltaire and Montesque gave birth to the world famous French Revolution. The words can encourage the people to take over and complete the tasks beyond their ability. On the other hand, the worlds can dis-spirit and discourage the people from doing even their routine jobs. Oral communication is vital to human relationships in every business organisation as well as in any other social organisation. The employees disclose their feelings to one another, they exchange their views and share each other's knowledge and experiences. Of course, there are many people who do not go about belabouring the world with their personal thoughts, feelings and ideas. But, as even the verbal battles are useful when they serve to clarify certain messages, there is no need to speak about the importance of talking out the differences by breaking the barriers of silence. We talk with other people for many purposes. We may talk in order to escape boredom, to get acquainted with a newcomer, to warn the subordinate about his misbehaviour, to suggest novel ideas to the superior, to instruct the workers, and for a number of other purposes. Much of the professional and business communication through oral media takes place between two people. The success of the business organisation depends to a large extent on managing the formal and informal oral communication between two persons. It is due to this fact, much face-to-face business communication takes place between two persons. The time factor and other difficulties that come in the way of arranging for a small group of busy people to take part in a meeting is also an important reasons behind giving stress on the oral communication between two people. Let us sum up the significance of the oral media in the words of Sir Walter Raleigh:

> According to Solomon, life and death are in the powers of the tongue; and as Euripides truly affirmth every unbridled tongue in the end shall find itself unfortunate; in all that ever I observed I ever found that men's fortunes are oftener made by their tongues than by their virtues, and more men's fortunes overthrown thereby also them by their vices.

Effective Oral Communication

Pronounciation

All the language units must be pronounced properly and clearly. The message cannot be intelligible without proper articulation of sounds. Sometimes, it happens that a person who is able to articulate a sound properly is unable to pronounce the words correctly. The words in English language must be stressed on the exact syllables.

Clarity, Conciseness and Completeness

It is essential that the message should be brief and concise, but complete in every respect. The brevity should not be achieved at the cost of clarity and completeness. Too much talking may lead to misunderstanding and overcommunication, but too little talking can lead to partial understanding and undercommunication.

Vocabulary

The communicator must have a good vocabulary. He should use choicest words to convey correct meaning. If the person who communicates orally has inadequate vocabulary, the listener will receive incorrect and confused meaning.

Self-Confidence

If the communicator lacks self-confidence, it is likely that he will not be able to impress the message on the listener. He must have a sufficient knowledge of the subject on which he has to talk. Secondly, he must plan his message carefully before imparting it to the receiver. The logical sequence of various ideas in the message is an outcome of organising and planning the message. Adequate planning, preparation and organisation of the message helps the speaker to raise his morale and self-confidence.

Variations in the Intonation Patterns

There are three intonation patterns, viz. (1) rising pitch, (2) falling pitch, and (3) dividing pitch. It is essential to use the correct pitch of sound. The variations in the pitch sounds can help the speaker to create interest and hold the attention of the listeners.

Tone and Style

The message must make appeal not only to the intellect but also to the heart of the listener. The words impart the intended meaning when they are spoken with the tone and style that suit the occasion. The 'tone' of the voice gives the listener an idea about the 'feeling' associated with the words.

Advantages of Oral Communication

Adjustment of Message

The speaker gets immediate feedback from the receiver which helps him to find out how he receives the message and how he reacts to it. The immediate feedback not only lets the communicator to know the kind of response from the receiver but it also helps him to modify his message in such a way that it becomes readily and favourably acceptable to the receiver.

Immediate Clarifications

The communicator can clarify certain ideals in his message which are not properly understood by the receiver or which might leave some doubts in his mind. These doubts or the queries (in the mind) of the receiver arise from the defective message and these are communicated to the receiver in the form of feedback.

Time

Oral messages can be transmitted through telephone almost immediately whereas the written message take more time to reach up to the receiver by post. The written message takes comparatively longer time because it may require consulting, dictating, drafting, typing, posting, etc., which the oral transmission does not require. When immediate action is required, the oral communication is the best media.

Persuasion and Control

The speaker can judge the replies of the other party and can change his arguments in such a way that thereby he can influence the attitudes, feelings, opinions and beliefs of the receivers. The oral directives and instructions are effective in controlling the employees and the situations in order to ensure the fulfilment of the objectives.

Formality

Oral communication is less formal than the written communication. Informal talks can help in building friendships and personal relations between the communicator and the receiver.

Cost

Oral communication is not as costly a process as that of the written correspondence, especially when the message is to be communicated within the organisation.

Group Communication

Oral communication is a convenient and reliable media for communicating in committees, conferences and meetings where a number of people come together for discussion.

Disadvantages of Oral Communication

Future Reference

The oral message cannot be referred back in future if they are not tape-recorded. As compared to written messages, oral messages do not constitute permanent record. Therefore, it has little or no value for legal procedures. It cannot become legal evidence in case of future disputes or law-suits.

Speaker's Preparedness

Oral communication cannot be good and effective if the communicator is not a good speaker. He requires to be lively, enthusiastic, vital, earnest and keenly interested in the subject.

Lengthy Message

Oral communication is not a suitable media for any lengthy official message that constitutes minute details.

Distortion

The oral message is more likely to be received in a distorted meaning by the receiver due to his misunderstanding and misinterpretation of it. It is found that people tend to have trouble in recalling correctly the main ideas and the factual details which are communicated to them orally.

Retaining the Message

It is found that people tend to have trouble in recalling correctly and completely the main ideas of the factual details which are communicated to them orally. Due to imbalanced mental state of the listener or due to the listening barriers, the receiver may not understand the message completely and he may even forget the major part of the message after a long time.

WRITTEN MEDIA

> Reading maketh a full man, conference a ready man; and writing an exact man.
>
> – Bacon, *Essays*, "Of Studies"

Increasing Specialisation and the Need of Written Media

The old-style business entrepreneurs were not particularly concerned with labour relations, advertising, quality control, income taxes, sales taxes, engineering, technology and many other aspects of modern business. They would converse with their employees almost daily and instruct them regarding the job requirements. The number of the employees working in the business houses of those days was relatively less as compared to that of the today's large business organisations. They could easily inspect, direct and judge the work of the employees. But today, the business houses require a team of specialists and each of them is trained, experienced and most qualified person to carry out his specific assignment. They may be research people, purchasing agents, scientists, technicians, personnel people, sales executives, accountants, psycho-analysts, tax consultants, traffic experts, physicians, etc. These specialists and experts have to communicate their ideas to one another and also to the management. They assist the management in decision-making process. Their findings, advice and instructions are vital to business success. This flow of information which helps to operate the business is necessary to be maintained through written media because of the mounting complexity of business activities. The written media is like the human sensory organs and memory power which receives, analyses and records the information for the purpose of decision-making in future. Especially, the written reports are like the memory of the business. The management scrutinises the information, acts on some part of it and stores up the remaining of it for future reference.

Written media helps to coordinate the knowledge and work of the staff specialists and the research specialists. The increasing research activities in every phase of business and the development of large organisational structures has made written media almost indispensable in every business house. The management has developed itself as a professional occupation. They need accurate written information to carry out their managerial duties related to different business and professional activities, which can be summed up under the following heads:

> Sales, quality-control, accounting, purchase, wages and salary, complaints, machinery, production, absenteeism, company

relations, supplying agencies, raw material storage, overtime, retirements, shipments, transportation, appraisal and assessment of the employees' work, education and training of the employees, advertising, grievances and adjustments, disciplinary actions, credit, finance, tradé union relations, sales, reports, market surveys, requirement of new branches or plants, material handling, packing, customer study, compensations, productivity, motivation of the employees and customers, product analysis, business research, etc.

The Art of Written Communication

A communicator who aspires to get mastery over the techniques of written communication, must keep his writing tools in enough of work and practice. The action-oriented people may have the ability to get the things done, but they may find it difficult to put their thoughts in written words, because they occupy themselves in their selected activities rather than in the practice of writing. He may have the ability to think logically and clearly and he may express his thinking through oral media. He may organise, analyse and evaluate the ideas of his own and those of others also, and he may really deserve to acquire the mastery of written media, but he would certainly require some of his devotion, time and practice to acquire it.

Everybody possesses the tools of the written media, but they have to learn to make effective use of their priceless possession. The tools of written media are used by all the individuals in the field of business, industry, science, education. These tools of written media are as follows:

(a) Memory,
(b) Imaginative power,
(c) Power of observation and study,
(d) Units of language like words, phrases, sentences, etc.
(e) Ability of thinking,
(f) Ability of collect and analyse the information, and
(g) Ability of writing.

A good writer is an artist who knows how to write a specific message effectively by making use of the above mentioned tools. He must keep his tools in good working order. It usually takes years of struggle and hardwork to learn and master the art of writing.

A wide and vast storehouse of information is the capital of writers' trade. It gives them the depth, perspective, balance and insight into the subject matter. He should always be alert to all the sources of information, which are related to his selected field of knowledge. He should also read widely the literature, which does not belong to his limited field of specialisation. For example, a manager must know broadly the socio-economic trends, problems and changes; the labour problems, government regulations, taxation, changes in politics, etc. Good reading indirectly helps to improve the skill of writing. A good writer can judge and evaluate the written message with ease and accuracy.

Besides reading, the business correspondent or the reporter should try to find a world of information with an inquiring mind and discerning eye. He can learn a great deal by asking some questions to the workmen performing an operation. They can give a piece of practical solution to your problem. Some of the basic problems that confront the business and industry can be understood when one tries to do things for himself and works with his own hands. The main purpose of written communication is to move, motivate and mould the minds and behaviour of the people in the organisation. It is necessary for the communicator to study the people with whom he works. Finally, he should know the history, policies, procedures, hierarchy, regulations and customs of the company in which he works. It must be remembered that the art and skill of writing depends on the competence and knowledge of the communicator. Besides all this, the communicator should prevent his feelings from dictating his thinking and should organise his thoughts which are based on factual information.

Advantages of Written Media

Permanent Record for Reference

Written message can be kept in files as a permanent record of the general. affairs, transactions and agreements of the business organisation. It remains as an evidence of the company's performance which is useful for future reference. It forms a basis for new policy decisions and also for the fresh measures for the development and expansion of the business.

Legal Evidence

Written message provides tangible evidence of the agreements signed between the two parties. It also gives a proof of the stages in which the transaction was carried out. It can show how the mistakes were committed in carrying out the transactions by either of the parties involved in it.

Accuracy

Usually, the written messages are organised more carefully than the spoken messages. The communicator uses standard language and tries to avoid colloquial words and expressions. As compared to oral messages, the written massages are more accurate in grammatical structures. Accuracy in language helps to prevent any misunderstanding or misinterpretation of the message.

Lengthy and Complicated Messages

Written media is especially more suited for lengthy and complicated messages. The receiver can read it repeatedly till he properly understands it. Secondly, it assures retaining every vital detail of the lengthy and complicated message.

Correspondence

Postal correspondence has given a really wide access to written media. This facility is available to almost all the communicators and receivers in the nooks and corners of the world.

Limitations of Written Media

Access to Literates

The access of the written media is limited to the literates only. There are millions of illiterate people who cannot use this media.

A Costly and Time-Consuming Process

In an organisation, a number of people get involved in the process of collecting information, consulting, drafting, typing and posting the messages. It takes the total cost of a business letter to not less than thirty rupees. Secondly, the oral message reaches almost instantaneously on the telephone, whereas a letter may reach to the receiver after 2/3 days.

Formalism

Usually, the written communication is more formal, and rigid than the oral communication.

Delayed Feedback

The communicator has to wait for the reply from the receiver. In oral communication, the feedback is almost immediate.

NON-VERBAL MEDIA

Meaning and Importance of Non-verbal Media

Verbal media can be used to communicate almost any thought, feeling or idea, but the non-verbal media has comparatively very limited range. Especially, it communicates feelings of likings and dislikings and reinforces the feelings expressed through verbal media. Occasionally, it contradicts those feelings which are expressed verbally by the communicator.

There are five major forms of non-verbal media like, spatial, kinesic, chronemic, paralingual and artifactual.

1. Proxemics (spatial)
2. Kinesics
   - Facial expressions,
   - Postures,
   - Body movements,
   - Gestures,
   - Eye contact
   - Haptics
3. Chronemics (temporal)
4. Paralingual (vocal cues)

5. Artifacts (objective language).

These different forms of non-verbal media help us to judge different degrees of feelings and also the contradictory kinds of feelings, which contradict the verbal message of the communicator.

Charlie Chaplin, Harold Lloyd, Harry Langdon, Buster Keaton reached the non-verbal communication media to almost perfection in their silent movies. Though each of these silent comedians had their own style of wordless communication, they were all able to communicate the complete sequence of human behaviour along with the isolated ideas. The managements and the employees may not be as well-skilled in silent, wordless or non-verbal communication as these actors, but much of the communication which affect their behaviour in the organisation is never verbalised. They transmit their messages by their movements like a smile, frown, handshake, etc. The non-verbal media is the most suitable means for the expression of the emotional messages. The manager's view regarding the suggestions of the employees become more clear by this attention and actions rather than by his words of encouragement for dropping the suggestions. The employees are motivated more by the manager's actions than by his words. Jurgen Rhesch and Weldon Kees say that we communicate non-verbal messages in three languages; sign language, action language and object language. Sign language is deliberately used to replace words, numbers or punctuation marks by the gestures. Action language includes all the movements which we do not use exclusively as signals, i.e. walking, running, eating, etc. Most of these actions are intentional non-verbal stimuli. Object language can be either intentional or non-intentional display of material things, i.e. clothing, jewellery, art objects. All these non-verbal languages help the communicator to talk without words. They give us the cues for interpreting human behaviour, cues for transmitting messages and the clue about intentions, emotions, views, social status and personalities of the people.

Often we spend a great deal of time in organising verbal messages. It indicates that effective oral or written communication requires conscious efforts. We spend years together in learning how to read, write and speak. Non-verbal communication does not require that much conscious learning efforts. It is usually learnt by imitation. It also happens that many people are often unaware of their own non-verbal communication behaviour. Silence is a form of non-verbal communication which usually goes unnoticed. Manager's silence over the achievements and hardwork of an employee makes the latter feel discouraged.

Kinesic Media

(a) Facial expression,
(b) Posture,
(c) Body movements,
(d) Gestures,
(e) Eye-contact,
(f) Haptics.

Facial Expression

Face is the best non-verbal conveyor of the messages among all the other non-verbal aspects of kinesic importance, there are four component parts of the face, which are capable of independent movements. These movements produce a number of signals that carry a variety of messages. We can look into the face of a person to know his real sentiments and reactions. One cannot command the expressions on his face as one can command his language.

Face can be divided into four parts: (i) upper face, which includes eyebrows and forehead; (ii) middle face, which includes the eyes, eyelids and foot of the nose; (iii) the lower face, which includes mouth and chin; and (iv) the sides of the face including cheeks. Facial expressions can communicate happiness, anger, surprise, embarrassment, boredom, fear, sadness, disgust, apology, favour, liking or disliking, etc. Sometimes different facial features require coordination in order to convey some message. Human face is so mobile that we unconsciously and effortlessly convey love, affection, sympathy, anger, boredom, disapproval, or surprise. All this is possible because of the proper coordination of the facial features. A smile at the lips is reinforced by smiling eyes. Half-raised eyebrows indicate worry. Half-closed eyes indicate boredom. An up-curved mouth indicates happiness and a down-curved mouth indicates unhappiness. But the eyebrows, eyes, cheeks, lips, etc., indicate a particular emotion through their simultaneous collective movements. In 'the expression of Emotions in Man and Animals', Charles Darwin says that most of the human expression actions are instinctive and not learned. Darwin further argues that even those born-blind children blush from shame. The facial movements are instinctive, spontaneous and are, to a large extent, beyond our control.

Posture

Posture gives us an idea about the attitude of the bearer towards the other persons involved in the process of communication. A good deal of relaxation in posture indicate disrespect, dislike and disinterest in the other person. A less relaxed posture indicates respect and linking for him. Generally, posture indicate superiority, fear, aggressiveness, confidence, rejection and anxiety. Anxiety, fear and lack of confidence is indicated by the total lack of relaxation in the posture. Superiority, higher status, confidence and even aggressiveness are generally indicated by a relaxed posture. For example, a man who sits expansively and stretches out his legs in front indicates that he is confident. There are some postures like looking down, slouching, bending head or biting one's nails, etc., which reveal anxiety, nervousness and the feeling of insecurity in the person. There are postures like forward leaning of the body or possible touching the other person which usually indicate nearness, intimacy, affection and other positive feelings, towards the other person. We can communicate many moods through postures. Hunching shoulders and keeping head down can be one's way of telling others to leave him alone. Crossing arms may indicate that one is not ready to accept what the other is saying. The effect of impressive clothing, good grooming and other items of dressing is lost when one is not careful enough about proper posture. The traits of character or personality are also revealed by the postures. One is supposed to be lazy if he sprawls when sits. Resting all your weight on your one leg while standing indicates that you are tired. But the postures do not tell the whole story. A man standing and resting his weight on one leg may not be tired and exhausted but such is the impression that his posture gives. A man who sprawls in the chair may not be lazy but such is the impression derived from his posture. A man standing tall, erect and straight may be tired and even exhausted, but he seems to be enthusiastic, self-confident and prepared to do something.

Body Movements

The individual tends to increase his body movements as the intensity of a particular emotion in him increases.

Gestures

The individual tends to increase his body movements as the intensity of a particular emotion increases in him. Every man or a woman is enabled to do a variety of works through his or her flexible hands. Flexibility of the human body and especially that of our hands is very useful in communicating a wide range of gestures. People can communicate their moods and 'talk' loudly with the movements of their hands. Sometimes, hand gestures can be substituted for the verbal communication. For example, one can give an order to another person to leave the room immediately solely by means of hand.

The hand gestures also play a significant role of supplementing the verbal message of the speaker. An unexperienced public speaker often does not understand the way of using hand-gestures effectively. He seems to ignore those two arms attached to his shoulders. He pays very little attention to them, because he feels very awkward with them. He tries to hide them by putting them both behind his back. He does so merely because he is just ignorant about its use in communicating gestures. Sometimes, he tries to hide his useless hands in his pockets or folds them over his chest. Gradually, he comes to know that the hand gestures are not only supplementary to the verbal messages but they can also be the substitutes for written or oral media. A system of hand-signals used to communicate the messages to the deaf-mutes is so comprehensive that it is literally a substitute for the spoken language.

The hand signals used in that system are as arbitrary and conventional as those used in our verbal languages. The words which are used as the linguistic signals are culturally determined and they do not have meanings but they represent the culturally accepted meanings. Similarly, the hand signals or gestures represent the culturally attached meanings and they carry different messages in different cultures.

It is possible to feel confident in using the gestures by practicing them at home in front of a mirror. We can learn to move out hands to express the ideas with suitable gestures. While practising gestures in front of the mirror, the movement of the entire arm up to the tips of the figures must be ensured. It is also essential to verify which gestures add to the meaning and which gestures distract and divert the meaning of the message. The movements of the entire body like stepping forward, pulling backward, crouching, hunching shoulders, turning on one side or another, etc., are the body gestures, which suggest non-verbal message of certain mood or feeling. The managers should observe the gestures of the people in the organisation. He also needs to observe how well the gesture clusters fit in with facial expressions and verbal messages.

Eye-Contact

> The eye speaks with an eloquence and truthfulness — surpassing speech. It is the window out of which the winged thoughts often fly unwittingly. It is the tiny magic mirror on whose crystal surface the moods of feelings fitfully play like the sunlight and shadow on a quiet stream.
>
> – Henry Theodore Tuckerman

The area around the eyes is one of the most expressive part of the face. The eyes hold the place of most significance among all the body expressions. Eye-contact gives us the cues to reveal a good deal of truth about the traits of someone's personality. Probing into the individual's eyes helps us to guess his mood. For effective management, the insights about effective eye-contact are essential. A research study in the role of eye contact in communication has found that we spend about 45 per cent of the time in eye contact with others during groups discussions, though twenty per cent of the eye contacts last only about a second. Some insights about eye-contact are as follows:

1. A looker's frank gaze can be interpreted as his positive attitude towards the other person.
2. Repeated mutual eye contacts indicates friendship, love and intimacy.
3. Generally, eye contacts are interpreted as the signs of honesty, confidence, interest, openness and friendship.
4. The embarrassed or nervous people try to avoid eye contact.
5. Seldom, avoiding eye contact indicates dishonest and deception.
6. Those who seek eye contact are usually well-disposed towards the other.

7. It is easier to maintain eye contact at public distance than at closer range.
8. Usually the persons who seeks eye contact are regarded as more believable, trustworthy and earnest.
9. Speakers, especially the teachers, tend to believe those who look at them as being sincere to their purpose than those who do not care to look at them.
10. If the short and intermittent gazes are replaced by constant and longer gazes during conversation, the receiver tends to perceive that the assigned work is less important than the personal relations between the communicator and the receiver.
11. A constant gaze or staring at another person can be interpreted as an invitation for interaction.
12. To avert the eyes of the looker is interpreted as a rejection of the looker's invitation for interaction.
13. Negative or poor eye contact of the audience results in poor performance of the speaker.
14. Eye-contact have a number of different cultural associations in different countries.

Haptics (Touch)

The observation of physical contact gives revealing cues of non-verbal messages. Haptics is the study of how physical contact or touch is used to communicate the ideas and feelings. The Americans interprete positive or negative feelings from the quality of the touch through a shakehand. A *limp* shakehand indicates lack of interest or friendship for them.

Proxemics

The term 'proxemics' refers to the study of how we use space to communicate message. Halt Edward describes human relationship in terms of four kinds of distances:

- intimate,
- personal,
- social,
- public.

Intimate distance of six inches or less lends itself to non-verbal communication and the subject discussed between the two persons involved in communication is usually some top secret. The intimate distance of six to eighteen inches is used to discuss the confidential matters. Personal distance, ranging from 1.5 to 4 feet is a distance for close relationship and friendship. Social distance ranges from four to twelve feet. It is a suitable distance for business discussions or meetings in business office or conference room. Public distance ranging from twelve feet or more is suitable for public meetings.

The way people communicate with one another depends upon the proxemics of where the people are in relation to one another. If the chairman of the conference is the employer and the other participants are his employees, he keeps some distance from the participants in order to indicate the status different between them. The observation of the way people sit at a meeting can reveal a good deal of secrets about who likes whom and who is competing with whom for position, profit or influence. Participants leaning backward or forward in the chair or his turning and pulling away from the speaker indicates his acceptance or rejection.

The distance maintained between people during communication in houses, offices and elsewhere throw light on their relationships. The appropriate distance between a communicator and a receiver depends upon the communication situation. The appropriate distance for communicating with colleagues need not be the same as the appropriate distance for talking with the superior. The structure and use of space conveys a non-verbal message for itself. The authority, powers, position and status can be indicated by the location of the office and its furnishing. The space speaks also when individuals come physically closer or maintain distance between them. They move closer with those whom they like and maintain distance from those whom they dislike. A greater distance is usually maintained from the people with high status.

Chronemics (Use of Time)

The use of time is an important non-verbal element, which is also known as chronemics. Time can be considered as a commodity that can be saved, wasted, earned or spent. Chronemics is concerned with out study of how human beings communicate through their use of time. Almost everyone is usually sensitive and concerned about his use of time. In business world, time is money for everybody and every successful businessman seems to be very time conscious.

Delay in replying to a personal or business letter; a phone call early in the morning, late entrance at a committee meeting; meeting of a friend after long interval; and innumerable other examples of this kind communicate certain non-verbal messages. Use of the watches or time clocks throughout the working hours; agendas, setting completion dates for projects and allotted work, time scheduling, etc., show the importance of time in business organisations. Completing the work of a project within a specific recommended time communicates sincerity, hardwork, loyalty and reliability; whereas frequent late coming and absenteeism may communicate unreliability, laziness and disinterestedness of the employee. The conception of time and its associations vary from culture to culture. Indian host may politely invite the American or British guest to come at any time to his home. But the European guests would misinterpret this "any time". They might believe that the Indian host does not expect them to visit. They may not pay a visit to the house of the Indian unless he states a specific time for the visit. Most of the non-verbal communication by the chronemics depends on 'late' or 'early' arrival time and departure time. A participant arriving late for a meeting of the executive committee may communicate disinterest and lack of respect for the Chairman and other committee members. If he arrives ahead of time for the meeting, it may communicate interest and respect for the Chairman and committee members. The employees are never expected to arrive late for an appointment with the employer.

Paralanguage

Paralanguage refers to something in addition to language itself. It distinguishes the verbal message from the vocal message. It makes distinction between what is said and how it is said. But it is concerned with how something is said rather than what is verbally said. Paralinguist studies the voice qualities such as intonation pattern, pitch stress, intensity, range, rhythm, tempo, articulation control, resonance and some vocalisations such as sighing, yelling, yawning, laughing, grunting, crying, giggling, etc. The study of vocalisations and voice qualities gives us the vocal cues which differentiate emotions and gives us an idea of the speaker's social standing and personality traits. Every human being possesses a distinctive and unique contribution of voice qualities. A combination of paralinguistic vocal characteristics help many people to make some judgement about the personality of another person, which, in some cases, turns out to be accurate and reliable . Deep-throaty voice of men indicate sophisticated and mature personality. But the same throaty voices in women indicate boring and ugly personality. Nasal voices indicate nagging and unpleasant personality in men and women. Breathy and high-pitched voices indicate pretty and feminine qualities whereas the breathy voice of a man may indicate his unmanly personality. Flat monotonous voice indicates the personality of the man who lacks interest in life.

Artifacts

> All that is good in art is the expression of one soul speaking to another, and is precious according to the greatness of the soul that utters it.
>
> – Ruskin

Artifacts refer to the object language which can either be intentional or non-intentional display of material things. Artifact means any article which is made by employing skill or craft. The artifacts include tools, implements, ornaments, utensils, religious objects, clothes, folk material and other art objects. They communicate the owner's cultural economic and social background as well as the style and standard of his living.

Exercises

(1) What is meant by 'media of communication'? How can the media of communication be classified? Described the scope of the classified media.
(2) Explain the need of — (a) Written media, (b) Oral media, (c) Visual media and (d) Audio-visual media in business communication.
(3) What are the forms of written media? What are the merits and limitations of written media?
(4) What are the essentials of effective written communication?
(5) Show how oral communication differs from the face-to-face communication.

(6) Discuss the merits and limitations of oral communication.

(7) Show how to overcome the defects of oral communication. What are the essentials of effective oral communication?

(8) Briefly discuss the working and utility of face-to-face communication in business organisation.

(9) What are the forms of visual communication? How are these forms useful in business communication?

(10) What are the forms of audio-visual communication? How are these forms useful in business communication?

(11) Compare and contrast the relative merits and limitations of oral media and written media.

(12) Why does a businessman make use of a combination of the various media of communication?

A. Introduction

B. Language and Semantic Barriers

(1) Lack of Common Language

(2) Semantic Barriers

(3) Poor Vocabulary

(4) Poor Know-how of Grammar and Punctuation

(5) Round about Verbiage

C. Organisational Barriers

(1) Hierarchical Barriers

(2) Specialisation of the workforce

(3) Wrong Choice of Medium

(4) Communication Load

D. Physical Barriers

(1) Noise

(2) Time

(3) Distance

(4) Age

(5) Sex

E. Socio-Psychological Barriers

(1) Status Barriers

(2) Attitudes and Values

(3) Different Perceptions of Reality

(4) Inference

(5) Abstracting

(6) Allness and Closed-mindedness

(7) Distortion, Filtering and Editing

(8) Post Experience

(9) Bad Listening

(10) Emotions

(11) Halo Effect

(12) Inattentiveness

(13) Resistance to Change

5

BARRIERS TO COMMUNICATION

INTRODUCTION

If one has to become a consistently successful business communicator, one has to develop his ability and skills of doing so effectively. But, his planning, preparation and practice of communication will be incomplete and unsuccessful unless he identifies and understands the barriers to communication. These barriers are physical, sociological and psychological obstacles that interfere with the planning, organisation, transmission and understanding of the message. There are a number of such obstacles that can occur in the process of communication. The natural result of such obstacles or interfering factors is the misunderstanding of the message.

These factors interfere with the self-confidence, self-disclosure and self-consciousness of the communication senders and receivers. The managers must contend with these barriers. They have to use communication in the managerial functions of planning, organising, staffing, monitoring and controlling. The barriers to communication are dangers to any business organisation if they are not removed in time.

When the communicator transmits the idea in an unchanged and undistorted form to the receiver and the receiver responds to it, then, the process of the communication is supposed to have been perfect. But this process of 'perfect' communication can never exist due to the number of factors which stand in its way as the barriers. The communicator has to identify and understand the reasons for poor communication in order to communicate effectively. Unless he knows the ailments he cannot seek the remedies. Understanding the process of communication is the first step towards improving the abilities and skills of communication; but understanding the factors that prevent us in transmitting the exact meaning is very essential for effective communication. The executives may spend ninety per cent of their time in communication but a substantial part of their message is misinterpreted and misunderstood. In large-size complex business organisations, messages get lost before they reach the receiver. The messages get distorted by the sender himself or by someone who carries the message or by the receiver or by the external environmental factors. There are lots of ways to go wrong and to misunderstand the messages, but attempts must be made to remedy the situation.

LANGUAGE AND SEMANTIC BARRIERS

Lack of Common Language

Language uses oral or written arbitrary symbols to transmit meanings from one person to another. Every human language has its own vocal symbol system and its own grammatical structures. If the communicator and the receiver belong to different language groups, their ignorance of each other's language or the lack of a common language will be a barrier to communication between them. It is not possible for them to communicate with each other unless they know some common language which is properly understood by both of them. An English speaking boss and a Tamil speaking worker will not be able to communicate without a good knowledge of each other's language. If both of them known a common language, say Hindi, their knowledge of Hindi word, inflections, phrases, clauses and sentence-structure should be adequate to express their thoughts and feelings.

Semantic Barriers

Words are said to have no meaning but they represent arbitrary meaning associated with it. A word may have a variety of meanings and the meaning attributed to a word by the communicator may not be the same as that of the receiver's attributed meanings of that word. A word can have different meaning to different people at different occasions. It is found by the experts that people attributes 14,000 different meanings to 500 commonly used English words. Therefore, the sender and receiver are many a times likely to attribute different meaning to the same word. Sometimes, they may use different words to communicate the same meaning. There are many words in English such as light, cheap, etc. which can be used with favourable as well as unfavourable connotations. A word can stand for its positive or negative connotations. Sometimes, the intended meaning of the sender's word is wrongly entered by the receiver by attributing negative meaning to it.

Poor Vocabulary

Poor vocabulary makes our message more difficult and less effective. Our pen falters and tongue fumbles when we probe into our brain for a suitable word or phrase. The words have different connotative and denotative meanings. The communicator needs to know them clearly in order to use them with clarity and precision. Words stand not only for their meanings but they are also charged with action and emotions. When the communicator and the receiver understand these word-associations, they are capable of using them as living entities. Poor vocabulary does not allow the communicator to write or speak effectively. It does not allow the receiver to understand the message clearly and completely. If the receiver does not understand the words, the sentences cannot be properly comprehended by him.

Poor Knowhow of Grammar and Punctuation

Poor knowledge of grammar and punctuation is a barrier to verbal communication. A good vocabulary is useless unless the communicator acquires the knowledge of how to use it in a sentence. More than ever before, the job applicants, business report writers, business correspondents and all those who are involved in written and oral communications today must have superior grammar skills because an understanding of grammatical structures provide excellent basis for effective writing, speaking, listening and reading skills. If the communicator is nor able to choose the correct verb form that agrees with a given noun or pronoun; if, he is not able to use nouns and pronouns precisely to indicate who does what; if he is not able to select exact adjective or adverb; if he is not able to use conjunctions and prepositions to join words correctly, he will not be able to communicate his ideas, thoughts and feelings fully and correctly. In addition to a good grammar, a knowledge of punctuation is essential for effective communication. Many of us do not pay adequate attention to it. But it must be remembered that the faulty and improper punctuation can change the intended meaning of the sentences. The absence or misplacement of a common a period can prove misleading to the reader.

Roundabout Verbiage

Roundabout verbiage consists of the usage of overworked, troublesome and exhausted words and phrases which usually cause a considerable amount of misunderstanding and confusion. It is a long winded way of saying the meaningless padding. By avoiding such roundabout verbiage, we can add a good deal of liveliness and simplicity of expression to our written as well as oral communication. For example, instead of saying 'in the majority of cases' or 'in a number of instances', we can say 'some' or 'usually'; instead of saying 'commence', we can use 'start' or 'begin'; instead of saying 'prior to', we can say 'before'. Roundabout Verbiage should be avoided to achieve clarity and simplicity of the message. By omitting such words and phrases, we can save our message from hollow pomposity.

ORGANISATIONAL BARRIERS

Hierarchical Barriers

In an organisation, communication transmission must flow through certain formal channels which are established by the organisational hierarchy. The employees are expected to contact the superiors and the subordinates through their immediate superiors or subordinates. This often results in hardships and difficulties in maintaining free flow of communication. Some managements disapprove with the barriers of hierarchy and propose that everyone in the organisation should be free enough to communicate directly with anybody else who can help him to solve his problems.

Usually, the subordinates do not find it easy to communicate their problems to their superiors. They experience an awe of authority in communicating with their superiors. Sometimes, the upward communication is deliberately distorted and suitably edited in order to make it pleasant, palatable and acceptable to the loss. The long lines of hierarchical communication are responsible for the loss of information and also for exaggerations and understatements.

Frustration is caused among the employees when their communication is restricted to the formal channels only. They try to find the resources of the informal groups which communicate through informal channels of communication like grapevine.

Specialisation of the Workforce

In large-size complex business organisation, increasing specialisation of the workforce is posing a serious barrier to effective internal communication. The tasks are specified and the procedures are structured in such a way that the workforce can hardly come out of their compartments to communicate with the people in other functional groups. They look only at those things that need to be done by a functionalised group. Everyone of them is assigned with a special kind of job. This makes if increasingly difficult to see and coverse with the people outside one's specialisation. In such organisation, the right hand can never find access to know what the left hand is doing. So far as possible, the works of each employee is confined to a single function. But this is not always possible. Therefore, generally the people who are involved in related functions are grouped together in the form of a functional department which is headed by a common superior. This separates the group of people belonging to one department from the people belonging to other departments in the organisation.

Wrong Choice of Medium

There are many ways and devices of communication. It may be oral communication through interviews, conversations, speeches, telephone talks, conferences, radio speeches, etc. It may be face-to-face communication, written communication or non-verbal communication. All these ways or media of communication are suitable for communicating at different times and for different purposes. Therefore, it is essential to think about their relative merits and limitations, before selecting one of the media for communication. The sales manager must think over if it would be better for him to hold a face-to-face talk with the prospective buyer than talking to him on the telephone. The oral communication may be a wrong medium for the smuggler at certain occasion and he may communicate safely and quickly by flashing a torchlight as a signal.

Again, the oral media will be wrong one for a policeman who should blow his whistle or use hand gestures to stop the vehicles. Audio-visual media vehicle better to instruct the uneducated workers, especially in rural area rather than using the written media for that purpose, which is merely an audio-aid to communication. Sometimes, it is better to communicate on telephone than to write a letter but there are certain messages which are more effective if they are communicated through written media.

Communication Load

Communication load is one of the major barriers to communication. It refers to the amount and the complexity of messages received by the receiver. The increasing specialisation and complexity of the modern business world has resulted in our growing needs of boundless information. Through the astonishing variety of communication media, we are continuously bombarded with messages from morning till night. In a busy organisation, a person who is connected with all the formal and informal channels of communication, is bound to be very busy in receiving and imparting the messages rather than a person who is supposed to receive the messages through a single channel. He has to process a large amount of information. He can handle an abundance of information, provided it consists of routine and simple messages, but it is very difficult to handle the information, which is relatively more complex and unpredictable. Even communication underload can be a barrier to communication. An employee who is undercommunicated gets bored because of his uninvolvement and ultimately starts communicating with the help of gossip, rumour, chitchat, etc., which may prove harmful to the organisation.

PHYSICAL BARRIERS

Noise

It interferes with the transmission of the signals. It also refers to the 'unwanted' signals of messages which interfere and disturb the reception of the wanted signals. This disturbance is usually in the form of sounds, but it need not be always the sounds. It can be in visual, audio-visual, written, physical or psychological form also.

There are many people who communicate with a little signal and much noise. In fact, they communicate extraneous matters which may diminish the interest in the receivers or may even annoy them. Anyway, they tell the receiver something more than they are required to communicate. Their extraneous distracting signal can be the result of their wandering minds–it can be because they try to communicate something more about themselves.

Technical or physical noise refers to loud noise of the machines or blaring noise of the stereo and such other noises which makes it difficult for any listener to receive the 'wanted' message. Visual noise can be experienced when a committee member arrives late at the meeting hall and all the committee members are distracted by his arrival. Poor telephone connections which interrupt conversations, mudged typescripts and bad handwriting are some examples of the technical noise.

Time

The frequency of communication encounters affects the human relationships and the intensity of human relations is affected by the amount of time that passes between these encounters. If the employee does not communicate with his superiors for a long time, or if husband and wife stay away from each other for a long time, it may create a communication gap between them which may affect their relationship. Time can act as a barrier to communication in some other ways also. A guest who arrives at midnight will not be able to communicate well with the host who might feel embarrassed or disturbed in his sleep. Time will now allow two communicators to talk with each other if they work in different shifts. A phone call at midnight can irritate or embarrass the receiver. A husband who keeps his wife waiting for a long time will not find it easy to communicate with her.

Distance

The distance between the communicator and the receiver can be a strong barrier to communication, if the technical devices of communication such as telephone, telex, etc., are not available to link them. Faulty sitting arrangement in the office can create a kind of communication gap which can be eliminated by adjusting the distance. Distance between the workbenches in the offices or in the modern production departments and half partitions between them are the distance barriers which severely limit the communication among the employees. By minimising the physical distance down to the personal distance that ranges from 1.5 to 4 feet. The boss can minimise the status difference between himself and his employees. A friend or a colleague who ceases to maintain the personal distance, i.e. 1.5 to 4 feet, and keeps himself always beyond the distance of 12 to 25 feet is a friend who keeps communication gap.

Age

The age, maturity, educational background and the eras in which a person grows up make a generation which inevitably comes in the way of human communication. The generation gap becomes obvious in their use of vocabulary and style of speeches and the values of life to which they stick or adhere. Considering his age and maturity, we tend to apply different standards of judgement to judge the statements of the speaker. In an organisation, older workers gradually form their social groups, which often remains apart from the younger workers. Their likings and interests are different and they take less interest in sports, cocktail parties and movies. Gradually, the older workers feel socially isolated and insecure because of the widening gap of communication between the older workers and the younger workers.

Sex

Men and woman communicate with one another according to their sex. When they work together in a group, men tend to be more assertive, acquisitive, self-confident and aggressive than the women. This may be because a five year Billy is encouraged to 'hit back' by his father, but Billy's sister is told that girls 'don't fight'. Thus, sex stands as a barrier to a direct, honest and appropriate expression of a female's thoughts, opinions and beliefs. On the other hand, man is more assertive of his thoughts and opinions. It is also found that women are more likely than men to express their emotions and feelings about a situation. But, it must be remembered that these are general tendencies of sex-typed communication behaviour and not the rules. The girls tend to be less aggressive because they receive negative results such as rejection, criticism for such behaviour. They are brought up with the feeling that assertiveness is unfeminine. A girl who is brought up with such feminine conceptions about herself may try to avoid a frank eye-contact with the interviewer and may even speak in a voice that is almost inaudible.

SOCIO-PSYCHOLOGICAL BARRIERS

Status Barriers

Status is a position or social rank of a person in a group. It depends on the person's abilities, amount of pay, job-skills, seniority, type of work assigned, age, etc. When the employees are status-conscious, it becomes one of the major barriers to communication. The high-status employees within a group enjoy more power and influence than the low-status employees. Thus, status reflects the degree of power, authority, importance and responsibility placed on an individual by the other people in the organisation. The subordinates are usually afraid of communicating unpleasant and unfavourable information to the high-status people. They get scared of entering into the air-conditioned cabins with runs on the floor and a number of telephones on the table. They become conscious of their own status in relationship with the status of their superiors. This status consciousness is harmful in the process of upward communication. The employees fear that the unpleasant facts communicated to their superior might bring adverse effects on them, if the information displeases the superiors. They are reluctant to communicate their problems, shortcomings, mistakes and other unfavourable information to the higher-ups because of their fear that the superior might consider them incompetent and unworthy to do their jobs. They do not show courage of offering suggestions and plans of improving the organisation and its procedures for the fear of being called arrogant by their superiors. The high-ups too are strongly conscious of their status. In order to safeguard the dignity of their status, they avoid accepting suggestions from the subordinates and presume that their higher status stands for better knowledge and competence than any of their subordinates. These assumptions prove serious barriers to communication between them. Therefore, it is essential that every superior should encourage his subordinates to talk freely. If he creates confidence, it can later on help him to earn the respect from them.

Attitudes and Values

The attitudes serve the personal needs of the people. They provide need satisfaction to the individuals. When the message is unfavourable to the receiver, he cannot be easily persuaded by it. The messages are interpreted by the people in terms of their attitudes and values. Their attitudes and values are different not merely because they are physically different but also because they have different backgrounds. They deal with the individuals and events according to their attitudes and assumptions. Their personal attitudes, values and opinions are the barriers to an effective communication. The most agreeable information for anybody of us is the one which is favourable and palatable to our opinions, values, norms and attitudes. The message which runs contrary to our views and beliefs is not easily acceptable to us even when it is factual and true. We promptly accept the government policy if it is favourable to our business, but we express our strong resentment towards it if it adversely affects our business. Even the process of interpreting the message is consistent with the existing attitudes and values. It is due to the fact that our thinking is coloured and characterised by our attitudes and values. Sometimes, these attitudes and values can have emotional basis. Such attitudes are extremely difficult to change.

Different Perceptions of Reality

Francis Bacon has said, "Man prefers to believe what he prefers to be true". The individual experiences and their interpretations are never identical because their perceptions are different. If two friends see a movie together, their interpretation, of the events and the characters in it will certainly be different. The communication barrier arises as a result of different selective perceptions of the same object or idea by two or more people. Our physical senses like hearing, sight, taste, touch and smell are our contacts with the physical world. Some people have limited rage and power of their senses, whereas some people have very acute and strong senses. These physical differences are also responsible for different perceptions of the existing things. Human needs are strong motivating factors which can very easily alter his perceptions. Poor children tend to estimate a coin of 50 paise to be physically larger than the children coming from the rich families. We create our own reality through selective perception which hides certain things that are there and see certain more things than are there. If a salesman treats all his customers, colleagues and others as if they were the same, then he is sure to get into a real communication difficulty. He should remember that his communication difficulties arise because his perceptions differ from those of the other people, and that each of them conceives a different picture of the reality.

Inference

Our everyday life is full of various activities based on inference. When we get up in bed at 8.10 a.m., we infer that mummy might have already started her housework. When we sit down at a table to write, we infer that the chair will support our weight and ink will flow from the pen. Thus, the statements which are based on the facts and go beyond the facts are inferences. We may have good reason to expect that our inferences will be correct, but they may prove incorrect due to some unpredicted probability. As inferences go beyond the facts in making certain statements, they can give wrong signals also. We are to interpret symbols on the basis of assumptions which usually prove correct, but we must be aware of the probability that they may sometimes prove incorrect. When we travel in the state transport bus, we infer that we may reach safely at our destination, but this inference may not prove correct if the bus is caught in some accident. The inferential statements involve certain amount of risk, but in every imaginable context, we cannot avoid them. The inferences drawn by the specialists are many a times reliable because they are based on verified facts, but the inferences of the non-experts should be accepted after receiving more feedback from the concerned people. If a girl comes out crying from the defendant's room and she has her dress torn and cheeks bruised, one may infer that the girl and the defendant had been brawling. But this inference may not be the actual fact. Therefore, it would be risky to accept the above inference without verifying the facts.

Abstracting

We use language to communicate our experiences and feelings, but we cannot communicate every detail of it. We cannot communicate every detail of our experience to others. "Because off its symbolic nature, language is a poor substitute for the realities which it attempts to represent. The real world is more complex, more colourful, more fluid, more multidimensional than the pale words or over simplified signs used to convey meaning." Daniel Katz, ('Psychological Barriers to Communication', from the *Annals*, Vol. 250, 1947). Secondly, we focus our attention on some details and do not bother about the rest. We prepare a business report on our observation of the various events in the market. While preparing it, we abstract the reality and report only the valuable characteristics of the market. We observe partially and communicate partially because our experience of the event is also partial. When we try to convert our observations and experiences into words, we further abstract it by using selected words, which involve leaving out the details. If we try to completely describe a simple object like 'shoe', we would require several volumes for it which would still be insufficient to describe the object.

Allness and Closed-Mindedness

A person may close his mind to communication receptions, if he considers himself to be a person who knows 'all' about a particular subject. It is very difficult to communicate with a man who has deeply rooted prejudiced mind. Such a man is not prepared to receive any message on a subject about which he assumes to know everything. His mind is closed to new ideas, facts and revelations. If an employee approaches his closed-minded boss with some suggestions to improve the work of a business unit, the boss would not entertain the suggestion, but, on the other hand, he would retort the employee by saying that he knows better than the latter regarding what should be done for the betterment of the organisation. Perhaps, he may further warn the employee that the latter should never try to teach him again. Thus, he completely rejects the information and recommendations of the communicator even before he knows the real facts. The reason behind his closed-mindedness is his deeply rooted prejudices. He may preclude all possibility of communication unless he humbles himself down and admits that he has a great deal to know about himself, his occupation and also about the other people and their occupations.

Distortion, Filtering and Editing

When a message is transmitted through translations, interpretations, explanations and simplifications, some part of it gets distorted or lost. The legally worded resolutions made in the management committee meeting cannot be transmitted in the same words to the operator on the machine. It requires translation of it into simple language. It does not exactly replicate the idea of the message on the receiver's mind, but, on the other hand, it interprets and simplifies the message for him. The accuracy of the message is lost and the transmission becomes imperfect as the message goes through the filters of translations and simplifications.

The upward communication also tends to be distorted and filtered. Most of the employees bear in mind what their boss would like to hear from them and shape their messages accordingly. They are reluctant to communicate the information which might expose their faults and inefficiencies. The horizontal channel is also subjected to such distortions and filtering. The negative effects of the informal channel like grapevine are due to distortions and filtering. No one knows where it begins, but everybody seems to be anxious to repeat and impart it to others. The message in grapevine receives fresh additions with every repetition until it gets worst. Thus, often the original information communicated through formal or informal channels gets lost or distorted to a large extent and very little of it is retained.

Past Experiences

Our manners of thinking, feeling and acting are influenced by the way of our living and also by our experience in the past. Even the attitudes and values depend on our background of experiences. Every human being has his own set of experiences. His style and way of living and personal background separates him from the rest of the society. If the individuals do not have similar experiences and expectations concerning any given communication situation, they will not attribute similar meaning to the symbols of the message. The experience and expectations attached to the language symbols by a farmer are bound to be different from those of the doctor, banker and a scientist. The process of communication between them becomes hard and difficult because they cannot exchange each other's ideas and feelings quickly, smoothly and readily even though they use the same language.

Bad Listening

Bad listening is one of the major communication problems. Misunderstanding and conflicts can be reduced if people would listen the message with enough of attention. Most people do not listen very well due to various distractions, emotions, excitement, indifference, aggressiveness and wandering attention. One of the major reasons for bad listening is an individual's continual thinking about his own problems and worries. The poor listeners always feel that the thought in his mind is more interesting than what the speaker is saying. A college student involves himself in thinking about his girl-friend rather than listening to the lecture of his professor. Bad listening can also be due to some strong reason for worrying. An employee may get engrossed in worrying about the sickness of his daughter rather than listening to the instructions given by his departmental manager. Some listeners mentally argue with the speaker before comprehending the complete message. This usually leads to misunderstanding and conflict. Their impatience to talk out their thoughts and their lack of interest in the message contents are strong barriers to communication.

Emotions

Negative emotions are obstacles in the communication. Emotions are our feelings about the world around us. Usually, the positive emotions such as joy, love or affection do not interfere with communication, but the negative emotions act as strong barriers to effective communication. Emotionally excited communicator is unable to organise his message properly. His excited or nervous state of mind does not allow him to think clearly. He expresses his blurred thoughts with gesticulations and keeps on repeating the same words. He cannot even grasp the message sent by the communicator in its true sense. This is especially true when one's negative emotion is uncontrolled and misdirected. It makes him blind to reason. When everything seems to go wrong with someone on some bad day, he gives vent to his negative emotions. Almost anybody who comes across such an irritated person becomes a victim of his unfocused negative emotions. The perplexed, nervous and excited state of mind never allows smooth flow of communication.

Halo Effect

The halo effect is a psychological barrier to the listener's trust or distrust of the speaker. Trust is an essential dimension of all human encounters. What two people would say to each other and how they would interpret it depends on the level of trust between them. If the psychological climate between two people is uneasy, there would be more distortions and misinterpretations of the messages communicated between them. Distrust distorts mutual understanding and takes away pleasurable and acceptable aspects of communication. It may even interfere with the efforts of introducing attitude changes and motivating actions. If we trust the speaker, we may change our attitudes easily and readily according to whatever the speaker proposes. Our readiness to change our views and values is a result of our acceptance of the speaker's statements as reliable 'truths' or 'whites'. If we distrust the speaker, everything that he says can motivate no action from us, nor can it bring any change in our attitudes, views and values. Our negative reactions are the result of the fact that we do not accept whatever the speaker says as 'true' or 'white'. The picture of our life is multi-coloured and it should not be painted just in black and white. We must be sensitive to its mixed tones and tunes. We must try to see and understand the 'grey' tones (the halo effect). If a departmental head believes that his subordinates are dishonest and will take disadvantage of him if they can, his communication with the subordinates will be characterised by suspicion and distrust. If he believes that people are basically honest and helpful he will communicate with trust and confidence.

Inattentiveness

The communication receivers are inattentive to the message that have no emotional value for them and the message which they do not expect to hear. As such, messages are likely to be transmitted by many communicators, in which the barrier of inattentiveness can be found frequently. A receiver can exercise a considerable voluntary control over what he has to receive. However, selective attention is not always a conscious process. We are inattentive to certain messages even without our conscious efforts of controlling the reception process.

If we do not like the exposure to the message which does not support our views and opinions, we prefer to be inattentive. But in face-to-face communication, it is somewhat difficult to be directly inattentive. When it comes to a theater show or TV programmes it is easier to walk out of the theatre or to turn off the television set if we dislike the performance or the programme. Distractions are also responsible for inattentiveness of the receiver. A clerk may not be able to concentrate his attention in his work if he is distracted by some appealing movements of a lady typist. A person can be inattentive because of his tiredness, anxieties, worries and sleepiness which may not allow him to concentrate his attention on the message.

Resistance to Change

If we receive a message which proposes a new idea, we tend to be inattentive to it. The new idea is rejected consciously or sometimes unconsciously if it conflicts with beliefs, morals, values, attitudes and opinions of the receiver. The average adult human mind ignores the new idea, especially when he feels insecurity and uncertainty about its aftermath. He feels that the things go along just fine with him and he would be insecure if the changes are introduced. He is also suspicious about its success in future. Because of its uncertainty, he hastily concludes in his mind that the proposal would not be successful. He even further feels that the proposal would make things worst for him. The new idea is considered as a drastic proposal which is not needed. Thus, the average human mind which resists change does not accept the new ideas from the communicator.

Exercises

1. "In reality there is no such thing as perfect communication". Discuss.
2. Describe the factors responsible for miscommunication in business organisations.
3. What are barriers to effective internal communication in business organisation?
4. How does language act as a serious barrier to effective communication?

5. How does the 'failure to use multiple communication channels' result in poor communication?
6. What are the psychological barriers to effective communication?
7. How do the personal attitudes and prejudices act as the barriers to effective communication?
8. What is meant by 'Status Blocks' or State Consciousness'? How does it act as a barrier to communication?
9. How does 'Faulty transmission and poor retention' affect business communication?
10. "All the barriers to communication are psychological". Discuss.
11. What are the semanuc barriers to communication?
12. Write short-notes on the following:

    (i) Abstracting
    (ii) Prejudices and distrust
    (iii) Emotional state of mind
    (iv) Status consciousness
    (v) The closed mind
    (vi) Inattentiveness
    (vii) Slanting
    (viii) Allness
    (ix) Wrong choice of medium
    (x) Inferring
    (xi) Noise
    (xii) Time and Distance
    (xiii) Different interpretation of words
    (xiv) Denotations and connotations
    (xv) Bypassed instructions
    (xvi) Different perceptions
    (xvii) The Halo Effect

(1) Positive and Pleasant Approach
(2) Appropriate Tone, Pitch, Quality, Force and Intensity of Voice
(3) Clarity of Purpose and Objective of Communication
(4) Clarity of Thought and Expression
(5) Adequate Knowledge of the Subject
(6) Adequate Knowledge of Communication Receiver
(7) Objective and Realistic Approach
(8) Self-confidence and Conviction
(9) Organisation of Message
(10) Proper Selection and Use of the Media
(11) Proper Selection and Use of the Channel
(12) Appropriate Formality
(13) Patience in Listening
(14) Adaptability
(15) Attentiveness
(16) 'You' Attitude
(17) Courtesy
(18) The Time Factor
(19) Conciseness and Relevance
(20) Correctness
(21) Completeness

6

THE ESSENTIALS OF EFFECTIVE COMMUNICATION

> Communication is effective when the stimulus, as it was initiated and intended by the sender, corresponds by the receiver.
>
> – S.L. Tubbs and Sylvia Moss, in *Human Communication*

An effective communication is the key of sure success in the modern world of commerce. The increasing specialisation and the expansion and complexity of today's tradefare have also brought about a revolution in the systems of communication. The businessman who wants to survive in the competition has to develop his communicating skills. He must know how to communicate with the help of new and speedy technical devices of communication. The efficient management executives spend more than ninety per cent of their time in communication. Their efficiency depends on their skills and effectiveness of communicating with others. He has to communicate with other traders and dealers for purchase and sell. He has to communicate with his superiors in order to decide the objectives and directives. He has to communicate with his subordinates in order to their get their cooperation and improve the productivity. He has to deal with banks, transport agencies, government officials, legal advisors, insurance companies, experts, customers, etc. The delay and lack of effective communication can result in heavy loss of money for any businessman. Therefore, it is very important for every businessman to know the art of how to communicate effectively.

'How we say' is equally important as 'what we say'. We want that people should listen to what we say; they should understand it, believe in it, appreciate it, and finally, get activated by it. The response of the other party depends upon how our personality is judged by them. It is the judgement of our manners, outward appearance, dress neatness and it is also the judgement of our style, tone, clarity, completeness, correctness, consciousness, objectivity, integrity, attractiveness, purpose and of many other essentialities of effective oral and written expressions.

The essentials of effective communication are:

1. Positive and pleasant approach,
2. Appropriate tone, pitch, quality, force and intensity of voice,
3. Clarity of purpose and objective of communication,
4. Clarity of thought and expression,
5. Adequate knowledge of the subject,
6. Adequate knowledge of the communication receiver,
7. Objective and realistic approach,
8. Self-confidence and conviction,
9. Organisation of message,
10. Proper selection and use of the media,
11. Proper selection and use of the channel,
12. Appropriate formality,
13. Patience in listening,
14. Adaptability,
15. Attentiveness,
16. 'You' attitude,
17. Courtesy,
18. Time Consciousness,
19. Conciseness and relevance,
20. Correctness,
21. Completeness,

Positive and Pleasant Approach

A positive and pleasant way of oral and written expression can easily build a goodwill in the customer-company relationship. With it, any businessman can win good reputation and friendly relations for his organisation. There are always many occasions when a businessman is likely to lose his temper. He has to refuse certain offers and requests of the people. Sometimes he disagrees with the people in his organisation and also with the outsiders who are in someway linked with his organisation. Sometimes, he finds imperfections and mistakes in the business transactions. Sometimes, he has to suffer inconveniences and even financial loss. Naturally, he has to complain against some people. In these circumstances, the businessman stands on trial. It is very easy for him to become plainly negative in his approach towards these people. But, his anger and impatience might bring adverse results because nobody likes the negative approach and harsh words.

He can tactfully use the sugar-coated words to express his regret, disagreement and complaint. People accept these words with smile and without any grumble. When a businessman has to refuse something, he is likely to break the goodwill of the party. He can retain the goodwill even after his refusal by the only way of his positive and pleasant approach. He should never spoil the atmosphere of goodwill by using bitter words and complaining undertone. A businessman should look at every situation with optimism and should try to make the best of it. He may not find everything agreeable, he may come across several problems, but he should always believe in the fact that every situation can have the advantages of its own. He has to find out those advantages. Michael E. Adelstein says:

> It is not a matter of overstating or overselling, but of accentuating the positive, and minimising the negative. Every cloud may not have a silver lining, but there usually is some sort of hopeful or optimistic prospect in a business transaction.

Appropriate Tone, Pitch, Quality, Force and Intensity of Voice

A small child is always conscious of the fact that the voice he listens does not always say what the words mean. He often experiences this fact when he is remonstrated by his parents. He looks into the eyes of his daddy or mommy and judges what the tone of their voice means. It is clear that words have meanings, but a different tone of voice conveys a different shade and colour of the meaning, which comes from the emotional involvement of the speaker. The tone of voice gives an idea of the depth and intensity of the emotions. The facial expression, gestures and postures are complementary to the tone of voice in conveying exact meaning to the communication receiver. The sound symbols (words) carry the ideas but the tone, pitch and force of voice communicate emotions of love, affection, hate, jealousy, fear, anger, etc. The pleasant and acceptable quality of our voice depends upon our emotional control. Pitch variations in our speech help us in emphasising certain points, whereas vocal monotony is useful in short formal speech. There are some people, who tend to speak rapidly. They find it difficult to change the pace of their speech. This monotony of pace is tiresome to the listeners. The variation in vocal pitch and rate helps the communicator to hold the attention and interest of the listeners. It must be remembered that the tone of our writing and speech invariably gives a cue to our personal attitudes. The receiver not only receives the words of the communicator but he also realises the mood of the conveyor between the lines. While listening to a public speaker, we first listen to the tone of his voice and then to the meaning of his message. Therefore, the communicator must strive to sound natural, friendly, sincere and pleasant.

Clarity of Purpose and Objectives of Communication

Communication is maintained at various levels of organisational hierarchy for the achievement of several objectives, but all these objectives originate from the purpose of achieving the general welfare of the organisation. The manager cannot plan, organise and control, if he does not communicate effectively to get the information about the facts and circumstances relevant to his daily responsibilities. If he has to take correct decisions, the information received by him must be complete, correct and concise. The administrator must be very clear about the exact purpose behind his communicational needs. In an organisation, he has to use communication media for the objectives like issuing orders, and warning, raising the morale, giving advice and suggestions and for some other purposes of persuasion, education and instructions, etc. He can motivate his workers effectively, if he tries to satisfy their basic human needs and healthy social relationships. Warning is very effective means of communication, but it ought to be used discreetly and sparingly. It should not be given to a person in the presence of others. The morale of the labours can be raised if the superior appreciates their good work, encourages them and gives them a sense of belonging with the organisation. The order can be very effective authoritative communication, if it is clear, complete and given in a friendly manner. In an organisation, an advice is effective, if it is related to a particular work of the worker. It should not create in him the feeling of inferiority. Suggestion can be used as a mild and subtle form of communication. Workers are to be encouraged to drop their suggestions in suggestion boxes. Persuasion is always better than repression and compulsion in order to change views, beliefs, attitudes, habits and actions of the people. The persuasive art is usually effective and successful as it is suggestive and the appeal is indirect.

Clarity of Thought and Expression

The cycle of communication starts at the origin of an idea in the mind of the communicator. It is the origin and source of the message to be communicated. The communicator must be very clear about all the aspects of the idea in his mind and about the purpose for which it is to be communicated. Next to it, he must be clear about the selection, suitability and usage of the medium. The signals of the encoded message must be carefully composed of and transmitted. It must be clear enough to replicate the exact meaning in the mind of the communication receiver. The words and sentences must be short, simple and common, so that the message is understood easily and readily. The clarity of thought and expression cannot be maintained if the communicator himself fails to understand his subject thoroughly. Sometimes, he may know his subject but he may fail to distinguish between its major and minor aspects. In order to maintain the clarity of thought and expression, the communicator can discard the use of well-turned phrases, elegant sentences and utopian-luxurious language. Good language should not call attention to itself. On the other hand, it should strive to transfer ideas and thoughts from one mind to another. The communicator need not desire to captivate the receiver with the prose but should see whether his message is clear or not. The message must be so clear that even the dullest man in the world should readily understand it. It should not consist of any ambiguities or misleading meanings. It should not be faulty and it should not produce any confusion in the mind of the receiver. It should be free from syntactical errors. The communicator must plan and organise his material before communicating it to the receiver.

The encoded message should be grouped under the major and subordinate heads. While placing related ideas together, there should be no fault in punctuation and pause in the written and spoken communication respectively. The special trade and professional language which is popularly known as jargon is difficult to be understood by a common man. If we avoid jargon, it adds to the clarity of the message. These precautions should be taken before transmitting the message. When our objectives, thoughts and expressions are clear and simple, the imparted message becomes easier to be understood by the receiver and the purpose of communication is effectively served.

Adequate Knowledge of the Subject

An adequate knowledge of the subject matter is essential for effective communication through both oral and written media. Before writing a letter or delivering a speech, the communicator should thoroughly know the subject on which he is going to express his thoughts, ideas and feelings. A salesman who works in a TV shop must have some knowledge of the TV sets. He will be able to raise the interest in the mind of the customers and focus their attention on the various points of merits in every TV set kept for sale in the shop. He must know how to operate the sets and how to make different appeals in order to generate interest in different types of customers. In generating interest and creating desire in the mind of a customer, the salesman has to dwell at length upon the various advantages and merits of the article he has to sell. The salesman should know not only the advantages of the product, but he should be able to compare it with other similar products available in the market. He should also know the facts and figures pertaining to the product. This statistical information can make an effective appeal to the educated. He should be able to judge the economic status and ability of the customer. In case of rich customers, he should make appeal to their pride of possession; and in case of the lower and middle class customers, the instinct to economise appeal is more effective. All this knowledge is essential to the salesman if he has to communicate effectively with the customer. An administrator, in a business firm, must know the background and policies of the firm. He requires the knowledge of buying, making and selling the articles. He also requires the knowledge of why to communicate, what to communicate and how to communicate with different agencies, banks, insurance companies, government officials, etc., in order to be effective in his communication with them.

Adequate Knowledge of the Communication Receiver

A communication receiver has a very important place in the communication cycle. When the receiver is absent, the communication situation itself cannot exist. Therefore, the message must be prepared by keeping in view the type of person who is the receiver of it. It is very essential to see that every attempt is made to get maximum information regarding his educational qualifications, his status and designation, the nature of his work and responsibilities, his intellectual level and other aspects of his personality. The communication sender has to organise his message in such a way that it becomes pleasing, suitable and acceptable to the receiver. The language of the communicator must be persuasive, adaptable and intelligible to the receiver. The colloquial and informal language is likely to be unsuitable while communicating with the superiors, but it might, sometimes, be more acceptable while communicating with the equals and subordinates. The style, manner and content of the language must be carefully used to create goodwill in the mind of the receiver. It must be remembered that we should not use the same language with the illiterate worker and office clerk and with the manager of the organisation.

The Objective and Realistic Approach

The mental set, attitudes, opinions and prejudices of the receiver towards the sender and towards the organisation have a marked effect on the meaning of a message. The hostile, suspicious and prejudiced receiver is likely to draw a negative, slanted and distorted meaning from the message. It is, therefore, very essential that the message should be objective, factual and realistic and it should exclude the emotional expression of the sender. The sender should not allow his opinions, attitudes and emotions to distort the objectivity and factuality of the message and at the same time, he should be aware of the feelings and responses of the receiver. Adequate care should be taken by the sender that the information provided in the message does not mislead the receiver or hurt his feelings. A high level of trust and mutual respect between the sender and the receiver facilitates clear and objective communication.

Self-Confidence and Conviction

Lack of self-confidence can be a critical barrier to effective communication. A person must have the self-confidence to communicate his achievements, his personal capabilities and his prospects. The communicator must build and develop in himself a justifiable self-confidence. The feelings of anxiety and worry are closely associated with the low self-confidence. A person with such feelings perceives himself unable to communicate with the people in any situation. He feels it difficult to face the different faces in his practical life. Anxiety is a negative emotion. It is natural that a person with negative emotions reacts negatively to the situations. In business, such a person tries to avoid the situations of challenge in finance, marketing, personnel management, etc. If he is in the management body of the organisation, he would give little time for communicating on unfamiliar and difficult problems. He would spend more time in dealing with the problems of which he is confident to find the solutions. The self confidence is essential to generate positive outlook in the person.

It is also essential that the manager should make some efforts to build the self-confidence among his subordinates, Stanley Coppersmith has suggested three conditions to which high self-confidence is related: (i) total acceptance of subordinates by the manager; (ii) clearly defined and enforced limits; (iii) managerial respect for individual action within the defined limits. The manager should be attentive to the needs of the people working in the organisation. When he shows the concern about the welfare of his subordinates, the total acceptance of the subordinates by him is communicated. The manager has to inform his subordinates about his expectations of work from them. Thirdly, the manager has to motivate and encourage the subordinates to act freely within the structure formed by him, the high self-confidence among the people working in the organisation can establish social relationship which is conducive to effective communication.

Organisation of Message

The message is transmitted through the signals of vocal and written symbol system, which is also accompanied by the non-verbal signals. The organisation of message involves the selection of suitable media and the composition of message by the systematic arrangement of symbols. When a message is to be communicated through written media, the words, phrases, clauses and the sentences must be simple and correct so that it may replicate the exact meaning to the receiver. Secondly, the handwriting, typing or printing must be orderly, neat, attractive and in suitable format. The sentences must be properly punctuated to bring clarity and to avoid ambiguity. The paper on which the message is written should have pleasant appearance. The appearance and the form of the letter is as important as the contents of the message in it. While communicating orally, the voice must be loud enough to be heard easily and clearly. We are to make use of the pauses to stress some ideas. The tone must be confident, vibrant and enthusiastic. The pitch of the voice should be suitable to the situation and to the content of the message. It is also essential that the message should be brief and concise. In face-to-face communication, the non-verbal aspects of communication like eye-contact, body posture, gestures, facial expressions, touch, silence, etc., are very effective in revealing trustworthiness, sincerity, intensity of emotions, enthusiasm, etc., of the persons involved in the process of communication.

The message must consist of an introduction, a body and a conclusion. The message can be organised in chronological pattern. The messages consisting of the historical accounts and the description of processes can be organised in a chronological order. The message can be organised in cause and effect pattern also. In this pattern, the communicator moves from the cause to effect or from the effect to cause. The third pattern of message organisation is that of a spatial order. In it, the message is organised by space, i.e. top-bottom, left-right, east-west, etc. The fourth pattern of message organisation is that of comparison. It points out the similarities and differences between the items under the study. Problem-solution pattern is often used in the business communications. It describes the problem, describes the solution, discusses the advantages and disadvantages of solution and finally proves how the proposed solution is better than the other. Analytical pattern of message organisation analyses or divides the subjects into parts and sub-parts. A well organised message is always systematic and effective.

Proper Selection and Use of Media

A manager can communicate through a variety of media. The media available to him can be divided into four groups: (i) audio-visual, (ii) non-verbal, (iii) oral, and (iv) written. Audio-visual communication includes television, video casettes, cinema-films. Visual communication includes gestures, facial expressions, graphs, charts, diagrams, slides, posters, etc. The oral communication includes telephone conversation, face-to-face communication, interviews, seminars, conferences, group discussions, meetings, speeches, etc. And written communication includes a variety of letters, reports, memorandums, circulars, telegrams, minutes, questionnaires, etc.

All the communication media have their own advantages as well as disadvantages. Before selecting the media, it is essential to think over its relative suitability in communicating the message. If the manager has to communicate certain directives to the departmental heads, it would better for him to convene a meeting rather than talking with them over telephone separately. If he wants to inform common policies of the Company to the employees, it is better to use circular notice-board rather than announcing them in a public speech. While communicating with the departmental or assistant manager, he can talk face-to-face with him, or he may talk to him over telephone. If he is desirous to record the message for future reference, he may send a memorandum to the assistant manager or to any other concerned authority in the company's hierarchy. He has to communicate with the local government officials also. He can get some clarification in certain matters by talking with them over telephone. But he has to communicate with the government authorities, insurance agencies, banks, etc., mostly through written correspondence.

Audio-visual media which is most suitable for mass communication is very suitable and effective in educating and training the workers. When the manager wants to communicate with the general public, he can reach up to them through advertisements on television, video tapes, cinema-films, radio, newspapers, magazines, etc. The silence also can be an effective media of communication in certain circumstances. Silence talks loudly when a beloved blushes and indicates her consent to the proposal of her lover. The visual media can be effective only when it is used in combination with other media. The charts, diagrams, maps, etc., are to be associated with the written media, and the facial expressions, postures and gestures, etc., are to be associated with the oral media in order to be effective in communicating the message.

Proper Selection and Use of the Channels

A communication channel runs along with the hierarchical line of authority in every organisation. The employees have to follow these prescribed channels if they are to communicate with one another. These prescribed channels are official or formal channels. They are grouped in four divisions: (i) upward, (ii) downward, (iii) vertical, and (iv) horizontal, for effective communication. It is almost obligatory to select a proper channel and abide the regulations associated with it. The downward channel is used by the supervisors to give directives to the subordinates, to assess and appreciate their work and to explain the policies of the organisation to the concerned employees. This channel can be effectively used if efficient care is taken to avoid under communication and over communication. The upward channel is useful in passing necessary feedback and constructive suggestions by the subordinates to their superiors. It can be effectively used if the employees do not have the awe of authority. Both the channels are ineffective if the hierarchy is ignored and the authorities are bypassed. The vertical channel is the combination of the upward and downward channels. The horizontal channel is effective when it is used for promoting friendship, understanding, cooperation and coordination among the equals. The horizontal channel is found most effective through oral media. The written media seems to make them status-conscious. Grapevine is an informal channel of communication which spreads in any direction. It does not follow any set pattern of the formal channels. The grapevine indicates the solidarity among the employees. If the manager carefully listens to it, he can judge and control the morale and behavioural trends of his employees.

Appropriate Formality

In almost every organisation, there are always some people who prefer to communicate with 'people' rather than with 'positions'. Formality in communication connects positions and not people. The unplanned informal channels of communication are convenient for many people to interconnect them for a variety of reasons. Informal communication is essential in the organisation because it bridges people closer together and helps them to share their work experiences and common problems among themselves. But, if the group which had come closer by informal communication does not trust management, the morale of the organisation is threatened. The formal communication brings about some obligatory discipline by its network which sets the lines of communication with the lines of authority as they are structured by the management. The message passes formally and slowly from managers to departmental heads, departmental heads to supervisors, etc., and the communication links between the positions are maintained. But, in the organisation, when the people work near each other and share each other's experiences, and problems, they are likely to come together for common purposes. when they come together, the informal group is formed. In order to coordinate and control such groups, the informal channels are more effective. The formal and informal ways of communication must go hand-in-hand in every business organisation.

Patience in Listening

The ability and patience to listen is a managerial skill which helps the manager to improve his relationships with the people in the organisation. To him, the auditory source of essential information is an important requirement for effective decision-making. The reception of information and its further processing are the important elements of communication circle. Therefore, it is obvious that effective communication requires effective listening. When the listener carefully listens to the message, he can understand, judge and evaluate the contents of it in a better way. Effective communication is impossible if the receiver does not listen to the message and does not comprehend it thoroughly. The receiver must be able to concentrate on the information imparted by the communicator. He must not be carried away by the distractions. It is likely that he might be distracted by the manners, etiquettes and physical appearance of the communicator. He must be positive and open-minded towards the communicator. He should not let his mind wander away from what the communicator is saying. Thus, if the receiver is a patient listener, with positive and flexible mind towards the speaker and understands the message by keeping himself mentally alert, the communication is bound to be effective.

Adaptability

A person must give adaptive responses to the changing

circumstances. In any business organisation, the successful implementation of the technological as well as economic innovations are possible if the significant flow of information is involved. The adaptive responses of the receiver facilitates the incoming flow of the information at various levels in the organisation. The communicator also has to adapt his communication to the needs and requirements of the receiver. He has to adapt it to the intellectual, academic and linguistic competence of the receiver. The receiver's state of mind and overall psychological make-up also deserves adequate consideration.

In our 'struggle for survival' with the other species on this earth, we have survived not only because we have faster birth rate, nimble body and teeming brain but because we are more adaptive to changing circumstances, In human society and especially in our complex business world today, adaptability is an essential factor in effective communication with the different people in different circumstances.

Attentiveness

The receptivity of our mind decides our attentiveness and concentration on the message which is either to be composed, written and transmitted by the sender or to be read, listened and seen by the receiver. The sender must be attentive enough in composing the message correctly, clearly, precisely and completely before transmitting it to the receiver. And the receiver must be attentive enough to listen and see every aspect of the message received by him. A successful businessman keeps his eyes and ears open to keep himself abreast of the knowledge in his field. He must keep his mind open to new ideas. But in practical life, it is found that people are inattentive to receive a message if it contain a new idea, they are half-attentive or inattentive to the message which is against their belief and unsuitable to their taste and likings, they are also inattentive to the message which seems monotonous and boresome to them. Inattentiveness is actually an ignorance of the message. When the message is ignored, the communication circle remains incomplete. When the message is received, the receiver is attentive to it. He can send the feedback to the communicator if he attentively comprehends the message. There cannot be effective communication unless both the communicator and the receiver are attentive to each other's message and feedback.

'You' Attitude

We must remember that the receiver is primarily interested in himself and in his gains. His own achievements, success and well-being is more important to him rather than those of his communicator's. If he is a businessman, his main goal will be to make profit for himself. Therefore, our communication is effective only when we communicate from the receiver's point of view. Our message must be organised in such a way that it makes appeal to the issues of his own interest. While organising the message, we must not forget the truth that the receiver loves his name, his position, his property, his status, his fame and his profits. By adopting the 'You' attitude, a business communicator must look at the things as the receiver does. If he does not view the things from the receiver's point of view, his arguments will not be effective. The word 'You' is magnetic and highly effective in both the oral and written media of communication. The listeners as well as the readers of the message like themselves personally addressed by the communicator. We can make our communication effective and persuasive by using the word 'You' as many times as possible and by trying to avoid the pronouns 'I' and 'We' in our message.

Courtesy

Our personality is understood by the style and tone of our language and by our overall behaviour. Our communication can be effective if we are courteous in our language and conduct. Courtesy can be defined as the considerate, friendly and sympathetic approach towards others. In order to be courteous in our language and conduct, we must not become sarcastic, unfriendly, impatient and irritated. In business, the important objective of communication is to build goodwill by establishing better customer-company relationships. We can create the new customers and hold the present ones by our courtesy. By our courteous and thanking nature, we shall not only be able to create new friends in the business world but we shall also be able to avoid enmity and wrath of others. Courtesy is a matter of polite tone, good manners and thanking nature. A courteous man neither criticises the other party for their mistakes nor uses harsh and bitter words in his speech. He maintains goodwill by keeping 'You' attitude in his mind and on his tongue. When the 'You' attitude is kept in mind, a courteous tone naturally comes in written as well as oral communication. He wins the trust and reliability of the other party by promptly attending to their complaints and requests. He wins their favour by using the sweet sounding words like 'thank you', 'please', etc.

Courtesy is obviously an important factor for both the verbal as well as non-verbal media. A businessman can never afford to ignore courtesy in his manners and etiquettes. While writing a business letter, the importance of courtesy does not need to be mentioned. We can say that a businessman should not write a letter unless he is in a right frame of mind. In fact, when he is in an irritated and perturbed state of mind, he is likely to write in an unfriendly and insulting manner. His discourtesy may be quite unintentional, but the reader will fail to realise that it was unintentional and unsought.

The Time Factor

In business, no matter how busy you are, you must communicate promptly and at appropriate time. It is essential to answer a business phone after first ring. In written communication, the promptness in answering the business letter is a matter of courtesy. This timeliness may not be always possible but the communicator and the receiver must make the effort to be prompt and timely. Any businessman cannot afford to abandon his customer by not attending the phone call. He is likely to suffer the loss of goodwill and money, if he does not reply promptly to the letter of enquiry and order. Therefore, it is important to reply the letters and answer the phonecall promptly and courteously. A reply to the letter may be delayed sometimes, because the writer may require some clarification and explanation from some other concerned people. He may also require the consent of his higher authority. But whenever possible, a reply must be transmitted within 48 hours. When some more time is needed to make inquiries and to collect information in order to give full and satisfactory answer to the enquirer; atleast an acknowledgement receipt must be sent immediately. The promptness in replying is essential in business because it creates a goodwill and friendliness.

The message must be communicated at the appropriate and suitable time. If it does not reach its receiver at an appropriate time, it may not bring the expected and desirable results. If the receiver is seriously occupied with some other work, he will not be able to pay proper attention to the message. If a message is passed at the time when the receiver has lost his temper on some irritable issues the communication cannot be good and effective.

Conciseness and Relevance

Conciseness is an important factor in effective communication. It means saying all that needs to be said and no more. The aimless verbiage, unnecessary details and heavy paragraphs make our communication ridiculous and ineffective. We must omit those words and sentences from our message which are not likely to bring good results. The message which can be expressed in fewer words is more impressive and effective than the same message expressed in a number of words. It must never ramble on and on unnecessarily. It cannot persuade the receiver to take action if it bores him by its length and heaviness. The communicator must organise his message in such a way that every word in it is meaningful and of interest to the receiver. There should not be needless repetition of the same ideas and words. Even a single word or a sentence which does not contribute to accomplish the purpose of the communication should be carefully omitted. As time is precious in the business world, the businessmen do not have time to read irrelevant details. Brevity, which is a part of conciseness is desirable, but it must not be achieved at the cost of clarity and completeness. To be concise means both to be brief and to be complete. The message should be as short as possible, but it must consist all significant ideas and necessary details. By conciseness, it also means that only relevant ideas should appear in as few words as possible. The message must consist of only those sentences which are related to a specific unit of thought. The communication receiver should not feel that he is wasting his valuable time in receiving the lengthy message.

Correctness

Business communication must be correct on various levels. It must be correct in tone and style of expression, spelling, grammar, format, contents, statistical information, stress-unstress, intonation pattern, etc. There should not be any inaccurate statements in the message.

Efforts must be made to avoid the errors of typography, capitalisation, spellings, punctuation, etc. The incorrect written documents lower the readers' confidence in the writer. In the same way, the incorrect statements and other miscellaneous errors of the speaker lower the listeners' confidence in him and it may tarnish his image and reliability too. When communication receiver finds one error he suspects that there can also be other errors in the message. Then he starts searching for other mistakes almost automatically. Therefore, a businessman must give every detail correctly in his message. The external as well as the internal communication can be considered effective only when it brings good reputation, status, profit and goodwill to the communicator. The errors in business message may bring down the status, profit, reputation and goodwill of the communication. The decisions taken by a businessman will be wrong and disastrous if he receives incorrect information from internal and external sources. Therefore, it is essential that the sender should verify the correctness of the information before transmitting it to the receiver. And before accepting the information for important decision-making, the receiver should clarify his doubts regarding the accuracy and correctness of the message.

Completeness

Completeness is an essential factor for effective communication. A message must be organised appropriately in the sense that it must include all the important ideals and its details. The contents of the message must be checked in order to verify that there is no omission of the relevant details. An incomplete message can do little to convey the information and to persuade the receiver. All the aspects of the message must be grouped and brought together in logical sequence to prepare meaningful thought units. The communication effort can be more fruitful and effective if the receiver easily reacts to the sender's message. The successful business communicator provides complete message with all its necessary details. When the message is fully understood, it becomes easier for the receiver to give prompt reply. The incomplete message may create doubts in the receiver's mind. It necessitates further inquiries and correspondence. The incomplete message is difficult to understand and many a times it results in misunderstanding. The receiver of the incomplete message feels angry, confused and irritated by it. The completeness adds to the clarity of the message. An incomplete information can be provided when the communicator strives too much for brevity. In such cases, another letter or inquiry is needed to get the necessary details. It results in delay and more expenses on further correspondence. Clarity and completeness of message save time, money and energy of both the parties.

Exercises

1. How do the clarity of thoughts and clarity of expression help to increase the effectiveness of communication?
2. Write brief notes on the following principles of effective communication:

   (a) Clarity,
   (b) Completeness,
   (c) Correctness,
   (d) Conciseness,
   (e) Completeness.

3. Give illustrations to show that the messages must be objective and also adaptable to receiver.
4. How does attentiveness enhance the effectiveness of communication?
5. What principles should govern the formal and informal channels of communication?

A. Diction

   (1) The Extent of Vocabulary and Choice of Appropriate Words
   (2) Colloquial, Dialectal and Slang Words
   (3) Efficacy of Words in Business Communication

B. Sentence

   (1) Variety in Sentence Structure
   (2) Repetition of Words, Phrases and Clauses
   (3) Giving Special Emphasis
   (4) Conversational Tone

C. The Paragraph

   (1) Organisation of Thoughts and Ideas
   (2) Coherence
   (3) Length of Paragraph

D. Punctuations

7

SHARPENING THE TOOLS OF BUSINESS COMMUNICATION

DICTION

The Extent of Vocabulary and Choice of Appropriate Words

The extent of vocabulary and choice of appropriate words are important factors in one's ability to communicate effectively on a given subject. The use of words depends not only on the given subject but also on the occasion, media, the type of communication receivers and the conditions under which a person communicates. The essential vocabulary for discussing a technical problem in an engineering industry will be different from that which is used for a similar purpose in an agricultural industry. A communicator can be found using different vocabulary for the oral and written media. Similarly, he will use different vocabulary while expressing his thoughts before the people in different walks of life. In every communication situation, his choice of appropriate words aims at adapting them to the understanding of his receivers. In some cases, typical businessmen tend to use difficult, long and unfamiliar words. Their aim is to talk over the heads of the receivers.

The usage of words must be based on their appropriateness in different situations. Technical vocabulary may be essential for discussions on technical problems among the group of professionals; but, if such vocabulary is used before the general public or in a letter to a layman, it will not be properly understood. Every business field has its own jargon which cannot be easily understood by the common people. This jargon is intelligible only to the people working in that particular field. The technical words used by them become a part of their everyday vocabulary. Though such words are so common for them, they can sound strange and even misleading to the people working in other fields. Though jargon can be aptly used in conversation and correspondence with the people working in the same business line, its overuse makes the reading hard and slow. Every business jargon consists some strong and vigorous words, but instead of overusing them, they should be used moderately. Standard vocabulary is generally used by the journalists, good writers and speakers. It is appropriate for all occasions and for all the people belonging to that language community.

Colloquial, Dialectal and Slang Words

Colloquial words and expressions can be used in informal communication situations, especially in informal social groups; but, it can be objectionable in formal speech and writing. Slang is a vocabulary which consists certain widely current but ephemeral words having eccentric humour. It also refers to violent and abusive use of words in a language. It is commonly used in talk but it is unsuitable for good writing and speech at some formal occasion. The social level occupied by slang is lower than colloquialism. Dialectal vocabulary refers to provincialism or localism. Dialectal words are those which are currently used by the people in particular province. Like colloquialism and slang, dialectal vocabulary is also unsuitable for formal speech and writing. Obsolete vocabulary refers to the words which are out of common use. The archaic words gradually become obsolete words. Generally, colloquial, dialectal, slang, obsolete and archaic words are not used in business communication.

Efficacy of Words in Business Communication

In business communication, apart from the technical vocabulary used in particular field, most of the words used in letters, reports, memos as well as in the business meetings, interviews, seminars and conferences are common, familiar and everyday words. Therefore, for effective business communication the speaker or the writer need not depend on his highflown, complex and utopian vocabulary. The strength and efficacy of his communicative competence depend on his skill of selecting from among familiar everyday vocabulary. While writing a business letter or delivering a public speech, the communicator need not seek to impress the receiver by using unfamiliar, abstract and long words.

A successful communicator carefully selects the words which have positive connotations and denotations. He is keenly aware of the receiver's potential reactions to his words. He anticipates the possible interpretations of the words by the audience or the reader who receive the message. He uses concrete words that carry specific and clear meaning instead of using abstract words that carry vague meaning. He avoids the biased, overused and negative words and chooses appropriate, conversational and positive words. He avoids pompous words and uses simple everyday words. He does not attribute virtue to the words simply because they are short or long. But, if two words, one short and the other long, express the same idea, he would prefer the short one. He avoids awkward combination and careless repetition of words. He avoids unintentional use of the planned rhyme and alliteration which are techniques of poetry and not a part of the language to be used for business communication.

Positive words used at the beginning of the message, or at the time of greeting someone face-to-face, can create warm, friendly and comfortable atmosphere. On the other hand, negative words bring negative and unpleasant reactions. When a business communicator greets the receiver in written message with some pleasant and positive words, he prepares his reader to receive the message attentively, carefully and positively. He knows that the cold and irritating words may not bring the favourable response and, sometimes, it may make the problem worse. Negative words make readers defensive. Similarly, a lengthy message can have its negative effect on the receiver. In business, most people value their time. They are likely to be annoyed by the wordy message in speech as well as in letters and reports. A good business communicator organises his message effectively by cutting unnecessary words from his speeches, letters, memos and reports. He tries to adapt the arbitrary meaning of his words and concepts to the receiver's competence and understanding of the language. In adapting his communication, he visualises the language competence and the cult of the receiver's mind. Having visualised the competence and cult of the receiver's mind, he selects appropriate words and phrases to express his thoughts and feelings.

SENTENCE

Along with the words selected in a particular sentence, correctness in grammar, spelling and tone of a sentence, variety in sentence pattern, special emphasis on ideas, conciseness of expression, tautology, length of a sentence, repetition of words and phrases in a sentence, repetition of the same sentence pattern, and the style of speech and writing are some of the important factors to be studied for achieving effectiveness in sentences.

Variety in Sentence Structure

Variety in sentence structure is required for effective speech and writing. In order to avoid monotony, the successive sentences should be written in variety of sentence structures. A business letter or a public speech which is prepared and imparted only in simple sentence structure, will certainly sound boring, dull and childish. While drafting a business letter, the communicator should not begin a number of successive sentences with the same word like — We, This, The, etc. Repetition of the same word or phrase at the beginning of every sentence results in monotony. Similarly if every sentence follows the same pattern, the message will be dull and monotonous. By using variety of sentence patterns, the communicator can help the receiver to keep in step with him. It stimulates the receiver's interest in the message and thereby helps him to read the message carefully and to understand it thoroughly.

Repetition of Words, Phrases and Clauses

A series of sentences, each consisting co-ordinate clauses connected by 'and', 'or' and 'but', can result in a monotonous message. To avoid monotony, the communicator should try to avoid repetition of such co-ordinate clause pattern. He should try to acquire knowledge of the various possible ways of expressing an idea, and, should make himself familiar with them. Careless repetition of the same sentence pattern is often a result of communicator's limited vocabulary and inadequate knowledge of phrase and clause structure. It may also result from his unwillingness to make efforts for findings a substitute sentence pattern to express the same thought or feeling. In order to avoid the repetition of certain words belonging to a certain part of speech, the communicator has either to change the sentence pattern or has to substitute the word with a synonym. A word can have several shades of meanings, but the same word should not be used in two or more different senses in the same sentence.

Giving Special Emphasis

Though it is not fair to attribute virtue to the length of a sentence, a short sentence can be a means of effective expression if it is used properly. If a thought or an idea is to be given a stand of prominence, it can be conveniently placed in the pattern of a short simple sentence. In making a rapid summary or in emphasising a series of important ideas, a series of short sentences are more effective than the long ones. But, the habitual use of short sentences usually results in a jerky style of speech of writing. In order to avoid the habitual use of short sentences, care must be taken to restrict the use of short sentences for the purpose of giving special emphasis on a particular thought or idea in the mind of the communicator.

While emphasising certain idea in a sentence orally, the communicator can make use of the variations in his voice and gestures; but, while emphasising it in a written sentence, he can underline or capitalise certain words, phrases and clauses. He can also use some other techniques and devices to provide emphasis on the desired words. He can position the key word at the beginning of the sentence to draw attention of the reader to the key idea. Naturally, the most prominent positions in a sentence are the beginning and the end, and such position can be reserved for placing key words. The use of dash signal in a sentence results in a pause and the pause in its turn results in making the key word emphatic. Thus by transporting a word from its normal position to the beginning of the sentence, the writer places the word on the stage. Similarly, he can end a sentence with a worthwhile emphatic word or phrase.

Conversational Tone

To build and foster good business relations, the communicator must use pleasant and positive conversational words in the sentences constructed in active voice. The active voice sentences are more direct, more forceful and thereby more conversational than the sentences written in passive voice. The passive voice statements sound less personal. Passive voice can be used when a statement may seem more threatening and negative if it is used in active voice. A common fault in the effort of achieving conversational tone of a sentence occurs when the communicator uses pet words and phrases to describe people, places, actions, occasions and objects. He should avoid pet expressions and should learn how he can used other words and phrases in a sentence which fit whatever he is describing. He must eliminate the unnecessary, overused and superfluous words and phrases, like 'you know', 'you see', 'so to speak', 'to tell the truth', 'do you get my point', 'naturally', 'frankly', 'if you see what I mean', etc. from his sentence.

THE PARAGRAPH

A paragraph is a group of related sentences that deal with a distinct unit of thought for a specific purpose of developing the subject of an article. Each sentence in paragraph presents a smaller division of thought and each paragraph, as a part of an article as whole is concerned with a different unit of thought that contributes to the development of theme.

Organisation of Thoughts and Ideas

Every sentence in a paragraph has definite purpose of contributing a smaller division of thought to the development of the topic. The first sentence of a paragraph usually opens with the main idea and the following sentences are used for presenting supporting material. In business letters, memos and reports, the straightforward and direct approach of starting the main idea at the opening of the paragraph, and presenting the supporting ideas in the following sentences, is a most suitable way of paragraph organisation. Presenting the relevant facts at the beginning and announcing the main idea or final decision at the end is an indirect approach pattern. In sensitive writing assignments the writers softens the blow of he negative decision by citing factual details first. He aims to show that the decision follows in a logical manner from the factual details presented earlier in the paragraph. The end of the paragraph comes logically after the discussion of the main and supporting material of the paragraph. It rounds up the discussion and brings out a logical conclusion which is based on the factual details provided by the writer. Sometimes it restates the topic statement sentence with which the paragraph beings. Third way of paragraph ending is to paraphrase the topic by giving an exact statement of the ideas covered in the paragraph.

Coherence

There must be logical relation between any two successive paragraphs which consists two different phases of thoughts. In the succeeding (second) para the discussion in the previous paragraph is completed. From the beginning of the letter or an article, there should be an orderly sequence of thought from one paragraph to the next. This enables the reader to follow the discussion with ease. Ordinarily, the first paragraph gives a general discussion on the purpose of theme of the article. The general discussion is followed by the discussion of factual details. The paragraphs which are closely and logically related in thought are grouped together. The logical sequence between such paragraphs is indicated by using the transition devices between them. For example, a paragraph indicating results of the discussion in the preceding paragraph begins with 'consequently', 'Accordingly', 'Therefore' etc. Though such devices are not always necessary they can be effectively used when they are needed to make the relation clear and logical.

Length of Paragraphs

The length of each paragraph in a letter, memo or report can have its visual impact on the reader. Besides the cognitive effect of its thought content, the visual effect of the length of a paragraph, can be a controlling factor of the reader's reactions. The heavy blocks of long paragraphs certainly discourage the reader to continue his reading. The short paragraphs, on the other hand, break up the heavy look of the reading material. The visual impact of too many short paragraphs is as negative as that of the overly long paragraphs. A business letter or a report having several short paragraphs makes a choppy appearance. When the content of one paragraph is divided into two or more groups, it loses its coherence, and consequently the reader finds it difficult to understand. The thought in short paragraphs can be more readily grasped than that in the larger ones, but, each paragraph in itself should have sufficient importance to be treated as a separate and properly developed paragraph. Even a single brief sentence, if it has a sufficiently important statement, can be treated as a separate paragraph; but, such a sentence is used only occasionally to give an extra prominence to it's thought content.

PUNCTUATIONS

Introduction

In oral communication we use pauses, intonations, gestures, volume and non-verbal body language to help the receiver to see the 'points of division' and the 'relation in thought' between the words, phrases, clauses and sentences. But, these and many other tools of oral communication are not available to us in written communication. In a written message, punctuation helps the reader to understand the points of division in the sentences. Punctuation marks allow us to tell the reader about the pauses and points of divisions that further indicate the relation in thought between those groups in the sentence. Punctuation bridges or breaks the thought content of the words or word groups in a sentence. If the appropriate punctuation marks are not used, the writer will not be able to impart clear message to the reader. When the punctuation marks are used in wrong manner, it shows false division and wrong relationship between the groups. It can ultimately lead to misunderstanding and confusion of the reader. The rules of punctuation are merely the statements of general practice, therefore, they are required to be used intelligently. Occasionally, he should be ready to deviate from the rules and should vary the punctuation to suit different thought contents of the sentence.

Marks of Punctuation

1.	Period	.
2.	Question Mark	?
3.	Exclamation Point	!
4.	Comma	,
5.	Semicolon	;
6.	Colon	:
7.	Hyphen	-
	Dash	—
8.	Quotation Marks	" " ' '
9.	Parentheses	( )
10.	Brackets	[ ]
11.	Apostrophe	'
12.	Ellipses	. . .

Period .

Period is used —

(1) At the end of a Declarative and Imperative sentence.
   (a) They passed the bill yesterday.
   (Declarative)
   (b) Do not lead us into temptation.
   (Imperative)

(2) At the end of the indirect questions.
   (a) John asked me when the marklists would be prepared.
   (b) John asked Joseph whether he knew the last date of sending applications.

(3) At the end of the requests phrased as questions. [Will you please give your book.]

(4) After initials.
   T.S. Eliot
   W.H. Auden

(5) After abbreviations.

C.I.D.	Ph.D.	Jr. and Sr. College
M.P.	B.A.	a.m. p.m.
M.L.A.	M.Com.	Mr. Mrs.

Sometimes, the periods are not used between initials standing for organisations.

UNO MSEB UNICEF WHO BEST

Question Mark?

Question mark is used —

(1) At the end of a direct question.
   What is it?
   When are you going to London?
   Do you know his name?

(2) At the end of each item included in a series of questions.
   Are they agitating at Bombay? at Delhi? at Madras?

(3) At the end of a short direct question that follows a statement.

They are playing cricket, aren't they?
She is beautiful, isn't she?

Exclamation Point !

The exclamation point is used to express strong feeling or urgent command. It is used after a word, a phrase or a sentence.

Exclamation point is used —

(1) After a word.
Stop!
Watchout!
Congratulations!

(2) After a phrase.
The first man on moon!
A prophet in Chicago!

(3) After a sentence.
What a splendid idea it is!

Comma ,

The comma is used —

(1) For introducing a short quotation.
   (a) Taft said, "I don't see how I could have done differently from what I have."
   (b) He said to them, "It is I; do not be afraid."
   (c) He said, "I was not sent except to the lost sheep of the house of Israel."

(2) For separating the co-ordinate clauses of a compound sentence.
   (a) Surely oppression destroys a wise man's reason, and a bribe debases the heart.
   (b) The words of his mouth were smoother than butter, but war was in his heart.
   (c) Cast your burden on the Lord, and he shall sustain you.

(3) For separating a subordinate clause that precedes the main clause.
   (a) When shall I awake, that I may seek another drink?
   (b) If you faint in the day of adversity, your strength is

small.

(c) When you eat the fruit of your labor, you shall be happy.

(4) For separating an appositive.

(a) If you, Lord, should mark iniquities,
O Lord, who could stand?

(b) Mahatma Gandhi, the father of nation, has passed away.

(c) The chairman of the committee, Mr. Edward Bok, was late.

(5) For separating a long introductory phrase.

(a) With reference to your advertisement published in *Indian Express* 14th Sept. 1990, I have the pleasure to apply for the post of an engineer in your firm.

(b) After conducting the comprehensive survey of sugar industries in Kolhapur district, the committee presented their report to the Board of Directors.

(6) For separating parenthetical terms.

(a) However, they were happy.

(b) Furthermore, they may be allowed to resume their duties from tomorrow.

(c) As you know, the examination can hardly be passed in such a condition.

(7) For separating a series of words or word groups in a sentence.

All the men, women and children from India, Nepal, Pakistan and Bhutan arrived here by the special plane of U.S. Air Force.

(8) For separating two or more adjectives modifying the same noun.

(a) Carl is a strong, healthy athlete.

(b) She is beautiful, little girl.

(9) For separating the terms of direct address.

(a) Lord, help me.

(b) O King, tell your servants the dream.

(c) Peter, follow me.

(10) For writing figures in thousands.

(a) 5,000,000

(b) 3,508

(11) For indicating omitted words in a sentence.
Mr. Ben Smith gave seven lectures; Miss Mary Smith, five lectures.

(12) For separating the day of the month from the year.
(a) August 15, 1947.
(b) April 19, 1967.

Semicolon ;

The semicolon is used —

(1) For separating co-ordinate clauses of a compound sentence when the coordinating conjunction is omitted.
I will sing to the Lord as long as I live; I will sing praise to my God while I have my being.
He weakened my strength in the way; he shortened my days.

(2) For separating clauses that are punctuated by commas.
If someone says, "I love God" and hates his brother, he is a liar; for he who does not love his brother whom he has seen, how can be love God whom he has not seen?

Colon :

The colon is used —

(1) For indicating explanation or enumeration of a word, phrase or sentence.
These Presidents of United States are quoted in this book : A. Lincoln, F.D. Roosevelt, J.F. Kennedy.
Three trades of business : buying, making and selling are functionalised in their organisation.

(2) For introducing a direct, formal and long quotation.
He touched my mouth with it, and said : "Behold, this has touched your lips; your iniquity is taken away, And your sin purged."

(3) For separating hours, minutes and sometimes seconds.

5:30 p.m. 8:30 a.m. 9:20:47 a.m.

Hyphen - And Dash —

Hyphen is used -

(1) After these prefixes : pro, anti, ex, self, vice.

Pro-consul,	anti-national,
Pro-French,	anti-progressive
Vice-chancellor,	ex-serviceman
Vice-chairman,	self-service

(2) Between two adjectives.
three-room suite
first-class fare

(3) Between compound numbers written in words
fifty-five
One hundred and twenty-two

Dash is used —

(1) For separating — explanatory clauses and changes in expression.
   (a) And criticism is a dangerous spark — a spark that is liable to cause an explosion in the power magazine of pride.
   (b) "May God do so to Abner, and more also, if I do not do for David as the Lord has sworn to him — to transfer the Kingdom from the house of Saul, and set up the throne of David over Israel and over Judah, from Dan to Beersheba."
   (c) "When someone told me, saying, 'Look, Saul is dead', thinking to have brought good news, I arrested him and had him executed in Ziklag — the one who thought I would give him a reward for this news."

(2) For emphasising an appositive.
Then Jeremiah spoke to all the people — the men, the women, and all the people who had given him that answer.

Quotation Marks ' ' " "

Quotation marks are used —

(1) For enclosing an unusual word or phrase used with special trade meaning.

As I was young, I did not realise that I was witnessing an example of 'management by crisis' — which has been playing an increasing role in various sectors of our life.

The consultant also expressed his surprise at the clamour for 'private offices' in India.

(2) For enclosing direct quotations.

"The constitution of India can stand his talk", claimed the customer, "but my constitution cannot."

'You will share in the profits resulting from your own efforts.'

Never lead into a story with, "That reminds me of a story . . ."

Parenthesis ( )

Parentheses are used —

(1) For supplementary explanations.

For most people (above and below) a high rate of activity signifies a high level of efficiency.

Particularly where decision are likely to be unpopular, keep out of them (even out of the committees) by going on tour or on training or falling sick at the appropriate time. If they are in a line job, recommend a staff job to take full advantage of the creativity, analytical ability and imagination (displayed in creating rumours and spreading gossip).

(2) For enclosing enumerations.

It is distributed in four cities : (i) Bombay, (ii) Nagpur, (iii) Pune, (iv) Kolhapur.

Brackets [ ]

The brackets are used for enclosing added material in the direct quotations.

"If he [the kingmaker] wants to use five courses in a chart, don't show how you can do it with two."

Apostrophe

The apostrophe is used —

(1) For showing the plurals of figures, words and abbreviations.
The 5's, 10's, 15's, 20's and 25's are to be separated for analysis.
John's Men's, Girl's, Children's, anyone's, Peter's, M.B.A.'s, V.I.P.'s, M.A.'s, Ph.D.'s

(2) For indicating omission of letters in words.
I'm, I'll, I'd, We're, We'd, We'll, You're, You'd, You'll, He'll, She'll, It'll, He'd, She'd, It'd, they'll, they'd, isn't, it's, aren't, can't, hasn't, haven't, didn't, don't, wasn't, won't, weren't, shan't, wouldn't would've, etc.

Ellipses . . .

An ellipsis is used for indicating omission of words from quoted material.
"Picture in your mind the able, earnest and useful person you desire to be, and the thought you hold is hourly transforming you into that particular individual . . ."

"Remember the time you did this . . . and that . . ?"
"Reason was wasted on him and so were facts . . ."
"I will speak ill of no man," he said,
" . . . and speak all the good I know of everybody."

Exercise

(1) What is the significance language tools in business communication? Why should a businessman sharpen his language tools of business communication with persistent efforts?

(2) How does a businessman's choice of appropriate words and his strength of vocabulary play an important role in business communication?

(3) What is meant by — (a) colloquial, (b) dialectal, and (c) slang words?

(4) What is the significance of the following factors in achieving effectiveness in sentences?

(a) correctness in grammar, spelling and tone of a sentence.
(b) variety in sentence pattern

(c) special emphasis on ideas
(d) conciseness of expression
(e) length of a sentence
(f) repetition of words and phrases
(g) repetition of a sentence pattern
(h) style of speech and writing

(5) What is paragraph? What are the essentials of effective paragraph writing?
(6) What is the significance of punctuation in written communication.

A. Nature and Characteristics of Group Communication

B. Committees
   (a) Different Types of Committees
      1. Executive Committee
      2. Advisory Committee
      3. Permanent and Temporary Committees
      4. Line and Staff Committees
      5. Formal and Informal Committees
   (b) Advantages of Committee Meetings
   (c) Disadvantages of Committee Meetings
   (d) Factors Responsible for the Failure of the Committees
   (e) Essentials of Effective Committee Meetings

C. Conferences
   (a) Definition of a Conference
   (b) Significance of the Conferences
   (c) Conference and Committee
   (d) Essentials of Effective Conference Meeting
   (e) Essentials of Efficient and Effective Conference Leadership

[illegible] study [illegible]

[illegible]

Findings

Findings [illegible] main [illegible] the [illegible] proper [illegible] sequence [illegible] written [illegible] other [illegible] figures [illegible]

Conclusions

The report [illegible] basis of [illegible] findings [illegible] and their explanations [illegible] number of conclusions [illegible]. They should [illegible] descending order so that [illegible] the beginning.

Recommendations

Recommendations [illegible] findings [illegible] reports [illegible] or suggestions [illegible] and the recommendations are [illegible] short reports [illegible] five-six [illegible] reports the [illegible] the future [illegible]. The recommendations [illegible] are put as the [illegible] resolutions [illegible]

Appendix

The appendix contains [illegible] statistical data and other material [illegible] of the report. The details which are [illegible] body of the report are included in the appendix. [illegible] understand the contents of the reports without [illegible] through the details of the related [illegible], supporting [illegible] documents, he can find them in the appendix.

8

GROUP COMMUNICATION (COMMITTEES AND CONFERENCES)

From our birth to funeral ceremony, groups play a significant role in our life and communication is the basic tool for its smooth operations.

Group communication is a meeting of several human beings with different ideas, skills and interests who communication face-to-face in order to achieve a common goal. Though it is said that the group solutions are far less effective than those made by the individuals, we spend a lot of time as the members of committees, conferences and many other kinds of such small groups. If a business is conducted by the people who work in groups, they spend substantial amount of their time in interpersonal meetings. In small as well as large business organisations much of the interactions take place in the meetings. Usually, the small groups or committees in the organisation conduct meetings to solve the organisational problems.

NATURE AND CHARACTERISTICS OF GROUP COMMUNICATION

A small group with its common purposes and objectives, is an identifiable entity. It is composed of at least three members, but it is difficult to specify its upper size limit. If a group is composed of five or seven members, all of them can speak to one another. When the number of group members become larger, the group discussion centralises around a few people. A group with fewer than five members cannot present diversity of opinions, orientations and suggestions. It is also found that the groups, which consists the even number of people cannot function as effectively and successfully as the groups of odd numbers. The knowledge, ability and experience of the group members to communicate successfully in such groups determines their personal future and also the future of their organisation.

Some decisions that affect the procedures followed by everyone in the organisation, are usually made in group settings. They go through the process of problem solving and ultimately reach up to some decision which is taken collectively by the group. It is obvious that each of such group has some problem to solve and they have to determine the best way of solving it. Now-a-days the business organisations are making an increased use of group discussions to solve their managerial problems. The essence of these group is the deliberation and discussion made in it. A group member may act as a leader or as a participant, but he must influence the group and carry his share of the load.

There must be some formal or informal purpose for group interaction which brings people together to decide the best ways of fulfilling it. The routine as well as the unusual meetings may need to solve problems, make decisions or simply to keep the group informed, but anyhow there must be some purpose or reason for the meeting. If they gather without any purpose, it cannot be called as a group meeting. A group can have a meeting only when there is a purpose for it. A group cannot be called as a group if it has no purpose. A group meeting always develops its own pattern of interaction through its communication network. To accomplish their specific purposes, the group members use a certain communication network. This network results from the relationships of the status system within the group. This status system decides the patterns of communication behaviour within the group. Even the seating arrangement for a group meeting indicates the status system of the group.

The group communication follows the meeting procedure which is called as an agenda of the meeting. The group cannot communicate properly unless the group members follow certain norms of the meeting. The group plans the procedure which is obligatory to all its members. If the procedure is violated by any one of the members, the group cannot function effectively. If the group has some kind of power and authority, the decisions made by them are implemented. A group like the advisory committee does not enjoy any power. The executive body of the organisation decides whether to accept the advice of the committee or not.

COMMITTEES

Different Types of Committees

Executive Committee

An executive committee or the managing committee is the action group which makes the decisions and implements them. This committee is usually elected by the members of the organisation at its annual general meeting. The parent body of the organisation specifies the powers and duties of the committee. The parent body is the policy making group to which the executive committee has to submit the account of its performance at regular intervals. Usually, the committee enjoys the right to give orders and it has powers to exact obedience from the subordinates. The executive committee must keep before their eyes the objectives, goals, policies and traditions of the organisation while making decisions in day-to-day matters.

Advisory Committee

Advisory committee does not have power in decision-making and in implementing the policy decisions. The main objective of this committee is to give advice to the managerial bodies of the organisation. The business organisations have become so complex today that the management has to seek the advice from the experts and specialists in the advisory committee. Such committee usually consists of the experts in their respective fields. The members of this committee do not enjoy any right to vote.

Permanent and Temporary Committees

The permanent or standing committee is formed on a permanent basis. It is a kind of executive committee which enjoy the powers of making and executing decisions in the light of organisational goals. Finance committee, product committee, bonus committee, salary committee are some of the standing committees. These committees perform vital managerial functions for the organisation. The temporary committee or ad-hoc committee is created for special purpose and it is dissolved when the objectives are reached. Thus it has a short life span. Such committees are usually formed to explore certain possibilities for restructuring the present systems, or for preparing certain reports. Immediately after accomplishing the purpose, they are dissolved.

Line and Staff Committees

A line committee discusses the issues related with the duties of their subordinates and it has the authority to take decisions on those issues. The decisions taken by the committee are limited only for those subordinates who are responsible to it. A staff committee is a kind of advisory committee. It performs advisory function and also informs the management about the views of the employees regarding the management policies and procedures.

Formal and Informal Committees

Formal committees are delegated with specific powers and duties by the organisation. They function as a part of organisational structure. These committees are of a permanent nature and they are formally constituted. Informal committees are formed for group thinking and for solving a particular problem. They do not have any formal authority of decision-making. They do not have any fixed agenda. The recommendations and suggestions of the informal committee are regarded as advice and not as the formal decisions.

Advantages of Committee Meetings

Coordination: Interdepartmental activities require coordination. The committee meetings can promote greater coordination in the interdepartmental activities. A committee consisting of departmental managers can foster better understanding and coordination among various departments in the organisation.

Democratisation: Committees do not permit the authoritarianism. They do not allow the concentration of authority and power in the hands of one man. It distributes the power in the hands of all the members of the committee.

Training the Juniors: Committees provide training to the subordinates or the junior executives who get insight into the managerial problems faced by the seniors. The juniors pick up the knowledge and skills from the experienced senior executives.

Transmitting and Receiving Information: Committees transmit and receive valuable information. The information which is communicated in the committee can be properly understood by all the members because they can raise questions on the points which are not properly understood.

Uniformity in Information: A committee consisting of different representative members gather information from various departments of the organisation. If the representative members belong to the department which requires coordination among themselves the committee ensures the uniformity of the information gathered from all of them.

Giving adequate representation: In business, a committee can be formed of the representatives of all the people who are linked with that particular business organisation. A committee can give adequate representation to the share holders, customers, creditors, trade unions etc. which are very important groups for any business organisation.

Fostering labour participation: A committee can be used to foster labour participation in management. The labour representatives of various departments or a representative of the trade union can be included in a suitable committee to safeguard the interests of the employees.

Consolidating authority: The general manager or the top executive delegates the authority of decision making to the committee which is formed of the heads of the various departments. Thus through delegation authority is consolidated in a committee.

Raising morale: When the employees participate in the decision-making process, their morale is raised and their relationship with the employers is improved.

Receiving feedback: The management receives feedback through the committees. A committee can be very helpful to the management in receiving responses and reactions of the employees and other interested groups regarding the proposed policies of the organisation.

New ideas and suggestions: The members of a committee may conceive altogether novel ideas while discussing a problem. They can provide valuable suggestions on the future activities of the organisation.

Pooling of knowledge and group judgement: A committee consisting of the persons with different specialisations can pool their knowledge and experience. Different views and opinions are expressed by the members having different personal qualities. Such a group discussion finally evolves a balanced group judgement.

Disadvantages of Committee Meeting

A tendency to prolong the discussion: It is a matter of common experience that taking decisions promptly is not an easy task in almost every committee meeting. There is always a tendency among the committee members to prolong the discussion.

Delay: When the committee members talk on irrelevant and trivial matters, it unnecessarily causes delay in taking decision.

Lengthy Procedure: Forming a committee, giving a due notice, preparing the agenda, making the necessary arrangements and finally the prolonged discussion is a lengthy procedure of the committee meetings.

Minority domination: Sometimes a committee has to yield to the wishes of a minority group. A strong-headed Chairman or few strong members of the committee can make the decision which is usually accepted by all the members of the committee.

Self-interest of the members: A committee works in groups and every decision taken by the committee accommodates the self-interest of the members. Such decisions may not be in the interest of the organisation.

Expensive: The procedure and arrangements required for the committee meeting are expensive. A committee sometimes branches out in sub-committee. Their deliberations take a long time which may prove expensive.

Split Responsibility: No member of the committee really feels accountable for the decisions taken after deliberations because the authority of committee is divided among its member. Every member of the committee feels lower degree of responsibility for the decisions as compared to the decisions taken by the individual.

Avoiding Action: Committees are often used to postpone the action on various grounds. The managers can avoid decisions and actions on the grounds of receiving committee report.

Compromised solutions: Committees have to take decisions which compromise the views and opinions of many dynamic members in it. Thus the proposed solution becomes a compromised or diluted solution. Such solutions often suggest weak course of action.

Factors Responsible for the Failure of the Committees

Lack of effective control: The chairman fails to control the meeting while the members talk at random. He fails to give right direction to the discussion which results in irrelevant and trivial talking among themselves.

Organised pooling of ignorance: Organised pooling of ignorance is found to be the cause of failure of many committee meetings. If the members lack competence, knowledge of the subject and essential experience, the committee meeting is bound to be a failure.

Authoritarian leader: In a committee meeting, communication is choked up if the chairman is authoritarian who does not allow the members to talk freely. In this situation, the members under-estimate their ideas, views, opinions and feelings.

Formal procedures: Sometimes the secretary does not follow the formal procedures. For example, he fails to give proper notice of the meeting well in advance.

Too few or too many members: The inadequate representation usually results in inadequate variety of opinions. On the other hand, a committee which is crowded with members provide wide diversity of opinions which results in delaying decisions.

Essentials of Effective Committee Meetings

Suitable subject: The subject of a committee meeting must be suitable for group discussion. Some subjects are not suitable for the discussion in committee meetings. Certain subjects are suitable for individual decisions only. Therefore, only those subjects should be selected for a committee meeting which really need to be discussed there.

Authority and scope of the committee: The power and authority of the committee must be defined clearly. The committee members must know the committee terms of reference.

An effective chairman: The chairman has to control and guide the members of the committee. He has to allow the members to express their thoughts without fear or terror. He must not be authoritarian. He must remain impartial during the discussion. The must be able to give proper direction to the discussion. He has to control the dominating member. He must motivate the silent member to express themselves.

Competent and appropriate membership: The committee members must be selected carefully. They must be competent, positive and experienced. They should have adequate knowledge of the subject in which they have to contribute to decision-making. They must not be submissive or aggressive. In business, appropriate representation must be given to various groups, departments, employees and other people who are connected with it.

Correct size: The size of a committee must be adequate. It should neither be too small nor too large. It is found that the committee in which the membership is limited between five to eleven, gives best results. Too many members cause delay in decisions, whereas too small committee may not provide necessary deliberation.

Procedure: A committee meeting must follow the prescribed procedure. The agenda of the meeting must be prepared properly before the given date of the meeting. The date, time and venue of the meeting must be suitable to the members. The agenda must be circulated well in advance to every member of the committee. There should be provision for writing minutes of the committee meeting.

Preparation

(a) Every member of the committee must make proper study of the agenda.
(b) They have to understand and identify the problems before the committee.
(c) They have to collect all the essential information from various sources such as office files, periodicals, journals, house organs, interviews, personal observations, visits etc.
(d) They must analyse the problem and write down the possible solutions and other points of their speech.
(e) The chairman as well as all the member of the committee must practice their speech before attending the meeting.

Punctuality: All the participants must observe punctuality. The meeting must start and end at a given time.

Study of the committee colleagues: The participants must try to study the behaviour of the other members. It is essential to know their strong and weak points and the way they react to different ideas and isms. The participants must know the special interests of their colleagues.

Positive approach: Every member of the committee must try to be calm and composed when others lose equilibrium of their mind. It is essential to use reason while dealing with unreasonable person. Every participant must identify and control his negative impulses.

Flexibility: The members must be flexible enough to understand others' points of views and opinions. They must gracefully agree with the right views and ideas of their colleagues.

Well-timed speech: Though there are no strict rules laid down about timing speech, it is essential for every member to decide when his speech can be most effective. The creative, constructive and important ideas which are to be accepted by the members, should be expressed earlier.

Clarity: The members must have clear idea of the purpose of the meeting. There must be clarity in the thoughts and presentation.

Some Do's for the participants

(a) They must express their thoughts, freely, forcefully, confidently, clearly, briefly and completely.
(b) They must listen attentively to the other participants.
(c) They must always respect the authority of the chair person.
(d) They must accept the final decisions.

Some Do's and Don'ts of committee meeting

1. *Some Don'ts for the participants*
   (a) They should not interrupt the speech of the other participants.
   (b) They should not be closed-minded.
   (c) They should not sound dogmatic.
   (d) They should not lose temper.
   (e) They should not consider others as 'ignorant fools'.
   (f) They should not give long lectures.
   (g) They should not satirise or ridicule the other speakers.

2. *Some Do's and Don'ts for the chairman of committee*
   (a) He should start and close the meeting in given time. He should be firm about meeting schedule.
   (b) He has to direct the discussion according to the list of all items in the agenda.
   (c) He has to plan the order in which the items are to be discussed.
   (d) He must make himself sure about the pleasant and comfortable physical facilities in the meeting hall.
   (e) He must clearly specify the purpose of the meeting at the beginning of discussion.
   (f) His opening remarks should be brief enough to suggest the urgency of the problem.

(g) He must try to get everyone involved in the discussion. He must encourage them to participate.
(h) He should control the proceedings, especially in the event of conflicts and personality flare-ups by assuming an impartial and neutral position.
(i) He should not have prejudices.
(j) He should exert his leadership to control the troublesome members. He should not let them take over the meeting. He must use his techniques to control the obstructors from ruining the group process.
(k) If required, he must be prepared to alter his plans and the agenda. He must be flexible.
(l) He must observe the non-verbal expressions of the participants.
(m) He must be a good listener.
(n) He must keep the discussion moving. As a leader he must question, summarise and direct the members.

CONFERENCES

Definition of a Conference

A conference is an act of consulting and discussing to share knowledge, experiences, thoughts, feelings and opinions among a group of people who have common objectives. It is a kind of meeting at which people pool their knowledge, exchange their views and talk together to analyse information which is relevant to the topic set before them. A group of people involved in conference can discuss their individual as well as collective problems. By pooling ideas and experience, conference provides collaborative thinking to the problems.

As compared to committee meeting, a conference meeting may be less formal but its formality cannot be denied. It is formal because it needs to be planned and organised. The conference leader or the group has to determine its purpose and the objectives. The leader has to outline the procedure and pattern of the conference. He has to prepare the set of questions. He has to guide and control the discussion. All this makes conference a formal activity of consultation. The participants of a conference must have knowledge and experience about the subject matter to be discussed in the meeting. The well-informed, experienced and studied conferees can take active part in the discussion. If they are experts in a particular field of knowledge and have specific experience in the subject, the discussion can be profitable for the concerned business organisations.

Significance of the Conferences

The conferences play significant role in accomplishing development of analytical and questioning attitude. The conferees try to find out what really is the problem. To define a problem may seem easy at first sight but by defining a problem, the participants ascertain the depth, scope and the critical factors of the problem. They analyse the problem and suggest the alternative solutions. They also find out the limitations to the solution of the problem. They collect the essential information and classify the facts. They decide the type of information they have secured for decision-making and eliminate the irrelevant information. In business, it is rare to find out a problem for which there can be no alternative solutions. The conferees suggest alternative solutions which helps to make the best decision. Only the inexperienced and ignorant conferees base their decisions on emotions rather than on reasoning. The manager who participates or leads the conference can develop his ability of analysing a problem to take apt and sound decisions.

The conferences have educational value in business and also in other fields where negotiation, collaboration and collective thinking is essential. Within the organisations, conferences are held to give training to the employees. Conferences can also be used for modifying attitudes, opinions and feelings of the participants. A conference within a business organisation can provide necessary information of the policies, procedures, customs, traditions and objectives of the organisation to the conferees. The new employees can share the practical knowledge and experience of the elders and superiors through conference. The managements can use conference tactfully to correct the mistakes and misunderstandings among the groups, but is not a place for warning or reprimanding the individual participant.

An employee who attends the conference starts thinking in terms of the company as a whole. In a planned conference he observes that the information is collected, facts are assembled and studied, problems are defined and analysed, all the advantages and disadvantages of the alternative solutions are discussed and then attempts are made to arrive at best decisions. This demonstration of the problem solving approach is bound to have a positive and beneficial effect on the employee who attends the conference. His participation in the conference raises his morale and strengthens his confidence. He tends to give more thought to the coordinate activities of the organisation.

The conferences help the employees to think more effectively and more often about the objectives and problems of the organisation. A weekly conference of the sales department can help the salesmen to develop effective sales strategy for the next month. They share each others views and experiences which help them to improve their performance.

In some industrial conferences, the experts and delegates from similar concerns are invited to discuss their mutual problems and prospects. Such conferences stimulate the creative flow of ideas and information, pool knowledge, views and experiences, and suggest possible solutions to the problems. If the conference is hosted by some industrial concern, it enhances its prestige and goodwill. The industrial conferences can promote public relations and can direct the attention of the public as well as of the government on the problems and prospects of a particular industry.

The conference sessions are very important in bringing about a change in attitudes of the conferees towards the other persons and situation. An individual's attitude towards the other persons and situations is governed by his past experiences and also by the varied impressions to which he is exposed. In conference sessions he listens to interpretations made by the other conferees about the same persons and situations. The group interpretations of the person's problems and situations can destroy the misunderstanding, distrust and doubt in the mind of an individual conferee. This does not mean that the group discussions can change the attitudes of every conferee on every subject, but the average individual is often willing to adopt the group attitude.

Conference and Committee

Comparative Study

Both a conference and a committee are kinds of group meetings and the dividing line between them is very thin. A Conference is more informal in nature than a committee. If a conference has a purpose to encourage group thinking a committee may have a purpose of covering definite information about some problem. A committee is more specific, whereas a conference is more general. The purpose of a conference is less defined than that of committee. The scope of a conference is wider than that of a committee which is confined to the discussion of given problem. A committee has to follow its procedures strictly. Usually this procedure is governed by parliamentary rules which are obligatory to every participant. In conference, the participants enjoy free discussions which are usually guided by its leader. In a committee, the emphasis is laid on decision making but in a conference the emphasis is on discussion which may later lead to decisions. The suggestions and recommendations from a conference are not binding on the executives. The decisions of a committee meeting are made for implementation. In a committee meeting agenda is compulsory but it is not compulsory in conference. A committee has to strictly adhere the agenda but at a conference the discussion is of a general nature. If a conference has an agenda, it is not required to be followed strictly. The number of the participants of a committee can be up to fifteen but a conference may consist of a larger number. A conference enjoy only an advisory or consultative capacity and its decisions are in the nature of recommendations. The conferees do not enjoy the voting right like that of the committee members.

Essentials of Effective Conference Meeting

There are a number of conditions for the successful and effective conference meeting. The following conditions must be considered while holding a conference meeting.

(i) The objectives of the conference meeting must be stated clearly. The topic and purpose of the conference meeting must be clarified.

(ii) The agenda is necessary to be prepared and distributed among the conferees well in advance.

(iii) The conferees invited for the meeting must be capable of making valuable contribution in the discussion.

(iv) The conference leader must be competent, well qualified, expert and experienced in subject which is to be discussed in the conference.

(v) The conference leader and the participants must make adequate preparation for the discussion. They must be interested and enthusiastic.

(vi) The number of the conferees must be limited up to fifteen.

(vii) The conference hall facilities must be adequate and ought to be kept in order.

(viii) The essential conference material must be carefully prepared and well planned to meet the needs of the discussion.

(ix) The management must be interested in the conference discussion and conclusions.

(x) The management must support the conference. The decisions from conference ought to be followed up by the management. The people in the conference must be worthy of every consideration and respect for the management.

Essentials of Efficient and Effective Conference Leadership

(i) He must have a good knowledge of the topic, conferees, conference objectives and procedure.

(ii) He must be intelligent, clear and rapid thinker.

(iii) He must be able to command, respect and confidence of the conferees and management.

(iv) He must make adequate preparation and planning for the conference.

(v) He must try to acquire maximum knowledge of the subject matter.

(vi) He must remember that selection of the conferees is critical to the success of the conference. He must carefully decide whom to invite to the conference.

(vii) He must be thoroughly acquainted with the purpose and objectives of the agenda.

(viii) He must prepare the agenda. The agenda must be distributed among the conferees well in advance.

(ix) He must be able to use language freely, effectively and clearly. He must have ease and clarity of expression.

(x) He must be able to analyse the points of discussion and the contributions of the conferees. He must have the ability of analysing problems and its solutions.

(xi) He must be receptive to new ideas, methods and suggestions.

(xii) He must try to understand new problems.

(xiii) He must understand the viewpoints of the top management. He must help the conferees also to understand the viewpoints of the top management.

(xiv) He must give fair treatment and courteous hearing to every participant.

(xv) He must be impartial and impersonal. He must not permit his personal feeling to affect the judgement.

(xvi) He must be open minded and he must help the conferees to become open minded.

(xvii) He must help the conferees to understand the viewpoints of their associates, superiors and subordinates,

(xviii) He must be patient and active listener.

(xix) He must have tact and ability of dealing with people without offending them.

(xx) He must encourage and help the conferees to organise their thinking and expression.

(xxi) He must have self-restraint. He must not dominate the discussion by expressing his own thoughts and opinions.

(xxii) He must not make long speeches.

(xxiii) He must not underestimate the views and opinions of the conferees.

(xxiv) He must recognise his own limitations. He must do his best for self-improvement.

(xxv) He must develop a personality that attracts, appeals and commands confidence,loyalty and respect, but, he need not wish to become a superman.

(xxvi) He must have a good sense of humour.

(xxvii) He must predetermine the ways of creating and maintaining interest and enthusiasm.

(xxviii) He must know the group dynamics and ways of handling them.

(xxix) He must anticipate the situations and problems that may arise during the discussion.

(xxx) He must plan his questions carefully in order to open the discussion, to get individual participation, to develop subject matter, to change the trend of the discussion and to limit the discussion.

(xxxi) He must assemble the facts of the discussion and chart them on the sheet of paper.

(xxxii) He must get the minutes prepared and distributed among the conferees.

(xxxiii) He must be able to evaluate the facts quickly. He must be quick in his reactions.

(xxxiv) He must make use of the case studies, maps, charts, diagrams, pictures, films and other audio-visual aids if they are necessary to be used.

(xxxv) He must determine the plan of action. While summarising the discussion he must make the plan of action clear to the conferees.

(xxxvi) He must make a good ending of the conference meeting. The closing time limits must be observed. At the end of the meeting he must announce the next meeting and the topic.

Exercises

1. What is a meeting? What are the various advantages of the meeting?
2. What is a committee? How is it different from a conference?
3. What are the various advantages and limitations of the committee meetings?
4. What are the ways and means of making the committee meetings successful?
5. What communication problems are generally found in committee meetings?
6. What should be the optimum size of a committee? What are the disadvantages of a too small committee? What are the disadvantages of a too large committee?
7. What are the different types of committees?
8. What are the duties of committee chairman? What important points should be kept in mind to run the committee meeting efficiently and effectively?
9. "Conference is a kind of informal committee meeting". Discuss.
10. What is a conference? What are advantages and disadvantages of the conference?
11. What are the essentials of an effective chairmanship?
12. How should the participants prepare themselves to participate effectively in the meetings of the committees and conferences?

A. What is Listening?
B. Significance of Effective Listening in Business Communication
C. Active Listening
D. Some Do's for Listeners
E. Some Don'ts for Listeners
F. Obstacles to Effective Listening

9

LISTENING

"Listen to counsel and receive instruction,
That you may be wise in your latter days".
"Cease listening to instructions, my son,
And you will stray from the words of knowledge".

– Proverbs, 19:20-27, *Holy Bible*

What is Listening?

Listening is a process of receiving, interpreting and reacting to the messages received from the communication sender. Effective listening is an art of communication which is often taken for granted and ignored. Like any other art, listening requires to be cultivated consciously, carefully and systematically. Unfortunately, our education systems beginning from kindergarten up to college level do not pay proper attention to the teaching of effective listening. As listening is fundamental to all communication, poor listening can be considered as a mighty barrier to communication. It often results in losing messages due to improper functioning of communication. We often mistake hearing for listening. In fact, hearing, which depends upon the ears, is just a physical act, and except for the physically impaired person, everyone can hear without conscious efforts. On the other hand, listening requires conscious efforts of interpreting the sounds, grasping the meanings of the words and reacting to the message. Interpreting the sound signals is a cognitive act which depends on the listener's knowledge of the code signals and on his attitude towards the communication sender.

Active listening process beings when the listener pays attention to some audible sound signals and permits himself to interpret those sounds cognitively. It does not begin when he unconsciously permits his ears to hear the audible sounds. It is a conscious process. The sound signals which stand for some arbitrary meaning engage the listener's attention and demand for some kind of response from him. Every human being possesses the ability to select from the sounds around him. But the selective listening is not an automatic process like that of hearing. An individual may hear many sounds but he may listen to none of them. The process of listening which stands with the selective attending of the listener to some listener can evaluate the message and draw certain conclusions. His judgements on the received message can be in agreement with the sender or it may stand in contradiction with the views of the sender. Usually, when a proposal is rejected by the receiver, the sender feels that the receiver has not listened to it. But, in fact, the receiver already listen to it and draws certain conclusions which compel him to reject the proposal. The active listener evaluates the message and decides whether to agree with it or not.

Significance of Effective Listening in Business Communication

In business, effective listening improves the information outputs of the manager and helps him to make better policies, to take correct decisions, to solve the problems and grievances, to know various activities of his own organisation and to understand the activities of the competing and parallel organisations. The average managers spend about fifty per cent of their communication time in listening. They carefully listen to the message to feel the pulse of the employees, to understand their mood and reactions to the policies of the management and to find out if there is any false rumour which may cause damage to the organisation. They try to create a congenial atmosphere for listening which allows freedom of expression for the speakers. Effective listening to the speech of an encouraged speaker is extremely important for promoting understanding and co-ordination among various departments in the organisation. Lack of good listening can create the embarrassing situations which result in the lack of co-ordination and mutual understanding. Some authoritarian managers do not like to discuss their problems and its solutions with the subordinates and they plainly reject to listen to their suggestions and proposals. This kind of authoritarian approach is a strong barrier to listening and it provokes bitterness, indignation and misunderstanding among the employees. Effective listening is very essential for the success of open-door policy. People will walk into the managers cabin if he encourages them to speak and listens to them carefully. A manager who listens to the employees, gives them an opportunity to purgate their pent up emotions. Effective listening also helps the managers to get the constructive suggestions from the employees. There can be greater harmony and cohesion in the organisation if the management and the employees listen to each others messages effectively. It can raise the morale of the employees and the raised morale can bind them together with a sense of togetherness. The employees can introduce now schemes and useful suggestions to the manager if he allows their participation in the decision making process and listen carefully to what they say. The significance of effective listening needs to be properly understood by the managements as well as by the employees and enough efforts should be taken to acquire the skills of active listening.

Active Listening

We may 'sit back' and listen to a song sung by a little girl or to the music on a radio broadcast, but when we are to take part in communication, it is necessary to 'sit up' and listen carefully. It would be improper to think about how we can get other people to listen to us, but it would be certainly advisable to think about how we can get ourselves to listen to others patiently and carefully because half-listening is likely to result in misunderstanding and loss of time. The listener must show his interest in the speaker and the speech by his facial expressions, posture and by the questions and comments on the speech. The listener who asks questions and comments on the views of the speaker, encourages the speaker to express his ideas fully and enthusiastically. The bored, disinterested and silent listener discourages the speaker.

Listening to a speaker on radio or television can be a good preliminary practice to improve listening. We can try to concentrate our attention on various aspects of the speech and find out the main theme, supporting ideas and the digressions from the given subject. After listening to the speech, we can write down a paragraph in which we may reflect on his thoughts and evaluate his arguments. This practice can certainly help us to become a better listener.

While listening, it is essential to concentrate on what a person is saying, but it would be wrong to neglect his 'looks' because his 'looks' can supply us with physical and non-verbal signs. His physical appearance, movements of the head, hands and of the entire body, facial expressions, his posture, etc., are equally important to his words. Though non-verbal signs give us reliable information, the listener should not be carried away with the thoughts on the physical appearance of the speaker. If he is distracted by the mannerism of the speaker, he will not be able to listen to the verbal message with adequate concentration. The listener must understand properly the feelings and sentiments of the speaker. He should look at the message from the speaker's point of view, so that he may get some idea of the speaker's feelings associated with the message. As an active listener, the employer should try to know what the employee thinks and feels on a particular subject by sincerely paying attention to his ideas and interpretations. People in different positions and occupations have different outlooks on the various issues of life. They perceive and interpret the ideas with different meanings because those ideas may have different associations with their past experiences. When the listener understands that the speaker is tending to be hostile critic of him and he may even pass some direct or implied criticism, the listener tends to be inattentive. But a wise listener searches for the complaints, criticisms and other evidences of the speaker's dissatisfaction. A wise department head shows receptive and constructive attitude towards the criticism on himself and his department because it gives him an opportunity for the self-improvement. Usually we listen with interest the message which is to our advantage, but we should take equal interest in the speeches which consist a message to the advantage of the speaker.

When it is possible to hear a message clearly without any physical distraction, the listener must become active in attending the message. If noises interfere with the physical reception of message, the listener has to prepare his mind to concentrate on the selected signals, and should not allow himself to be distracted by the noises. A pretty typist sitting beside him may distract a clerk's attention but he must try to avoid the cause of his distraction with effort. He might not allow himself to get visually distracted by avoiding the temptation of looking at her but he might again feel difficulty in avoiding distraction caused by the sweet cosmetic perfume of his neighbour. In such situations, a good listener has to exercise a good deal of mental discipline over himself in order to concentrate properly on the message transmitted by the speaker.

The listener has to force his attention to stay on the speech. The concentrated effort of the listener to focus his attention on the message in order to understand its contents can surely help the listener to overcome his tiredness and fatigue. If the listener feels tiredness, his attention tends to wander. He has to keep a part of his mind aware about how he is listening to the message. When he finds himself losing interest, he has to pull himself back to the message. The listener who loses his interest in the speech would find the speech dull and his mind will be distracted in daydreaming. The speaker may also develop his idea in an interesting way. The listener can keep his mind alert to receive even a dull and slow speech by anticipating what the speaker would say as a next point in his speech. If he guesses correctly, it will arouse his interest in the subject. It can also help him to remember the speech. On the other hand, an incorrect guess would keep him engaged in thinking about why the speaker might have turned to the other point. There is also another way of listening to a boresome and slow speech. The listener can take a very quick review from time to time of what the speaker had said a shortwhile ago.

It is proved that the poor listeners usually listen and remember the specific facts presented by the speaker and tend to forget the central idea. For effective listening, the listener has to look for the main ideas and for the theme of the speech. If the listener listens for the factual details, he will not be able to recall the theme and many of the factual details because human memory tends to remember the 'pattern' or 'theme' rather than the isolated factual details. It is obvious that the isolated facts do not make sense if they are not associated with the main theme. The facts can be remembered but only as the logical supporting evidence to the main idea of the speech.

The listener can listen faster than the speaker can speak. This gives an excess time to the listener to judge and evaluate the message. He listens just a part of what the speaker tries to convey and goes on preparing his cross-questions, queries and replies. Sometimes, he gets so much involved in judging, evaluating and preparing his replies and cross questions that he fails to pay attention to what the speaker says further. He raises a question and interrupts the speaker at the first pause without listening the message completely. Such a listener keeps himself busy in forming his own comments. But it is always better to listen to the speaker completely. A careful listener never jumps to conclusions about what the speaker says till the latter completes his speech. For effective listening, the listener should wait for the entire representation to conclude. He has to begin his overall evaluation of the speech just after the speech is over.

The tired, bored and lazy listeners may pretend to be attentive by their postures as they usually rest their chin on hand or bend forward in the chair of show that they really pay attention to the talk, but in fact, they may get occupied with some other thoughts. They may drift away in pondering over their personal problems and worries. Some of the listeners pretend to listen as they make notes, read mail and do other petty routine activities. But, effective listening should not be considered as an easy and passive encounter. The listener requires mental preparedness and energy to concentrate on the speech and on the non-verbal cues of communication like body movements, posture, hand gestures, facial expressions, tone of voice, eye-contacts, etc. Therefore, a good listener always takes listening as hard, conscious and positive work which requires will power and attention.

The listener sometimes avoids the message if he feels it difficult to be understood or too hard to be followed. But he should try to be receptive even to the difficult subject and should take it as a challenge to his ability of listening and competence of understanding. It may be easier to listen to a humorous and commic talk as compared to a lecture on the laws of taxation, but the listener who makes strong determination of attentive listening can find even the complicated and complex presentation easy to comprehend provided he possesses average or good intellectual ability. In order to devote his time for training his ear in listening the difficult, complicated and challenging speech programmes on radio and television are useful.

A number of audio, visual and audio-visual distractions can distract our attention from the speaker. This interference of 'noise' can sidetrack the listener's attention if he does nothing to control his environment to filter out the distractions. A manager who has to listen to the complaint of an employee should not tap on the table or shuffle the papers. He must refuse the phone calls and should shut the door so that he can listen attentively to the complaints or grievances without getting distracted by noise or the intruders. Some workers are afraid to tell their grievances and complaints to their supervisors. But the superiors should try to convince the subordinates that they really want to listen to their complaints and grievances in order to settle them. It is essential to remember that people explain their problems to the sympathetic listeners. When they get an opportunity to tell about their problems, worries and anxieties to someone, they find the release of their emotional tensions.

Some Do's for Listeners

1. Keep quiet while listening.
2. Focus on what the speaker says rather than on his looks.
3. Control and screen out the distractions.
4. Show interest in the speaker.
5. Be friendly and patient towards the speaker.
6. Listen first and take notes afterwards.
7. Look for the main theme and main ideas.
8. Let the speaker finish whatever he has to say without interrupting him.
9. (a) Find an area of interest in the speech.
   (b) Look interested in the speech.
   (c) Act interested in listening.
10. Try to repeat the key-ideas during the slow and long speeches.
11. Avoid pondering on a single point.
12. Keep your mind open to every subject and speaker.
13. Choose a quiet place to listen, if possible.
14. Arrive early at the place of a seminar, lecture, talk or meeting.
15. Empathise with the speaker and try to understand his opinions, views and values.
16. Try to probe the emotions and feelings of the speaker.
17. Seek out difficult speech presentations to challenge your listening skills.
18. Observe the non-verbal signals, the body movements, facial expressions and gestures.
19. Try to look into the eyes of the speaker.
20. Try to relate the speaker's message with your personal experience.
21. Try to evaluate the speaker's message objectively.
22. Try to enrich your vocabulary so that you may understand the exact shade of meaning conveyed by the words of the speaker.
23. Accept criticism without losing your temper.
24. Communicate feedback to the speaker. Ask questions which may encourage the speaker.
25. Remember that God has given you two ears and one tongue.

Some Don'ts for Listeners

1. Don't interrupt the speaker.
2. Don't be impatient towards the criticism in the speech.
3. Don't be distracted by the audio-visual noise.
4. Don't be involved in daydreaming during listening.
5. Don't lose interest in the speaker and his speech.
6. Don't just pretend to pay attention.
7. Don't focus on the dress and appearance of the speaker.
8. Don't be late at the place of meeting or lecture.
9. Don't think too much about a single point.
10. Don't be closed-minded.
11. Don't hesitate to give oral or non-verbal feedback.
12. Don't listen to several people at a time.
13. Don't read your mail and don't entertain telephone calls while you listen to someone's speech.
14. Don't discourage the speaker by openly contradicting his statements or by pointing out his petty grammatical mistakes.
15. Don't be in the state of emotional excitement.
16. Don't listen with negative attitude towards the speaker.
17. Don't show your lack of interest in the speech.
18. Don't try to outline every factual detail.

Obstacles to Effective Listening

As listening is an art of communication, the communicator has to learn and acquire the skill of listening. While improving his listening, he must identify and overcome the following obstacles:

1. Listener's resistance to the new ideas in the speech.
2. Emotional excitement of the listener.
3. Inattentiveness to the lengthy and untimely speech.
4. Listener's distrust in the speaker.
5. Listener's status consciousness, especially when the listener is superior and the speaker is subordinate.
6. Closed-mindedness of the listener.
7. Conflict of the attitudes and values of the listener with those of the speaker.
8. Mental argument with the speaker before comprehending the total message.

9. Prejudices against the speaker.
10. Lack of empathy for the speaker.
11. Slow, dull and boresome speech.
12. Lack of interest in the subject of speech.
13. Tiredness of the listener.
14. Listener's impatience to talk.
15. Physical distractions or 'noise'.
16. Creative distractions like daydreaming or reading mail while listening.
17. Listener's responding to the dress and mannerisms of the speaker.
18. Listener's inadequate knowledge of the language used by the speaker.
19. Wrong perception of the message.

Exercises

1. How does listening break the barriers to communication?
2. Why should a businessman listen carefully and attentively?
3. Briefly discuss the significance of listening in business communication.
4. What are the obstacles to good listening? How can these obstacles be overcome?
5. How does listening improve the superior-subordinate relationship?
6. How can a businessman train himself to become a good listener?
7. What are the ways and means of cultivating the art of listening?

A. Understanding the Audience
B. Planning and Preparation of Public Speech
   (1) Deciding the Purpose and Objectives of Public Speech
   (2) Acquiring Adequate Knowledge of the Subject
   (3) Selecting Suitable Pattern of Arrangement
      (a) Topical Pattern
      (b) Chronological Pattern
      (c) Spatial Pattern
      (d) Causal Pattern
      (e) Problem-Solution Pattern.
   (4) Determining Sub-Points and Supporting Material
      (a) Analogies
      (b) Statistical Data
      (c) Examples
      (d) Quotations.
   (5) Outline of a Public Speech
      (a) Introduction
      (b) Body
      (c) Conclusion

C. The Language of Public Speech

D. Presentation of the Public Speech
   (1) What is Speech Delivery?
   (2) Modes of Delivery.
      (a) Impromptu Delivery
      (b) Memorised Delivery
      (c) Extemporaneous Delivery
      (d) Manuscript Delivery
   (3) Using Visual and Vocal Cues in Public Speech
      (a) *Visual Cues*
         (i) Eye Contact
         (ii) Facial Expressions
         (iii) Postures and Movements
         (iv) Gestures.
      (b) *The Use of Vocal Cues in Public Speech*
         (i) Volume
         (ii) Rate
         (iii) Pitch
         (iv) Articulation

10

PUBLIC SPEECH

> Half the world is composed of people who have something to say and can't, and the other half who have nothing to say and keep on saying it.
>
> – *Robert Frost*

UNDERSTANDING THE AUDIENCE

Though audience consists of individual listeners, they must have certain common characteristics which enable them to assembly for participation and reciprocity. The speaker has to find out those characteristics in order to determine his method and style of delivery. His correct judgement of the audience helps him to organise the details of the message in such a way that it becomes best adaptable to the audience. He has to consider the age, sex, occupation, education, religion, social status and economic level of his audience before preparing his speech for them. Such a consideration will give him some idea about the linguistic competence and academic background of the audience; and secondly, it will help him to draw inferences about the beliefs, values, opinions, interests and attitudes of the audience. He can use these inferences to change, mould and reorganise his arguments and to present them with good impact on the audience. He must take it for granted that the audience belonging to different social classes and occupations have different views and values. The formal language style can be of maximum impact for one class of the society, whereas it may not be favoured by the other. The speaker's use of language and choice of words must match the language competence of the audience. He has to use familiar terminology and the connotations of his words must be understood by the audience. If he uses figurative and utopian language style, he must think about its appropriateness for the audience. Before constructing his message with a persuasive appeal, the speaker has to determine how the audience members are likely to react about a given issue. There are always some people who resist to change their views and values, some are partly resistant to it, whereas others may have very low resistance. The speaker's persuasive argument is easily adaptable to those having low resistance and to those who are receptive to almost anything said by the speaker. It means that some members of the audience are more persuasible than others to almost any message. It is generally found that the persuasible persons give more respect to the opinions of others than to their own. They tend to have low self-esteem which does not allow them to form their own views, values and opinions.

PLANNING AND PREPARATION OF PUBLIC SPEECH

Public speech requires prepared and formal presentation. The speaker's strong feelings or attachment with the issue may give intensity to the expression, but it may not result in effectiveness. His deep involvement in a particular issue will simply bring out his passionate and intense feelings about it. Therefore, if the speaker has to ensure the optimum effectiveness, he must prepare and present his speech carefully. He need not consider the occasion of public speech as an ordeal but, on the other hand, it can be considered as a good opportunity to convey his message to others. He may develop inferiority complex if he concentrates on himself, his inabilities and his lack of experience. He has to improve and develop his communication skills and communication attitude by trying to concentrate on the message which he has to impart. Though the speaker must have sufficient knowledge of his subject, it would be useless if it is not planned carefully and with distinct purpose. The unplanned speech is more likely to lose his credibility. When a businessman has to speak on the business affairs, he must have sufficient knowledge of all the aspects of his business in order to speak confidently about it. He has to plan and organise the introduction, the main ideas, supporting ideas and the conclusion of his speech. Disorganised or poorly organised speech lowers the audience's opinion of the speaker. Therefore, the speaker has to organise elaborately and practice his speech material carefully.

Deciding the Purpose and Objectives of Public Speech

Almost every speech consists of an introduction, the body of message and the conclusions. All the aspects of the public speech are organised around the central idea of the message which the speaker wants to communicate with some definite purpose and objectives. The speech becomes manageable only after deciding its purpose and objectives. The speaker can prepare an effective speech if he narrows the scope of the topic according to the objectives set by himself. The topic must be narrowed down so as to fit it in the given time and this will enable the speaker to give adequate justice to each aspect of the message in his speech.

Acquiring Adequate Knowledge of the Subject

The speaker will not be able to communicate properly with the audience if he lacks adequate knowledge of the subject. The audience may not accept the message if it is not convincing, plausible and credible. After deciding the subject, scope and the limitations of the message, the speaker must find out the sources of information. He has to be selective about the gathered information. The selection of the related information depends on the purpose and objective of the speech and also on the topic itself. He has to obtain information about the preparedness, competence, aims and interests of the audience. If the audience are the workers of a business enterprise, the speaker ought to know about its establishment, hierarchical structure, procedures, goals, traditions and policies. There are many sources of information like books, journals, office files, interviews, personal observation, questionnaires, etc.

Selecting Suitable Pattern of Arrangement

The public speeches can be organised with multifarious patterns. Different patterns of speech organisation may suit for different topics, purposes and occasions of speech. There are five major patterns of speech organisation.

Topical Pattern

The topical pattern demonstrates how one topic is related to the other. In a systematic manner, the speaker develops his subject by moving from one topic to the related next. An outline of the topical pattern shows logical development of the subject along with the main and subordinate supporting ideas. From the outline of the topical speech pattern, it becomes obvious that the speech material or the subject gets divided according to its logical components.

Chronological Pattern

The speech material or the data of information is divided according to time sequence in chronological pattern. A particular course or sequence of events described through a speech which is organised in a chronological order, gives a historical sense to the audience. In such a speech, the speaker does not arrange his material topic-wise, but he arranges it item-wise. The time factor is used as an organising mechanism in chronological pattern. It helps the speaker to take review of the past course of events and further, it also helps him to discover its development into contemporary events. If desired, the speaker may guess, infer or project the future events on the basis of his knowledge and experience of the past.

Chronological Patterns of Speech Arrangement:

1. *Subject*: "Rise and Fall of the Maratha Empire".
   The Maratha Upheaval
   Shivaji, the Great, and the foundation of the Maratha State,
   The Rebirth of Maratha State,
   The Beginning of the Empire,
   The Empire under the Peshwas,
   Causes of the Downfall of the Maratha Empire,
   Conclusion.
2. *Subject*: England under the Destinies of King James II (1685-1989 A.D.):
   Accession of James II
   His Character,
   His Parliaments,
   Rebellions against James II
   The Glorious Revolution (1688)
   Causes of the Revolution,
   Nature of the Revolution
   Results of the Revolution
   End of his Regime.

Spatial Pattern

The data of information is divided according to physical or geographical location in spatial arrangement of speech material. When the speaker has to inform the audience about different regions or areas having their own unique and special features, the spatial method is the most suitable speech pattern for it. As this pattern uses space, location and distance as its organising principle, it is useful for planetary and geographical descriptions. For example, it would be well suited to describe military or trade routes and centres in different countries, environmental regions, linguistic regions, territorialities of the birds and animals, centres and regions of natural resources, etc.

Spatial pattern of speech arrangement:

Subject: 'Temple Architecture in Western India'.
Daidyasundar Temple, Lonar
Garuda Temple, Lonar,
Bagicha Temple, Lonar,
Wagh Temple, Lonar
Mor Temple, Lonar
Munglya Temple, Lonar
Narsimha Temple, Lonar
Mahadev Temple, Lonar
Vishnu Temple, Satgaon
Mahadev Temple, Satgaon
Mahadev Temple, Sakegaon
Mahadev Temple, Kothali
Siddheshwar Temple, Sultanpur
Rameshwar Temple, Sindkhed Raja.

Causal Pattern

The speaker uses causal pattern when he argues either from cause to effect or from effect to cause, especially while dealing with a social, economic or political problem. This method is most suitable on the occasion when the speech deals with a specific problem. By describing its effects, the speaker wants to inform the audience about the urgency, seriousness, vitality and reality of the problem. For example, a speaker might describe a problem of air and water pollution. He may start with the description of its deteriorating effects and later he may discuss its underlying causes. After discussing the causes, he may end his speech. But, usually such a speech ends with the suggestions, remedies, recommendations or solutions of the problem.

Problem-Solution Pattern

The speech material of this pattern is divided into two parts. In the earlier part, the speaker describes and analyses the causes and effects of the problem. After having analysed the problem, the speaker moves to the main objective of his speech, i.e. to suggest or propose solution to the problem. He may also try to show the worth of his proposed solution, evaluating it and by assuring its practicability and success. Obviously, problem-solution pattern is effective for a persuasive speech.

The body of the problem solving pattern may include:

1. Definition of the problem,
2. Explanation of its nature and scope of the problem.
3. Explanation of the causes,
4. Proposed solutions,
5. Explanation of the solutions.

Problem-solution pattern of speech arrangements:

Subject: 'Environmental Pollution.
Introduction,
Origin of pollution
Effects of pollution,
Types of pollution,
Types of pollutants,
Levels and Movements of pollutants,
Remedies.

Determining Sub-points and Supporting Material

The speaker has to express his point in a clear, simple and impressive language. In addition to effective and appropriate language, he must provide supporting material to the audience to clarify his ideas. The supporting material is nothing else but the norms of evidences that support the ideas being made by the speaker. Analogies, statistical data, examples and quotations are some of the important forms of the supporting material:

Analogies

The speaker can use analogy when he makes a comparison between two ideas, things or situations. He can show how one idea or a thing is like or unlike the another. This comparison is made on the basis of partial similarities between them though they can never be exactly similar in all respects. Contrast is another form of analogy in which two things having opposite aspects are compared. An analogy is useful for clarifying and dramatising a point. Abraham Lincoln was skilled in using analogies. Let us take one of its example: Abraham Lincoln was resting with his managers in a hotel lobby. As usual, the village duds had congregated there, and one, bolder than the rest, remarked, "Mr. Lincoln, your speech was good but there were some points quite beyond my reach". The simple Lincoln looked up and chuckled, "I am sorry for you; I once had a dog that had the same trouble with flies".

– Edmund Tisdel.

Statistical Data

Statistical or numerical facts are also important forms of supporting material. Numerical data provides a great deal of information in concise and concrete form. It conveys the speaker's authoritativeness in the subject. It classifies a given point with factual information. When statistics is used as supporting material, the speaker must verify whether it is taken from a reliable source or not. He should also ensure that it is accurate in every minute detail.

> "We are told that there are some millions of people in poverty and poorly nourished in this country, yet, here at Niagara is wasted the equivalent of 250,000 loaves of bread an hour. We may see with our mind's eye 600,000 fine fresh eggs dropping over the precipice every hour and making a gigantic omlette in the whirlpool".

– Edwin S. Slosson in
Daily Science News Bulletin

Examples

Examples are frequently noted as supporting material. Like statistical data, the examples can also add concreteness to the ideas presented by the speaker. The examples can also add dramatic presentation to the given idea. The audience believes the statement made by the speaker when it is supported by the specific instances and illustrations.

Quotations

The speaker can support his ideas very effectively if he uses the quotations or testimonies in his speech. It can enhance the eloquent qualities of the speaker. It must be remembered that in public speech, the speaker should use the quotations of the experts, thinkers or of the qualified people in their respective subjects. Secondly, it is essential to select those quotations which are particularly memorable and dramatic. Apart from the dramatic effect of the quotations, they are cited for many other reasons. They enhance the credibility of the speaker and add validity to his arguments. For example, we can quote the following lines from Shakespeare's "Kind Lear" and ask the speaker to prepare his speech carefully, "Mend your speech a little, Lest it may mar your fortunes".

While selecting supporting material, the speaker must know the interests of his audience. The audience may have special interest in certain topics, the speaker can choose something which refers to it. The audience generally gives response to the speech which does not bore them. Therefore, it would be improper to use a lot of statistics. The speaker can use relevant examples with dramatisation and humour if it suits the occasion and the audience. The irrelevant supporting material can spoil even a good speech. Therefore, the speaker has to use the facts, illustrations, analogies, examples and statistics which have a direct bearing on the topic being discussed.

The speaker has to select the supporting material which may directly appeal to the emotions and motivational needs of he audience. The audience instinctively tends to respond to their basic human needs. The basic human needs can easily motivate them for some action. The speaker ought to know some of the basic motivational needs such as those of self preservation, love, sex, beauty, social recognition, economic security, etc. The supporting material needs to be presented in such a way that it may strongly appeal to the motivational factors. These appeals should be made with different kinds of supporting materials. The speaker who wants to provide convincing proof through supporting material has to use the well-organised variety of the evidence in the form of illustrations, analogies, instances, statistical data, quotations, etc.

Outline of a Public Speech

Speech outline shows a plan of presentation. Therefore, it is an important aspect of speech preparation. It is a written form of the accepted pattern of arrangement. Though every speech represents individual thoughts, arguments and requirements, it consists certain common features like introduction, body and conclusion. Writing the outline of a speech helps the speaker to study and review the speech. It also helps him to see if it misses some vital factor which is essential for achieving better effects. While preparing an outline, the speaker decides what material he has to use, what to omit and how to order the material in a particular form to suit the topic, occasion and the public. It can also help him to predict the probable response of the audience to his ideas and to the style of presenting those ideas in his message.

Introduction

The speaker uses introduction to prepare the audience to listen to his message. His primary aim in introduction is to catch the attention of the audience, usually with some kind of dramatisation. Before bringing the problem home of them, he may take preview of the given topic to establish link or communication line between himself and the audience and also between the audience and the topic. After having established the communication line, his efforts turn to bringing the problem or the subject of speech home to the public. In other words, the speaker tries to establish a triangular link between himself and the subject, the subject and the public and the speaker himself. In doing this, he can make use of humour to catch the attention of the audience. It requires technique, practice and ease to tell a joke before the public, especially at the beginning of the speech. The art of dramatisation helps the speaker to tell a joke. It not only captures the attention of the audience but it can also neutralise their hostility. If the audience are not well-disposed towards the speaker, the humour can probably be a very good device to relax the tension between them. The speaker should try to avoid the outdated jokes. He can draw humour from the situation and also from the public gathered on the occasion. He can create humour by twisting and turning the words and phrases. The quotations from the literature, scriptures, thinkers, experts or famous persons are usually very effective for introduction. But a quotation must be relevant to the topic of speech. Like good quotations, most of the audience also love a good story or a parable at the beginning of the speech. The story to be used in the introduction can be true or imaginary; but the audience must be informed whether it is fictional or a true one. As compared to the length of the total speech, the story should be proportionately short, but it must be complete. The speaker can also make an introduction to his speech with a direct reference to the occasion or to the topic itself.

Body

The body of the speech includes the main points and the supporting evidences. It is a written form of the accepted speech organisation pattern discussed earlier. Different patterns of speech arrangement can be used to make the body of a speech. The speaker has to decide which one of them would be the appropriate pattern for the purpose in his mind. The speech purposes like analysing, informing or persuading, etc., can be achieved by careful selection and planning of the patterns like those of chronological, spatial, topical, cause-effect and problem-solving arrangements.

Conclusion

The conclusion gives the final impression of the speaker and his speech. In it, he summarises the main points of his speech. The experienced and eloquent speakers always plan the conclusion of their speech even more carefully than the introduction, because a well planned conclusion gives a sense of completion to the audience. The conclusion reiterates the purpose statement, which is usually made earlier in the introduction. For re-statement of the purpose of speech, the speaker may use different words but it must convey the same idea. The re-statement of purpose motivates the audience to take certain action or to change their views and outlooks. The speaker sometimes does not re-state the purpose, but merely summarises the main points of the speech. Usually, the summarisation is not followed in a persuasive speech, but it is supposed to be more effective when the speaker imparts information or instructions to the audience.

THE LANGUAGE OF PUBLIC SPEECH

Words are the smallest meaningful elements in the language and they are constantly assembled and reassembled to convey the messages. For effective oral communication, the speaker has to develop his own style of language usage. The style of the speaker involves a choice of form without changing his message. It acquires the speaker's selection of the right word at the right place in his speech. By locating and dislocating the words and phrases in the structures of the sentences, the speaker tries to achieve its desired effects on the audience. there are always some speakers who are exceptionally skilled in their individual style of finding a right word for conveying certain meaning. When the audience listens to the speech of a well-skilled speaker, they are delighted by the art of his word-play. The speaker gets immediate feedback when the transmitted meaning is received and clearly understood by the audience. Sometimes, he may find the meaning unclear or ambiguous to the audience. In such a case, he has to repeat and paraphrase his message. It is always a better way for him to ask himself what his audience might infer from his words and sentences. If the speaker has an inordinate liking for rhetorics, picturesque words and highflown phrases, his speech becomes impressive, emphatic and effective. His language not only carries a message but also holds the attention of the audience and pleases them. But along with his attractive way of saying, the content of what he has to say is also an important essential to capture the minds of the audience. Sometimes, the speaker repeats certain words, phrases or the sentences. If the repetition does not tone the things up, it can act as the barriers to communication. Sometimes, repetition may give a second change to the listener who might miss a part of the message for the first time. Overemphasis and repetition usually result in a kind of loudness which make the meaning of the words more clear and intelligible. When the intensifiers like 'so', 'very', etc., are unnecessarily used, especially before the absolute adjectives, the overemphasis becomes distinctive. For example, very devastating, very unique, so perfect, etc. In fact, many adjectives and adverbs become stronger if we do not put intensifiers before them; thus, 'unique' is stronger than 'very unique'.

The speaker may use the jargon or the technical vocabulary of a specialised field just to impress the audience with his knowledge of that subject. The effect of such a language on the audience in general is negative. They might feel that the speaker's language is embellished with incongruous words and affected phrases. If the speaker is successful in creating confusion by using extraneous connotations of the words, the audience may consider him childish, foolish and even pedantic.

PRESENTATION OF THE PUBLIC SPEECH

What is Speech Delivery?

Though speech is prior to writing, carefully written public speech in its appropriate pattern of organisation is absolutely necessary for a systematic delivery. But the delivery of the speech includes both verbal and non-verbal elements of oral communication. Certain linguistic factors such as style of language, uses of vocal variations in pitch, articulation, rate, loudness, etc., and certain para-linguistic factors like facial expression, posture, gestures, etc., also deserve adequate consideration. When we think about the methods of speech delivery, the speaker's goal of speech is not only the delivery of speech, but, on the other hand, he uses it as the means to achieve his goal. The goal of the speaker is to communicate his ideas, thoughts and feelings by means of effective delivery. The speaker is to be judged not merely by his dramatic and flowery style of delivery, but also by the merit of his ideas, word economy and rhetorical style. In the same way, speech delivery does not merely include the speaker's fluency of speech; on the other hand, it also includes his ability and skill of using the vocal and visual cues.

Modes of Delivery

The methods of delivery refer to the speaking situations, the amount of preparation and the type of presentation employed by the speaker. There are four major modes of speech delivery which are commonly used in public speeches. Each of them is appropriate for the different purposes and each of them has its own strengths and weaknesses. Each of them requires enough of practice for the perfect and successful delivery.

Impromptu Delivery

The speaker has to organise his speech material promptly and quickly for impromptu delivery because he does not get enough time for formal written preparation of his speech. In a meeting of the management committee, the Chairman may ask one of the members to report the major events in his sales during the past month. The assistant sales manager will have to respond immediately and he will have to prepare himself in a few seconds. As this method is sometimes unavoidable and does not allow enough of time for preparation, many people get unnerved and uncomfortable by it. In this method, the speaker has to stand before the audience without preparing the matter of his speech. He has to speak out his thoughts as they arise in his mind. The audience finds maximum spontaneity in such a delivery.

In impromptu delivery, the speaker quickly determines the central idea, main points and their order. His preparedness comes from his general awareness of the topic, its main points and the supporting material. It is always preferable to begin the impromptu delivery with some illustration of human interest. The speaker's ability to dramatise the story may increase the interest and involvement of the audience. The audience may even become curious about the purpose of telling the story at the beginning. The purpose should be to make them interested in the speech and to catch their attention for further listening. The speaker can prepare a list of various topics for impromptu speaking. Then he has to select any one of it and start speaking immediately on it. He can listen to himself and evaluate his own performance in private. The impromptu speaker has to remember that the audience does not expect a well accomplished or highly polished speech from him, because they know that he has not been given adequate time for preparing his speech in advance. The impromptu speech is usually assigned only a few moments before the speech. Mark Twain humorously remarks on it that, "It usually takes more than three weeks to prepare a good impromptu speech".

Memorised Delivery

Most of the speeches in business are not memorised. In a memorised delivery, the speaker plans the speech before hand. He writes the entire prepared speech and memorises it. As the speaker commits the speech to his memory, he does not require to read from the notes or manuscript. The memorised delivery does not sound natural or spontaneous without conscious efforts of the speaker to achieve it. Often, the memorised speech sounds as a mechanical or robot-like delivery. The speaker looks freely at the audience, because he does not look into the notes, but the speech loses its natural qualities. The speaker concentrates himself on recalling and reproducing the memorised speech. In this process, he cannot pay sufficient attention to the non-verbal communication which takes places through vocal changes, eye contact, gestures, postures, facial expressions, etc. On the other hand, he concentrates on the words which are committed to his memory. It would be advisable to such a speaker that he should concentrate on the thoughts, feelings and ideas of the message, rather than on the words that represent them. Secondly, he has to make use of the vocal expressions and other techniques of dramatisation in order to get the interest and attention of his audience. The robot-like memorised speech always carries a risk of forgetting some part of the message. If the speaker happens to forget some part of the message, the button of his mechanical speech gets automatically switched off.

Extemporaneous Delivery

In extemporaneous speaking, the speaker carefully prepares the speech outline and plans the supporting material. Neither does he write down the outline speech nor memorises it word by word. He may use minimal notes on a small card to help him to recall the main points of the topic. The minimal notes usually consist of the key phrases, titles and sub-titles of the main points, etc., which remind the speaker of the speech organisational pattern. The major issues and the supporting ideas in the notes are written in abbreviated form. The speaker has to make himself sure about the completeness of the message and also about its appropriateness of length. Careful speech preparation and rehearsal can make him feel sure about the completeness, clarity and appropriateness of the message, but the preparation does not go to the extent of writing out a complete manuscript. Extemporaneous style of speaking allows the speaker to be prepared, spontaneous and flexible. The speaker feels secure with extemperaneous delivery because the prepared material gives him self-confidence and he speaks before the audience with ease, directness, natural gestures and body movements. Majority of the public speakers prefer the extemporaneous method because most of the audiences give better response to it. Though it is well suited for the occasions of public speaking, the other modes are also required for different speaking occasions.

Manuscript Delivery

Manuscript delivery is the most formal mode of delivery. The speaker takes the copy of the speech manuscript and reads it before the audience. This method is necessary for certain occasions. When every word of the speaker is important and likely to be misconstrued by those who want to take disadvantage of it. Usually, the Prime Ministers and the Presidents of different countries make use of he manuscript delivery because every word of their speech reflects the national policy of the government. If they do not think out every work carefully, they may find themselves in political difficulty. The manuscript delivery is useful in business also. If the general manager has to make presentation on behalf of the board of directors before the workers of the company, the manuscript method would be the most suitable one for it. If someone misconstrues or misquotes some part of the message, the manuscript can prove what the speaker had exactly said. A good manuscript speaker's skill can be recognised when his audience remains unaware of the fact that he is reading the manuscript. The manuscript reading can be more effective if the speaker uses all the means of non-verbal communication skillfully and appropriately.

Using Visual and Vocal Cues in Public Speech

There are several means of non-verbal communication, but all of them can be grouped under the visual and vocal cues. The visual cues are the general physical appearance, posture, gestures, eye-contact, facial expressions, etc. The vocal cues are the vocal articulation, volume, pitch, quality and rate of speech, etc.

Visual Cues

Eye Contact: Direct eye contact may be the key element in establishing friendliness, sincerity and trust, but it is certainly one of the most important visual cues in public speaking. The use of eye contact is essential for an effective and successful public speech. If the speaker breaks off his gaze and looks away, it has a negative effect on the audience. If the audience dislikes the speech, the speaker can judge it in the eyes of the audience. Similarly, the speaker's eyes will be the mirror of his true feelings like confidence, sincerity, etc., for the audience. Therefore, it is advisable to the public speaker to maintain good eye contact with the audience. If he stares down at the floor or at the backwall of the hall, the audience would also avoid to look at him. The speaker should be able to maintain frequent eye contact even when he gives a manuscript delivery. People feel that the speaker who averts or shifts his eyes while speaking is trying to conceal something from them. A good eye contact makes the speaker and the audience feel comfortable. Staring at one person or one part of the audience for a long time is likely to make them feel uncomfortable. A good eye contact establishes personal and direct contact between the speaker and the audience.

Facial Expressions: The audience generally does not like the expressionless delivery. The speaker can project his emotions through facial expressions and this projection can create similar feelings in audience. In public speech, the speaker must not forget the distance between himself and his audience. His facial expressions must be displayed in such a way that every listener would be able to see them. His facial expressions should be more expansive than those used in the small group communication and in the face-to-face communication. He should not show tension or fear on his face, but on the other hand, he has to show his friendliness towards the audience by smiling warmly at them, especially at the beginning of him speech. It may also prepare him for imparting mobile and flexible facial expressions. The mobile facial expressions must reinforce the thoughts and ideas of the speaker. The speaker becomes self-conscious and thereby he loses self-confidence. When he loses confidence in himself and in his speech material, his facial expressions are likely to contradict his words. Therefore, it is essential that the speaker should not think about himself and his shortcomings. He must strongly believe in his knowledge, speech material and in himself.

Posture and Movement: The posture and the movements of the speaker helps to communicate his poise, confidence and the way he feels in front of the audience. While standing at the podium or while sitting on the stage, the speaker's posture should be relaxed and alert. If he lacks physical mobility and relaxed alertness, it will communicate his sense of being uneasy. His lack of alertness may reflect that he does not care about the audience. The speaker must stand tall and erect. He should not rest his weight on one foot. When he distributes his weight on both feet and stands straight, it conveys his self-confidence. The speaker may move from one spot to another. While making a transition from one point to the another, if he paces back and forth on the plateform, it displays his frustration and nervousness. His constant paces can also distract the attention of the audience from whatever is being said. Only those physical movements are permissible which reinforce the ideas in the speech. The speaker has to avoid both too little or too much physical actions in his delivery.

Gestures: Gestures of the arms, hands, shoulders and head are important ways of non-verbal communication. Gestures of hand are commonly used to reinforce the speech. Though gestures are deliberately used for effective speech communication, they must look natural and spontaneous. Hand gestures are communicative in themselves when they describe certain actions or the shape of things. Gestures can provide valuable information to the audience about the speaker's interest and emotional involvement in the subject. Secondly, they can provide a vent to the suppressed feelings of the speaker. The gestures should be natural, emphatic, meaningful, definite and large enough to be seen and understood by all the audience.

The Use of Vocal Cues in Public Speech

The vocal cues help the audience to differentiate emotions of the speaker and to form their judgements about his personality. The words, "I am glad to meet you" can give its verbal message and non-verbal message at the same time. The vocal cues can prove it either warm and affectionate or cold and insincere. The real emotions and feelings of the speaker can be easily identified by the vocal cues. Sometimes it may also show the feelings expressed by the verbal cues. The way in which the speaker sounds his verbal message is important both in public speaking and also in informal conversations. The speaker must remember that he can spoil his good impression by using substandard diction and pronounciation. The use of standard diction, correct pronounciation, fluency and authoritative voice can create impressive and favourable image for him.

The speaker usually tends to be self-conscious about his appearance and the visual impressions he might make on the audience, but he pays very little attention to the specific aspects of his vocal quality and production. He can look into the mirror to confirm his good appearance and the other visual impressions like proper gestures, postures, facial expressions, etc. But he cannot listen to his own voice as the others do. He cannot exactly listen and inspect his own vocal qualities such as range, pitch, resonance and articulation. He cannot examine the worth and working of his vocalisation such as laughing, crying, grunting, etc. unless he listens to a tape-recording of his own voice. The speaker must train his vocal qualities and vocalisations for effective speech delivery.

Volume: The speaker's message must be audible to the audience. If the audience are not able to hear the speech clearly, there will be no communication. The speaker's voice can be clearly and distinctly heard by all the audience if his voice has adequate volume. The volume is the relative loudness of the voice. The speakers having large volume can be barely heard by the listeners. The volume can be useful for emphasising certain ideas or to show emotional intensity of the speaker. We are very sensitive to the volume of the sound and it is obvious when we show serious concern with the noise pollution. The feedback from the audience should be used to check and adjust the volume.

Rate: The rate of speech is the average number of words uttered per minute by the speaker. The average rate of speech is about 120 to 150 words per minute. The speaker whose rate of speech goes above 140 words per minute should make conscious efforts to slow down the rate for better comprehensibility of his message. In order to minimise errors in speech and to maintain steady and even fluency, the speaker should not allow his speech rate to be too fast. Though every individual has almost stable speaking rate, his speech rate may get faster when he expresses his fear, anger or joy, but it may get slowed down while expressing grief, depression or sorrow. Many speakers find it difficult to slow down their speech rate unless they reduce intensity of the pitch and volume. When the speaker is possessed with certain emotions b .t tries to maintain control over his speech rate, the strain of it becomes obvious in other vocal and visual cues. The increased dynamism of the other vocal and visual cues are the result of the speaker's conscious efforts to maintain control over the rate. The speaker must always be careful that his rapid rate of speaking does not paralyse his audience. If his delivery is as rapid as that of he machine-gun, the message would be almost unintelligible. He has to insert more spaces between words and sentences if he wants to sound clear by using distinct articulations.

Pitch: Pitch is the frequency level of the voice. This frequency level is determined by the person's larynx. The pitch range of the speaker depends on the shape and size of the vocal cords or bands which are at the top of the larynx. Though many speakers use a high-pitch in public speeches, the audience like a voice which is varied in pitch. A voice without any variations in pitch sounds monotonous. The monotonous speaker who do not impart any information about his emotions by changing the pitch levels becomes quickly unpopular and the audience does not like to concentrate their attention on his speech. It has been also found that the speaker can even more be disliked by the audience if he exaggerates the pitch changes. The changes in the pitch levels must be spontaneous and the speaker should have maximum control over the pitch variations.

Articulation: We make use of the tongue, lips, palate, vocal cords and other speech organs to a articular different speech sounds. For the articulation of different sounds, the tongue takes distinct positions in the mouth cavity. The front or the back of the tongue can be raised high towards the palate. It can be kept low to interfere as little as possible with the flow of the air in the passage. Even the tip or the blade of the tongue is involved in the articulation of certain sounds; for example, the sounds such as /Ɔ/ in moth or /χ/ in that, etc. Lips are involved in the articulation of the sounds such as /p/ in pat, /b/ in bat, /m/ in mat, etc. In case of some sounds such as /m/, /n/ and /y/ in (giving), the air stream is checked in the mouth, but it passes freely through the nose. The sounds such as /w/ in win or /j/ in yet are consonants but they are made by the combination of vowels. /f/ in fan and /v/ in van are articulated by the contact of upper teeth and lower lip. Thus, different organs of speech help to articulate the speech sounds. When the speaker is unable to produce certain sounds, he just omits them or substitutes it with some other inappropriate sound. The omission of necessary sounds is not the result of mere inability of the speaker to articulate it, but it can also be due to careless articulation in rapid speech. Some speakers distort the sound by using wrong vowels; for example, they may use /i/ for /e/ or /o/ for /a/, etc. This may make their 'feed' sound such as 'fid', and 'harsh' sound like 'horsh'. The use of inappropriate and distorted sounds may irritate the audience and it may also result in misunderstanding of the message.

Exercises

1. Why is it necessary for a public speaker to study his audience?
2. Why should a public speaker decide the purpose and objectives of his speech? What is the significance of acquiring adequate knowledge of the subject?
3. What are the different patterns of public speech arrangement? How should a public speaker select suitable pattern?
4. How should a public speaker determine the arrangement of sub-points and supporting material?
5. How should a public speaker prepare the outline of his speech?
6. How should a public speaker plan and prepare his speech?
7. List the steps in public speech preparation.
8. What are the elements that determine how successful a public speaker you are?
9. What kind of a language a public speaker should use in his public speeches?
10. How should a public speaker present his public speech?
11. What is speech delivery?
12. What are the four modes of delivery?
13. What is the basic purpose of the introduction and conclusion of a speech?
14. What are the visual and vocal cues in public speech? How should a public speaker use these cues for effective speech delivery?

A. Introduction
B. Functions of the Interviews
C. Problems in Interviewing
D. Interview Strategies
E. Interview Questions
F. Employee-Selection Interviews
G. Need of Planning and Preparation for the Interviews
H. Self-Preparatory for the Interviewer
I. Self-Preparatory for the Interviewee
J. Guidelines for the Interviewee's Conduct at the Interview
K. Appraisal Interview

11

INTERVIEWS

"The greatest fool may ask more questions than the wisest man can answer."

– V.V. John

Introduction

In business, interviewing is a basic means of interpersonal communication. A person may come across a number of employment interviews while hunting for a job. He comes across a number of training and instructional interviews in which he is trained and instructed by his superiors to do his job properly and efficiently. The supervisor may also call his subordinate employees for job assessment and appraisal.

Interviews or interpersonal on-the-job communication requires planning and oral skills for talking with another person about the matters related with the job. To talk in an informal and casual way with the employee is a complicated communication situation, though the superiors do much of their managing through informal face-to-face conversations. If this conversation fails to bring about mutual agreement and understanding, the matter become serious for both the parties. When a superior wants to explain to his subordinates about what he requires to do to accomplish a given organisational task, he must keep in mind some of the basic principles of communicating with another person. A skilful communicator can resolve several conflicts through the process of interviews. This process is called as the conflict-resolving interviews. Almost all the interviews are arranged with the purpose of exchanging information between two persons. In order to handle the interview effectively, a person must know the obstacles in interpersonal communication, because all the interviews are face-to-face interpersonal communication situations. Both the interviewee and the interviewer have to find out the obstacles in interpersonal communication and they must try to overcome them.

Functions of the Interviews

The interviewer may come across a number of interpersonal interview situations for different purposes. The purpose of an employment interview is to exchange information. The interviewer as well as the interviewee seek information from each other. The interviewer tries to gather the facts, opinions and attitudes from the interviewee; in return, he may also feel the need of presenting information to the interviewee about the organisation and the job conditions. He may also give certain instructions to the respondent regarding the procedures, customs and requirements of the job. The interviewer who wants to sell the products of his company to the prospective buyer, has an objective of influencing the buyer's attitude and behaviour. Today, almost every business unit requires expert advice in many matters of business concern. The manager can have an interview with the expert to seek advice from him. The interviewer and interviewee may have an objective of problem-solving. Both of them make an attempt to identify the causes of a problem and together they may seek a possible solution. The general manager may call the department head of sales division to discuss the problem of declining sales during the year. Interview can also be arranged with the purpose of receiving complaints from the concerned people. The sales manager may talk directly with the customer about the causes of dissatisfaction or about the defective products and services. The interview which is arranged for receiving complaints gives the interviewer a chance to minimise the respondent's dissatisfaction by improving the quality of the product or by giving better services.

A manager who wants to review the performance of different departments in his business unit may arrange interviews with the departmental heads to evaluate their periodic performance. While reviewing the performance of the subordinates, the manager may not set fresh goals before them. He may give them specific instructions about how they can meet the set targets or goals by the next appraisal interview. When the superior wants to reprimand the subordinate, it is always better to do so in a private interview between them. The interviewer can discuss the issue privately with the interviewee and may reprimand him for his undesirable behaviour. He may warn the respondent for his unsatisfactory performance.

Problems in Interviewing

Though interview is a convenient vehicle for evaluating the employees, much of the research conducted on the methods and effectiveness of interviews has shown disappointing results, especially when the job predictions made by the interviewers are not fulfilled. The unfulfilled predictions of job behaviour are due to the lack of essential interview skills on the part of the interviewer or it can be due to some mistakes in the methods of interviewing. Predictive accuracy can be reached by the interviewer when he is adequately trained in the techniques of interviewing. The interviewer has to find out the problems or the difficulties in the way of effective interviewing. He has to identify the obstacles in the procedures of interviews and has to overcome them in order to make accurate assessment and prediction.

Self-Expression and Over-Communication

It is usually found that the interviewer dominates the discussion. In fact, he has to lead the discussion instead of dominating it. He must learn how to lead the discussion, how to direct it towards purposeful casual conversation and how to shift it from one topic to another. In order to be successful in this task, he is required to be a good listener. He has to show genuine interest in the views, opinions and comments of the interviewee. The interviewer may have very good verbal skills, he may usually enjoy communicating and expressing himself to the others; but, for interviewing the candidates, he must control his verbosity. By talking too much, he may feel comfortable simply because he commands the interview situation and dominates the discussion. But obviously, he receives little or no information when he himself goes on talking instead of allowing and encouraging the candidate to talk freely.

Drawing Inaccurate Conclusions

The interviewer's failure to evaluate the information heard or observed during the interview is a serious but most common problem of the interviews. The interviewer may encourage the candidate to express freely and he may have all the qualities of a good listener; but, if he fails to evaluate the information provided by the candidate, the interview is bound to be a failure. When the interviewers listen to the statements made by the candidate and observe the non-verbal clues of the message, they usually jump to some conclusions without trying to find out the other probable conclusions. Instead of jumping to conclusions, the interviewer should try to analyse and evaluate the information in a systematic way so as to maximise predictive accuracy. To judge a man's character in an interview of fifteen minutes is not an easy job for any interviewer. The interviewer may spend even more time in conversing with the candidate and yet he may not be able to predict about the candidate's future performance in the work situation. The information gathered from the candidate is to be interpreted by drawing some inference about the candidate's ability of job performance. From the facts gathered in an interview, the interviewer can draw several probable inferences, but he has to select the one which is most probable.

Halo-Effect Judgement

The candidate's dress, etiquettes and manners can show one aspect of his personality and his remaining qualities may remain untraced in the interview. A poor candidate borrowed new dress for an interview from his rich friend and was judged as dandy by the interviewer. The interviewer judged the candidate's entire potential for job performance on the basis of 'looks' of the candidate in a new dress. Such an error in the process of interview is termed as the halo-effect which occurs when the interviewer judges the candidate's nature on the basis of one of its characteristics. The candidate's pleasant smile, eye-contact, firm shake-hand, appropriate posture and up-to-date manners and etiquettes make him mentally acceptable even before the interview begins. Thus, the interviewer is likely to be misled if he uses the 'limited information' to form his opinion about the person's other characteristics. To avoid this error, the interviewer must try to find out and evaluate the other characteristics of the candidate.

Ignorance of the Job-Conditions and Job-Requirements

The interviewers often do not prepare themselves for the interview. An interviewer who does not have a complete description of the post to be filled is unable to find out a right kind of person for that job. An accurate appraisal of the candidate not possible unless the interviewer knows the critical requirements of a particular job. Often the interviewers do not know conditions of job performance. Their ignorance of the job conditions and job-requirements can result in the selection of a candidate who would be unable to meet the requirement of job performance. Therefore, the interviewers should obtain complete job-related information before the interview.

Casual Approach

An interview is a process of conversation that exchanges information. The interviewer asks a number of questions in a way to learn as much information about the candidate as possible. He asks questions beginning with how, why, where, what, describe, compare, etc., or with 'yes' or 'no' type of questions. Often the interviewers do not prepare a set of such questions. His lack of such preparation indicates that he does not want specific information about the candidate's background, knowledge, skills and interests. When the interview is conducted by the selection committee without deciding and dividing the kinds of questions among themselves, the selection decisions are bound to be poor. Sometimes, they do not integrate and discuss the information obtained from the candidate in a proper and systematic manner. Such a casual approach may save their time but it cannot serve the very purpose of the interview.

Poor Reputation and Lack of Goodwill

The organisation which suffers with a lack of goodwill and poor reputation finds it difficult to receive adequate number of applications for the posts to be filled. The interviewer's judgement regarding the comparative suitability of a candidate is often affected by the inadequate number of the available candidates. The interviewer cannot organise the various selection elements like resume, tests, etc., because of the pressure to fill the position. He lowers the interview standards and takes a bad decision.

Interview Strategies

The interviewer can select either the directive or the non-directive strategy for conducting the job interview. The alternative titles used for these strategies are "structured and unstructured", "patterned and unpatterned", "guided and unguided" and "directed and non-directed". In directive approach, the interviewer prepares a list of questions for the interview. He decides the order of questions to be asked and the topics to be introduced in the interview discussion. A list of such questions proves very useful to the untrained and inexperienced interviewers. The interviewer knows what to ask, in what order to ask and what to do with the information received from the interviewee. He uses the same pattern of reference for each candidate and carefully covers the same areas. He relies on the pre-determined set of questions and never deviates from it. He allows the candidate to talk only on those topics and questions which are introduced by him. He may interrupt the speech of the interviewee if he does not want to listen to it, or if he considers the speech irrelevant to the selected topics and questions. He controls both the upward and downward channels for the fulfilment of his specific purposes and objectives. He prepares the plan of the interview and tries to cover all the important matters according to time schedule. The rigid format of such interviews seems quite mechanical to some people.

The non-directive strategy is more flexible and more often used for counselling, grievance processing and for other interpersonal communications. This approach is suitable for the personnel specialists because it allows them to develop questions as the interview proceeds. Though such an interview is much like a friendly conversation, it lacks the reliability of a structured directive interview. A non-directive interview is largely unplanned. The interviewee is encouraged to do most of the talking and to reveal more of his thoughts, feelings, ideas, problems, desires and aspirations.

Though the directive interview approach does not allow the interviewer as well as the interviewee to deviate from a set of prepared questions, it has one distinct advantage. It gives the uniformity in response of the large number of interviewees. This uniformity comes because of the restriction that the interviewer should ask only a set of prepared questions as they are worded on the form. The interviewer cannot even change the order of the questions.

The second advantage of the directive approach is that even an inexperienced interviewer can conduct a fairly successful interview if the interview is properly structured. In non-directive approach, the interviewer can deviate from any of the prepared questions. He enjoys the freedom of pursuing any line of questioning. Thus, this approach gives considerable flexibility and latitude to the interviewer as well as to the interviewees. Though each of these approaches have their own merits, it is advisable to use appropriate combination and balance of both the techniques.

While conducting interview through directive as well as non-directive approaches, the interviewer must remember that not only he himself is in the search of a good employee but the interviewee is also in search of a good employer. Therefore, the employer must create his good impression on the interviewee by following certain etiquettes and mannerisms. Some hints of interview etiquettes are as follows:

He should welcome the candidate with a warm smile and friendly talk. Secondly, in order to put the candidate at ease and to earn his confidence, the interviewer must begin the dialogue with a discussion on a subject which is familiar to the interviewee. Thirdly, the interviewer must show that he is keenly interested in the information supplied by the interviewee. Fourthly, the interviewer should encourage the candidate to ask questions. The interviewer must give satisfactory answers to the questions asked by the interviewee regarding salary, job-conditions, etc. Fifthly, while parting, he must thank the interviewer for having come for the interview.

Interview Questions

At the beginning of an interview, the interviewer may ask open questions by which he may expect to get more personal information from the candidate. The second advantage of an open question is that the candidate feels relaxed when he is asked to respond without any restrictions. An open question like 'What is your opinion about the foreign trade policy of the Government?' allows the candidate more freedom in interpreting the subject at any length. On the other hand, a closed question like, 'Would you like to work in our Factory?' does not allow any latitude to the candidate in interpreting the subject. The closed question requires short, direct and specific answers. Almost all the closed questions expect the simple yes-or-no answers. When a closed question is emotionally charged, it is called a loaded question which puts the candidate on his guard. For example, 'Have you ever tried to satisfy your employer?'. A closed question can be asked to get the expected answer. For example, 'Are you capable enough to carry out this responsibility?'. A person who has come forward to carry out a particular responsibility would obviously answer 'yes' to the above question.

In a job interview, the interviewer may ask questions on the subjects such as the candidate's qualifications, training, aspirations, willingness to do the job, sociability, emotional balance, trustworthiness, physical fitness, attitudes, financial condition, interests, previous experience, reason for changing the job, salary drawn, etc. By asking these questions, the interviewer aims to judge the candidate's self-confidence, general knowledge, enthusiasm, professional attitude, ability to communicate, preparation for interview, his non-verbal reactions and his character in general.

Employee Selection Interviews

Interviewing is really an effective but highly complicated tool of selection. For an interviewee, if interview is the first step taken in the world of business, it should be considered as a vital turning point on which may depend the rest of his life. The process of interviewing is an oral examination with all its variations. The written examinations cannot trace the personal qualities, behaviour, habits and character traits of the candidate. Therefore, the interviews are used as supplementary means of the tests for finding out the suitable candidate. In order to find out a suitable candidate, the interviewer has to seek more information about the candidate through interview techniques. The second objective is to impart complete and accurate information about the job, and its terms and conditions. The interviewer can use it as an opportunity to inform the candidate about the background and policies of the organisation. The interviewer can verify the facts of the interviewee's past achievements and failures which help him to predict success or failure of the candidate in future. He has to perceive the qualities of the candidate and has to predict his performance in the work situation.

The employment interview is usually observed in terms of its long range effects on the employer, employee and the organisation. The applicant as well as the interviewer feel anxious because of the future implications of success or failure. This tension is felt while conducting interview, because the interview interviewee is just expected to do the required work and to get along with others in the organisation, but there can be no guarantee of its realisation and success in future. When the interviewers select a right person for the right job, the employment interview is successful. Though the employer usually gets the bio-data of the applicant before the interview, he has to evaluate the merits and weaknesses of the applicant's personality.

The major source of information regarding the personality and background of the applicant is the observation of the candidates non-verbal reactions and his general behavior during the interview. The information sources of secondary importance would be to get all the essential information about the applicant's performance and competence from his previous employer or from his associates. The information collected from other sources before the interview must be checked face-to-face with the applicant himself. The applicant may appear well-qualified and eligible on the papers of application, but it needs to be verified during the interview. The non-verbal reactions of the interviewee to the variety of questions asked by the interviewer may give clue to the applicant's personality features such as loyalty, honesty, self-confidence, maturity, hardwork, etc.

Need of Planning and Preparation for the Interview

Before meeting for an interview, both the interviewer and the interviewee have to make planning and preparation. Large business enterprises and corporations usually have their personnel departments consisting of experts in general psychology, organisational behaviour and in other systems of knowledge in business. They use highly specialised methods of finding and keeping the right employees for right jobs. They make careful planning and preparation for the selection of good candidates through interview. Many job interviews are failures because either the applicants or the interviewers lack the skills of planning for them. Not only the applicants, but the interviewers also require adequate preparation for the interview. The interviewer must have clear and detailed information about the post for which the candidates are to be interviewed. He should be in a position to tell the candidate the working conditions, details of job operations and other responsibilities. He has to make proper seating arrangement for the candidates in such a way that they may feel relaxed in the waiting room before facing the interviewer. He should know what type of candidate is required for the job. He must have the bio-data of all the candidates who might attend the interview. Similarly, the applicants too must prepare themselves for the interview situation. He has to know his own abilities in carrying out the responsibilities of the post for which he applies. He has to ask himself whether he really desires to do that work and if it is suitable for his talents. Secondly, he has to know the organisation in which he seeks the job. He has also to prepare himself for the probable questions which would be asked in the interview. Some specific instructions for the preparation of the interviewer and the interviewees are given below:

Self Preparatory for the Interviewer

1. The interview call latter must be sent well in advance to the candidates. It give sufficient time to the interviewees for adequate preparation.
2. If several applicants are to be interviewed on the same day, the time schedule must be prepared and the candidates should be informed about it well in advance so that all of them do not come at the same time and nobody will have to wait for a long time to be interviewed.
3. Considering the requirements of the post, the interviewer must know what kind of qualifications, training and experience of the candidates is essential.
4. In order to gather facts, opinions and attitudes of the candidates, the interviewer must prepare a set of questions to be asked in the interview.
5. The interviewer must decide the best order in which he may ask the questions or take up the main topics for discussion.
6. The interviewer can gather information about the candidate's character and temperament from his previous employer, references and associates by way of correspondence, telephone conversation or face-to-face meetings.
7. The interviewer must know the duties and responsibilities of the post.
8. The interviewer has to make proper seating arrangements for the candidates. If possible, the provision should be made for the newspapers, magazines, tea and light refreshments, so that the candidates who sit in the waiting room till the interview may feel relaxed and comfortable.

9. All the members of the interview committee should be given a copy of the candidate's bio-data.
10. The interviewer should know the kinds of certificates, documents and other papers which the candidates have to produce at the time of interview.
11. The interviewer should take care that there would be no interruption, disturbances or intrusions in the interview hall while the interview is in progress.
12. There must be proper seating arrangements in the interview hall. The interview can be conducted across the desk or while sitting on the adjoining sofa-set.
13. If the candidate is to be interviewed by the committee, each member of the interview committee should prepare questions in his specific areas. They should decide among themselves the type of questions which each of them would ask the candidate. They should decide their turns of asking the questions.
14. The interviewer must not allow himself to talk more than the interviewee.
15. The interviewer should talk with the interviewee in such a way that it will create an atmosphere of friendliness and mutual understanding. It will put the applicant at ease and he will be able to express his thoughts and feelings freely and naturally.
16. The interviewer has to initiate the dialogue between himself and the interviewee. He should begin the meeting with report and sympathy for the applicant.
17. The interviewer has to make full enquiry about the interviewee's knowledge, expertise, motives, interests and habits.
18. The interviewer has to give his full attention to the verbal and non-verbal expressions of the interviewee. He must remember that the facial expression, gestures, posture, eye-contact, tone of the voice, and body movements of the interviewee are as important as his verbal expressions.
19. The interviewer can acquire a variety of information from the interviewee, but he must decide which information he really needs to get from the applicant during the interview, because in an attempt to secure a variety of details, the interviewer may not be able to spare sufficient time for the major issues.

20. The interviewer should encourage the interviewee by using brief verbal responses while the latter speaks. The brief verbal responses like 'good', 'then?', 'tell me more', etc., will keep the applicant talking.
21. The interviewer has to anticipate the interviewee's resistance on certain issues.
22. The interviewer must keep his patience. He should never argue with the interviewee.
23. The interviewer's voice should be clearly audible to the interviewee.
24. The interviewer should use simple language which will be easily understood by the applicant.
25. The interviewer should not allow himself to snap the speech of the interviewee.
26. The interviewer must be receptive to what the interviewee says. He should never express his disapproval.
27. The interviewer must learn to respect the feelings of the applicant.

Self-Preparatory for the Interviewee

Acquiring Knowledge about the Organisation

The interviewee has to prepare himself for the interview in order to make good impact on the interviewers. He has to find out everything he can about the organisation and has to decide whether he really wants to become a part of it. He can collect information about the organisation from the business periodicals, chamber of commerce, business bureau, local newspapers and personal contacts. This information may give him an idea of the Company's public image. The information about a Company's financial status, its long-term projects, labour disputes, etc., can affect his desire to work in it. He has to get the basic information about the Company's recent developments its affiliated organisations, its main products or services, etc. It can enable the interviewee to give intelligent answers to the questions like, "Is he interested in working for that organisation?" "Why does he think that he would be successful in that organisation?" and "What does he feel about he course of work which may be allotted to him if he is selected for a particular post?", etc. The candidates acquired knowledge about the Company and his sincere interest in it can create a good and favourable impression on the interviewer.

Reflecting on One's Own Image

It is never an easy task to reflect and know one's own self, but it is easy to be honest with ourselves. We can look our own reflective image and think about how we come across others. The interviewee is motivated by a number of his primary and secondary needs which egg him on to find an employment. He seeks employment because he is motivated to get wealth, security, comfort, power, status and position in society through it. He has to find out his motives behind seeking the job. He must ask himself why he is applying for a particular job. He must introspect his aspirations and drives. He has to consider his capabilities, competence, skills, training, education, experience, talents and desires. After having introspected himself and his capabilities, he must consider whether the job for which he has applied is suitable for him or not. The interviewer may also want to know about all the dimensions of the interviewee's personality, therefore, the interviewee must be prepared to provide all the essential information regarding himself.

While reflecting on one's own image, the candidate should never think negatively about himself. He may think about his own image on the basis of his past experience with other. His judgement of himself may be based on what the others might have thought and said of him. If he might have been considered either shy or aggressive by some people in the past, he may think of himself in similar terms. If he thinks himself aggressive, he will project himself in an aggressive manner and the interviewer will naturally perceive him as aggressive. Therefore, the interviewee must never have any negative thought about himself. He should never have any inferiority complex and should never lose confidence in himself. Similarly, he need not exhibit the merits which he really does not possess.

Anticipating the Questions and Preparing the Answers

The interviewee can anticipate the questions which are likely to be asked in the interview. Generally, the question are asked about the candidate's academic and technical achievements, his aspirations, interests, hobbies, social relationships, family background, etc.

Therefore, it is easy to anticipate the interview questions and prepare its answers. The interviewee can participate effectively in an interview if he improves his ability of anticipating typical questions and practices answering them. The most commonly asked questions in job interviews are:

1. Why are you interested in this job?
2. What do you know about this job?
3. What are the requirements of this job?
4. How can you fulfil the requirements of this job?
5. What are your educational qualifications?
6. What are your plans for further education and training?
7. Which is the most interesting subject for you?
8. How did you participate in the extracurricular activities?
9. What are your goals and ambitions?
10. What are the reasons for leaving the pervious services?
11. What do you know about our organisation?
12. What can you offer to this organisation?
13. What are your expectations about the salary?

The interviewee must be clear in his mind about the answers he would be giving for the above open-ended questions. As these questions give freedom of self-expression for the interviewee, they cannot be simply answered with 'yes' or no'. He must prepare, practice and rehearse his answers and non-verbal responses. The interviewee also needs to prepare the questions which he would like to ask in order to get full information about the Company and the job.

Arriving for the Interview

While arriving for the interview, the interviewee must take care of his general appearance, scheduled time of the interview and of the certificates and testimonials required for the interview. The interviewee must remember to bring along with him all the essential certificates, testimonials and other documents, even though they are not mentioned in the interview call-letter. They may be required as the proof of his education, training, experience and good character. All the certificates and other documents must be filed in a proper order.

Though clothes do not make a person, the dressing, grooming and general appearance create relatively long-lasting impressions. The dressing or uniform of the interviewee tells a great deal about his rank and social status. His dress must be suitable for the occasion. It should not be pompous and showy. He must arrive at the place of interview fifteen minutes before the scheduled time. A late arrival violates standards of courtesy and discipline. A late entrance in the interview hall can have a disastrous effect, not just a dramatic one. If he arrives before the scheduled time, he may get its advantage to relax and prepare himself to face the interview.

Guidelines for the Interviewee's Conduct at the Interview

1. The interviewee must remember the fact that his first impression is the most lasting.
2. His general appearance must be neat.
3. He should arrive in time.
4. He has to bring all the certificates, documents, essential papers and other material needed for the interview.
5. He should enter the interview room with a straightforward and confident attitude.
6. He should not be nervous and agitated.
7. He should keep himself calm, composed and confident.
8. His expression should be pleasant.
9. He should greet the interviewer with confidence and politeness.
10. He need not wear a stupid smile while entering.
11. He should take the indicated seat.
12. He should not take the seat until he is asked to sit down.
13. He should sit in a relaxed but alert manner.
14. He should not play with the pin-cushion or the paperweight on the table of the interviewer.
15. He should not bend or lean on the table.
16. He must pay careful attention to what the interviewer says.
17. He must not interrupt the interviewer.
18. His posture must be appropriate.
19. His body movements must not indicate his nervousness or evasiveness. He should not clasp and unclasp his hands.
20. He must tell the truths, because his non-verbal statement will conflict with his verbal statements and it may reveal the fact to

the interviewer.

21. His answers must be relevant to the questions asked by the interviewer.
22. He should not boast of his capabilities and vast knowledge.
23. He has to present his strengths to the interviewer, but he must not pretend to be something he is not.
24. He has to retain his dignity while answering even to this annoying and repelling questions.
25. He must always remember that he has to present the best qualities of his character.
26. He need not agree with all the views of the interviewer. He may express his individual views also.
27. He must not annoy or offend the interviewer.
28. He must try to avoid distractions such as chewing gum, smoking, etc.
29. He must express his keen interest and enthusiasm for the job and the organisation.
30. All of his attitudes must be positive.
31. He need not criticise himself.
32. He should never become emotional and impatient. He should never lose his temper.
33. He should frankly answer the questions about his previous job.
34. He should not criticise his former employer and colleagues.
35. He should not try to look funny or serious-minded.
36. He should ask relevant questions to the interviewer in order to get essential information about the job and the organisation.
37. He must not emphasise the issue of what the organisation will do for him, but, on the other hand, he should tell about his potential service to the organisation.

Appraisal Interview

An employee has to face an appraisal interview atleast once in a year in which the supervisor discusses and evaluates his performance. Such an interview is also called as the assessment and training interview. It can be the occasion for both imparting and receiving criticism. If appraisal interview is structured carefully and carried out successfully, it may improve the job performance and the relation between employer and employees. It also helps to improve the downward and upward channels of organisational communication.

The purpose of appraisal interview is obviously to discuss, criticise, praise and assess the performance of the employees. Often, the managers try to point out the shortcomings of the employees in such interviews. The way of handling criticism is very important in appraisal interviews. In giving and receiving criticism, both the employer and the employee, must remember that it is very much a part of life on the job. The following guidelines will be useful for the participants of such interviews.

Some Guidelines for the Employers

1. The employer must try to create friendly and informal atmosphere.
2. It is better to start with the discussion of what the employee was doing for the organisation in the past.
3. Secondly, he has to analyse the past performance of the employee.
4. The third step would be to pick up the plus points of the employee and to praise him.
5. The fourth step should be to describe and to evaluate the present performance of the employee.
6. The last step is to tell the person what he should do in order to improve his performance.
7. While criticising, the employer should focus his remarks on the performance and behaviour of the employee and not on the employee himself.
8. The objective of the criticism should be always to improve the performance of the employee to bring about a change in the behaviour of the employee.
9. Before interviewing the employee, the employer must collect the correct and factual information about what had happened and what should be done at the next time. He should give the employee an opportunity to state his case.
10. He should never use the insulting terms while describing and criticising the behaviour of an employee. He should not use threats which may set up the style of ego-defensive arguments between them.

Some Bits of Advice for the Employees

1. The employee should take the criticism as a well intentioned comment.
2. He should respond properly to the criticism, for it may prove useful to the employee in future.
3. He should have positive attitude towards the employer and the criticism
4. He should not feel embarrassed if his weaknesses are pointed out.
5. He should not take the criticism personally, but should consider it as a comment on his work that needs to be improved.
6. He should express his willingness to learn and improve.
7. He should ask for the specifics of his mistakes so that he may correct them. He should try to understand where he had gone wrong.
8. He must carefully listen to the criticism and should try to understand its implications.
9. When the critic is angry and he makes personal attacks, the employee must keep his temper. He must control his emotions and asks for the specifics.
10. He must assure the employer that he would improve his performance in future.

Exercises

(1) What are the different types of interviews?
(2) How should interviewer prepare himself for the interview?
(3) How should an interviewee prepare himself for the interviews?
(4) What are the objectives of selection interview? How should the interviewers conduct the selection interview? How should a candidate behave during the selection interview? How should the interviewers and interviewees prepare themselves for the selections interview?
(5) What are the essentials of a successful selection interview?
(6) What is the significance of appraisal interview? Suggest some ways and means of making an appraisal interview successful?

SECTION II

A. Significance of Business Correspondence

B. Essentials of Effective Business Correspondence

1. Study of the Reader's Point of view and Interests
2. 'You' Attitude
3. Knowledge of the Subject
4. Planning the Letter
5. Appropriate Tone
6. Command of Language
7. Simple Language
8. Avoiding Monotony
9. Avoiding Jargon
10. Promptness
11. Completeness
12. Conciseness
13. Courtesy
14. Clarity
15. Correctness
16. Concreteness

C. Structure of Business Letter

1. Heading
2. Date-line
3. Reference
4. Inside Address
5. Salutation
6. Subject Line
7. Body
8. Complimentary Close
9. Signature
10. Enclosures and Postscript

D. Forms of Letter Layout

1. Indented Form
2. Full Block Form
3. Block Form
4. Semi-block Form
5. Hanging Indentation Form

12

NATURE AND STRUCTURE OF BUSINESS CORRESPONDENCE

SIGNIFICANCE OF BUSINESS CORRESFONDENCE

As a part of its routine work, a business organisation has to write a number of letters everyday. Almost every business involves a wide range of activities which require frequent communication links between the concerned parties. Many of these links are established and maintained through correspondence. It can also happen that a letter-writer who lacks knowledge and tact of writing a good business letter may not achieve his purpose, but on the other hand, he may hurt the feelings of the receiver and the communication link between then may get snapped. Business letters not only help the businessmen to build new relations and maintain the established ones, but they also help him to plan, manage and organise the business activities which are more diversified and specialised today than ever before. It becomes an indispensable job for him to correspond and communicate effectively with the customers, suppliers, associate organisations, credit agencies, employees and the government officials in order to survive in the business field and to achieve goals of progress and prosperity. The continuous flow of scientific discoveries and inventions, innovations of recent technological and mechanical devices, changes in market, challenges of rival companies, policies, rules and regulations of government and strengthening of trade unions have made business world very complex and challenging. The businessman has remained alert in receiving and imparting a good deal of information which enables him to meet the challenges successfully.

The legal implications of manifold business transactions add to the significance of drafting a correct, complete and effective business letter. The concerned parties get legally bound to the written commitments in the business letters. The business letters are signed by the responsible persons. The written commitments in it become an authentic legal proof of the transaction signed between two parties. In case of disputes, the business letter can be produced as evidence in the court of law. The legal function of the business letter is more significant especially when it contains offers and undertakings. Therefore, almost all the commercial organisations follow some procedure for keeping the record of incoming an outgoing letters. The record of the inward letters is maintained in inward registers which consist the name of sender, name of receiver, subject matter, reference number and remarks. The outward register keeps the record of the name and address of the receiver, reference number, subject matter and remarks. The registered Acknowledgement Due letters are also sent to obtain the signature of the receiver, which can serve as a proof of the receipt of the letter.

The most personal way of introducing a new product in market is writing a business letter. It is more useful and less expensive than sending a salesman to the prospective buyers. Comparatively, it is more direct and less costly than advertising. Usually, the sales representatives are sent to the prospects after sending a letter which creates favourable atmosphere for the both to meet and communicate effectively. Besides introducing new products or services in the market, the manufacturer can use the business letter for widening his the area of his business operations. Sometimes, he may find it inconvenient to send his sales representatives to all the prospects, associated business houses and other business connections. In such cases, a letter is the most convenient and reliable way of approaching the business connections. Business correspondence for the promotion of sales requires special type of drafting which results in expanding the sales of the existing product. Like a good salesman, the business sales letter can create, maintain and expand the market for the goods and services. It can arose interest and create desire in the mind of the customer to buy the product and services. The sales letters explain different features, specialities, novelties and usefulness of the products in such a way that the customer feels compelled to place the orders.

Persuasive sales letters can promote the sales, quicken the pace of turnover and thereby help the businessmen to gain the profits. Sales letters provide essential information about the quality and quantity of the products available with them. When the prospective buyer gets complete information about the products or services, it helps him to decide what kinds of goods and services are needed for him. The information regarding the merits and specifications of the products, the changes made in the design, quality and size of the product and the comparative price-list help the prospective buyers to select the products which suit their needs and tastes.

The business letters play an important role in selling the good reputation and goodwill of the company. It builds friendly relationships between the company and the concerned parties such as the customers, suppliers, creditors, expert advisors, government officials, etc. Business correspondence is naturally dominated by the profit motives, but it also has the social motives of building friendly and cordial relationships with the other concerns and the customers. It aims towards holding the present customers and gaining the new ones. It expects the positive response of the customers to the persuasive appeals made by the manufacturers, trade agencies and dealers. The positive response from the customers is not necessarily secured by personal visits but by the persuasive and polite business letters. The personalised contacts made through business letters add a moral-cordial touch to business transactions. A good business letter creates goodwill among the customers and up-grades and reputation of the firm. It reveals honesty and sincerity in dealings, balanced arguments, friendly and courteous tone and reliability of the sender.

Now-a-days the buyers and the sellers cannot meet actually at the market place to discuss terms, to fix prices and to do the business as it should be done, because the markets are no longer localised. They are spread over long distances, sometimes across oceans and continents. It has increased the complexity of the modern business world and it has made it necessary for businessman to use letters to exchange information of various type with different parties. There are various purposes served by writing the business letters. Placing order for goods, making enquiries, acknowledging orders, executing orders, applying for credit, complaining about delay, complaining about the mistake in the supply of goods, correspondence with government departments such as sales tax, income tax, local tax offices etc. and a lot of such matters require communication by letters.

Business correspondence is preserved for future references. In business communication, past references help the proceedings of the future transactions. The letters of transactions and agreements with the suppliers, customers etc. are frequently referred for future business transactions. All the points of innumerable transactions with a large number of persons cannot be stored in memory by any businessman. The letters provide valid written records for ready reference in routine administration and also in planning for future.

ESSENTIALS OF EFFECTIVE BUSINESS CORRESPONDENCE

Study of the Reader's Point of View and Interests

If the letter writer considers the reader's point of view and interest, he can establish rapport with him. The letter writer has to take the reader into confidence. He must assure the reader that all his interests and views are taken into account. When the reader is assured that his interests are safeguarded, he reacts favourably to the appeals made by the letter writer. The letter writer can create very good first impression if he tries to imagine the views, feelings and reactions of the reader about the message transmitted to him. It is essential for every letter writer to make querries about the needs, requirements, views, wishes, interests, problems and weaknesses of the reader and he has to find the ways to meet them. While writing the letter he has to imagine himself in the place of the reader. He should ask himself what would be his reactions if he receives a similar letter.

"You" Attitude

The letter writer cannot develop his "You" attitude unless he studies interests, views and feelings of the letter receiver. The 'You' attitude is used to make direct personal appeal to the reader. In order to make such appeal the writer must foresee and appreciate the probable expectations of the receiver. It is natural that the reader is primarily interested in himself rather than in the aims and objectives of the letter writer. The 'You' approach of the writer can be easily identified in a letter which repeats and emphasises 'You' rather than 'I' or 'We'. It must be remembered that the most pleasant sound to the reader is his own name. If the writer wants to appeal to the heart of the reader, he must use as many 'You's' in a letter as possible.

Knowledge of the Subject

The letter writer must have adequate knowledge of the subject on which he writes. A business correspondent requires the knowledge of past correspondence. He also must know the background and policies of his organisation. He must have adequate knowledge of his particular trade in the business line. If he lacks knowledge of the subject he will not be able to give satisfactory information required by the receiver. The letter writer must know what exactly he has to write and how he should present it in the letter.

Planning the Letter

By planning the letter, the letter writer does not leave things to chance. Planning of letter depends on the communication situation. The communication situations for business letters are manifold. The letter writer makes inquiries, asks for catalogue of products and its prices, places orders for goods, applies for bank loans etc. In order to meet different objectives and requirements each of these business letter consists different details and they are to be presented in different manners. The letter writer must plan these details and manner of its presentation. The routine business letters with their fixed format are comparatively easy to write and they do not require special planning and preparation, but other business letters which are written with different business purposes must be planned carefully. While planning for a letter, the writer must have clear idea of its purpose. Usually the matter related with the purpose are presented at the beginning of the letter. But, before making beginning of the letter, the letter writer must write down all the major and supporting points which he has to be covered in the message. Then these points should be arranged in successive logical order. This logical arrangement of all the jotted points gives clarity to the message. While planning the message, only relevant information should be included. All the irrelevancies must be strictly excluded from the message. The reliability of the gathered information also needs to be checked.

Appropriate Tone

The tone and style of the language used in the letter must sound sincere and natural. The tone of the letter must be appropriate to the need of the occasion. The style must vary to suit the communication situation. The appropriate tone, suitable style and natural expression helps the sender to build friendly and good relations with the receiver. We use various tones and styles of our language while talking with our parents, wife, sons, daughters, friends, employer, colleagues and sub–ordinates. In business correspondence too, it is essential to vary our tone which would suit the reader and the occasion. To adopt the right tone is to adopt the right way of influencing the person who receives the letter. The writer can adopt the sweet, serious, obligive, persuasive, firm or any other kind of tone in order to produce desired effect on the reader.

Command of Language

The reader understands the idea in the writer's mind through language. If the writer encodes his message in faulty language, the reader may misinterpret it and it may create misunderstanding between the sender and the receiver. Therefore, the writer must have command over the language which is used for the purpose of communication. He must know the various meanings represented by the words and also he must have competence to organise those words into meaningful message. The language used in the business letters must be appealing, forceful and convincing. The words used by the letter writer must be relevant and exact so that they may not create any ambiguities and confusion. He must have adequate knowledge of phrase, clause and sentence structures of the language.

Simple Language

Simple language is more effective in business letters than the language which consists long and complex sentences. Similarly, short and simple words are more effective in convincing the message than the long words. 'Disconsolate' is a more difficult word than 'unhappy'. The word 'tell' is simpler than 'inform'. It is always advisable to use 'words' for 'phrase and phrases' for 'clauses' if the words are simpler than the phrases and the phrases are simpler than the clauses.

Avoiding Monotony

The language of business letter must introduce variety and diversity in order to avoid the wearisome monotony by using short as well as long sentences and also by dislocating some words in the sentences for changing the normal word order. The short sentences are more suitable for business writing because they are simple and easy to understand. But a succession of short sentences creates uninteresting and wearisome monotony. If the sentences of different length and structures are used in the letter, it provides variety and creates interest.

Avoiding Jargon

Jargon was used by the commercial letter writers to say what they could have said in plain language. In modern business letters the overused and roundabout jargon is not appreciated. Though every profession has its jargon and there is nothing wrong for the specialists to use technical words to convey their meanings, the jargon is sometimes used by them to show their superiority and knowledge. Secondly, the complex thoughts which are expressed through jargon imply unintelligibility. Therefore, the letter writer must try to avoid the jargon which creates semantic gap. He must try to use the plain words which are more widely understood, to convey his thoughts. He can catch the reader's attention more easily by using short, familiar and plain words.

Promptness

A business letter must be answered promptly. The letter writer has to send the reply on the same day. If he requires information from other sources to give all the expected details in the reply, he may require some more time to collect the information and draft a full reply. But in such cases, before drafting a full reply, the letter writer should at least send the acknowledgement letter in which he should make it clear that the full reply would require few more days. The letter writer must draft the letter immediately after receiving the details and clarifications from the concerned authorities and different departments.

Completeness

A business letter must be complete in all respects. The letter writer must know the purpose and objectives of his letter. He must include all the details in his letter which are required to accomplish the purpose and to achieve the objectives. The completeness of message also helps to achieve clarity, precision and accuracy. If the letter writer has to draft a reply to the inquiry letter, the reply must be complete in the sense that it must give full and satisfactory information required by the other party. The letter writer can avoid the repeated inquiries and their replies, if his first reply is neatly packed with all the necessary details. The sales letter cannot be complete unless it gives all the particulars of the products or the services offered. The sales or purchase letters must include the complete description of the goods, their prices, credit facilities, discounts, packing, transportation etc. If the letter writer does not specify any of these essential details, the letter is likely to lose its effectiveness. In order to bring completeness in the message, the writer must know the definite purpose of the letter and the requirements of the receiver. Secondly, he has to collect the information from various available sources. The third step is to organise all the facts and figures which are necessary to accomplish the purpose. And finally, he has to review and check up the particulars provided in the letter.

Conciseness

The message can be effective if it is composed with no more words than are really needed by the writer to make the meaning clear. The superfluous words, phrases and sentences unnecessarily waste the time and energy of the business correspondents. Therefore all the business writing must be direct and to the point. While drafting a letter, the writer must be aware that the time of the businessman who receives the letter is invaluable and no effort should be made to compel him to go through a lengthy and tiresome letter. There should be no repetition of words and ideas because the repetition is tiresome, boring and nobody likes it. The letter writer should also try to avoid wordiness and verbosity. Often the adjectives, adverbs, phrases and clauses are used without thought and they do not add something to the sense. The letter writer must be careful about excluding the unnecessary verbosity of language. For brevity and conciseness of expression, he must use the appropriate words which convey the exact meaning. The conciseness not only economises the time and energy of writer and the reader but also reduces stationary and other charges. But the letter writer should not try to be concise at the cost of clarity and completeness.

Courtesy

The letter writer can show courtesy by showing sincere consideration for the receiver and by using polite language. It helps the writer to build and keep friendly relations which are necessary for future business. A letter with friendly and courteous tone keeps out all sarcasm, impatience, irritation and criticism. On the other hand, it shows sympathy, gratefulness and mutual understanding. A courteous letter writer never forgets to thank for services performed or for a works done. A courteous letter tries to avoid making any enemy. It always aims to win over the sympathy, friendliness, respect and understanding of the reader. A general quality of gentle-menliness displayed by the tone of courtesy makes the letter more likable and persuasive. Courtesy does not ignore the basic principles of social and business relationships. It shows regard for the feelings of the reader. Courtesy is helpful in producing favourable response by creating goodwill. It never displays anger, rudeness, roughness or arrogance and it never tries to hit back. A courteous letter writer is a civilised man who is always willing to recognise the feelings of the reader. He shows readiness to render every possible help to the reader who is caught in an unpleasant and odd circumstances. He is always prompt in sending replies to the letters of customers and the suppliers. He honours the psychology of the reader and remembers that he is self-respecting. He avoids self-praise but never loses an opportunity of appreciating the accomplishments and achievements of the reader.

Clarity

Clarity of thoughts is essential for clarity of expression in business letters as well as in public speeches. The clarity of expression helps the reader to understand the message precisely without any difficulty. For clarity of expression the writer should think before writing. If his thoughts are confused, his written message will lack clarity. The letter writer achieves clarity in his message when its meaning is effortlessly and easily understood by the reader. The letters lacking in clarity necessitate further correspondence for explanations, clarifications and inquiries. It can also irritate some readers who may totally ignore the message because of its confused presentation. Such letters adversely affect the goodwill, reputation and sales prospects of the business organisation.

The clarity of message implies that the reader perceives the same meaning of the message as the writer intends. Clarity gives effortless understanding of the contents and it aims at avoiding ambiguity and confusion of meaning. If a message lacks clarity, its contents will not be easily perceptible and intelligible to the average reader. The letter writer can achieve clarity if he thinks clearly before writing, chooses short and simple words, avoids jargon and ambiguities, organises his message, arranges the main and supporting ideas, uses short and simple sentence structures and presents the message in logical successive order.

Correctness

The layout or physical design, appearance and contents of a business letter must be suitable and correct. The correctness of a business letter is also expected in its spelling, punctuation and grammar. The style and diction should be also suitable to the subject. Correctness does not merely mean the absence of errors in language but it also implies that the letter writer does not make inaccurate or wrong statements. The errors in language divert the reader's attention and weaken the potentiality of the message. The incorrect letters make the readers doubtful about the firm's capabilities in handling business matters. Therefore, the letter writer must keep himself alert and careful in order to avoid errors in language, form, facts, figures and other particulars of the letter. The letter must be correct in physical design and make-up. The quality and size of the paper, letter head, typing must be correct and suitable. The letter writer must follow the accepted norms and standards of the layout. The heading, date, salutation, inside address, the body of the letter, complimentary close, signature, enclosures, etc. must be written at their apt places on the paper. The letter writer must be careful to avoid grammatical errors and mistakes in punctuation, spelling, capitalisation etc. The letter must not include false and unrealistic statements. There should be no mistakes in the quotations of price, description of the products, credit facilities, mode of payment etc. The presentation and analysis of the facts and figures must be accurate because it helps the letter writer to earn confidence of the suppliers and the customers.

Concreteness

The letter writer must use concrete words and expressions which create visual images. The concrete expressions make the message clearer and easier to be comprehended. Whenever possible, the letter writer should try to avoid the abstract words which often lead to vague, doubtful, and roundabout statements. The statements made by the letter writer must give definite message. Therefore, he must not make the generalised statement which require further clarifications and specifications. Instead of saying 'consignment will soon be despatched', it is better to say that 'the consignment will be despatched on 5th September'.

STRUCTURE OF BUSINESS LETTER

The structure of a business letter constitutes the following parts:

(i) Heading
(ii) Date
(iii) Reference
(iv) Inside Address
(v) Salutation
(vi) Subject line
(vii) Body
(viii) Complimentary close
(ix) Signature
(x) Enclosures

Heading

Generally a printed letter-head is used for correspondence by the business organisations. The letter head consists of the name and address of the company and it may also consist the telephone number, telegraphic address and telegraphic code, if it has any. Most modern business concerns use attractive design for letter-head. The letter sheets or pads on which their name and address is printed at the top expresses the personality of the firm. The attractive design of the headings are usually prepared by the commercial artists or the experts. Such a letter-head is intended to form a good impression of the writer's firm on the reader's mind. In a printed letter-head only date line is to be filled in by the letter writer at the time of writing the letter. The name and address of the firm in letter-head enables the reader to send his reply. The letter-head not only introduces the firm to the reader but it also conveys the nature of business carried by the firm. It gives the reader an idea about the goods and services in which the firm deals.

The style and design of the letter-head should be simple and clear enough to enable the reader to make out the name and address of the firm easily at a glance. The letter-head should not be used as a tool for advertisement. It should be proportionate to the size of the letter sheet. It should not occupy more than three inches or one-fifth space of the sheet at its top. The name of the firm should be printed in bold letters and the address below it is desirable to be written with appropriate indentions. The telegraphic address and telephone numbers should appear at the left hand corner below the address. If colours are used in letter head, they should be sober and pleasing so that the decorative design will not distract the attention of the reader from the main message.

SUNSILK PVT. LTD.
Textile Chemical Manufacturers
501, Timber Road,
Bombay-5

Telephone:
Cable: SUNTEX, Bombay

Date-line

The date-line has an important place in any type of business letter. It is typed two spaces below the last line of the letter head at right hand corner indicating the date, month and year on which the letter is drafted. The dates are written in various ways like (i) 5-12-77, (ii) 5th

December 1977, (iii) December 5, 1977 etc. Though all of these methods of date writing are acceptable, the correct modern practice of date writing is as "5th December, 1977". This method of date writing has a logical order of day, month and year. But in United States there is a practice of writing dates in the order of month, day and year which is less familiar to Indian letter writers.

The date-line indicates time consciousness of the letter-writers. The dates help the clerks to arrange and file the letters chronologically for future references.

References

Reference line is also an important part of the letter and it should be properly placed. Some letters contain two lines of references. These reference lines should be placed two spaces below the letter-head at the left hand corner. When the letter writer writes a reply letter, he has to give correspondent's reference number against "Our Reference : "and his own reference number against "Our Reference". The main advantage of placing the reference number at the top is that it helps the clerk to put the letter quickly in the proper file for further action. Some business organisations put the reference number of the correspondent in the beginning of the body of the letter. The reference lines are also typed in the cages meant for quoting them. The reference lines are written in various ways like:

(i) Your Ref :
Our Ref :

(ii) Reference No.

(iii) Please quote in reply
This Reference No.

(iv) Ref. No.

Telephone 412516
Telegram : BAYPLAST

BOMBAY PLASTICS PVT. LTD.
77, Tilak Road,
Bombay-7

Your Reference : Date : 7th July, 1977
Our Reference :

Inside Address

The inside address contains the name and address of the company or the individual who receives the letter. It is usually written two spaces below the date line and two spaces above the salutation. In the physical make-up of the business letter, inside address is an essential part. While writing the inside address, it should begin at the left hand margin and two spaces below the date line.

15th July, 1972

The Chief Executive Officer,
Kolhapur Zilha Parishad,
Kolhapur.

This can be typed in block form or in an indented form and it can either be with open or closed punctuation.

Indented form with closed punctuation:

The Director,
  Department of Education,
    Vidyabhavan,
      Poona-5.

Block form with open punctuation:

The Director,
Department of Education,
Vidyabhavan,
Poona-5.

The details of the inside address like the name of the person or the title of the firm and the address or the location of the firm etc. should not be written in abbreviation. If the letter writer is writing a letter to Mrs. Betty Jones, it would be bad manners to write her name as Mrs. B. Jones. Abbreviated name shows that the writer has little respect for the addressee.

The name of the person or the business organisation should be written in the first line of the letter. The following lines should consist the address which should not exceed more than three lines. The courtesy titles should be used before the name of the individual to whom the letter is addressed. The courtesy titles such as Shri, Shrimati, Miss, Mrs. Mr., Messrs, Mms, Esq., Sir, Doctor, Professor, Colonel, Reverend etc. should be carefully used. Though Mr. is the most appropriate mode of address in business correspondence Esq. is also used to certain individuals as a mark of social importance. When the addressee holds a special title such as Doctor, Colonel, Professor, Sir, Reverend etc., the courtesy titles Mr. and Esq. should not be used.

Dr. Donald Fry,
27, Main Road,
Hyderabad.

Rev. Sudhakar Parab,
All Saint's Church,
Shivaji Park,
Poona.

Col. Vikram Patel,
Madhav Housing Colony,
Madhavnagar,
Nasik.

Prof. Vinayak Godbole,
New College of Arts and
Commerce,
Aurangabad.

For a married woman Mrs. is used, and for a unmarried woman Miss is used. When the letter writer does not know whether the addressed woman is married or single, he can use Ms as an alternative for both Miss and Mrs.

Miss Mary D'Souza,
New English School,
Belgaum.

Mrs. Shanta Patil,
107, Vidya Colony,
Gokhale Road,
Pune-7.

Ms. Geeta Kulkarni,
Department of Zoology,
Bombay University,
Bombay-1.

Messrs. Laxmi Builders,
37, Main Road,
Rajarampuri,
Kolhapur.

M/s. Joshi Brothers,
Peshawe Park,
Pune-5.

If the name of the organisation already consist a courtesy title as in, 'Sir Richard Smith and Sons' the courtesy title Messrs should not be used. The title Messrs is also unnecessary if the name of the firm begins with 'The' as in 'The Rainbow Co. Ltd.'

While writing letter to the addressee in other countries the letter writer must write the name of the country because there are many cities and towns of the same name in the world.

Salutation

The role of salutation in a letter is to greet a person or the firm to whom the letter is addressed. It is the conventional and most integral part of every letter. It is the customary greeting or formal wishing for the addressee before drafting the subject matter of the letter. It is placed two spaces below the inside address. The name of the addressee in the inside address and the personal relations between the letter writer and the reader are the basis to decide the kind of salutation to be used in the letter. Though usual greeting in a business letter is "Dear Sir", there are other greetings also which suit the addressee and the relationship between letter writer and the reader. The other most common forms of salutation used in business letters are Sir, Dear Sirs, Dear Madam, Mesdames, Madam, My dear Sir, Dear Shri. . . . etc. 'Gentlemen' is the most commonly used salutation in U.S.A. The greetings such as Sir, Dear Sir, Madam, Dear Madam, Gentlemen, etc. are very formal and overused. The English business letter writers now rarely use those 'Very formal' salutations. They prefer more personal, friendly and warmer greetings such as, Dear Mr. . . ., Dear Ms. . . ., Dear Mrs. . . ., Dear Miss . . . etc. Such greetings are used when the letter writer personally knows the correspondent or if he had traded with him in past. The salutation 'Sir' is used especially, when the letter writer wishes to be very formal, especially if the officer addressed is occupying a high position in the organisation. The greeting becomes a little less formal if the letter writer writes surname of the addressee as 'Dear Mr. Tiwari', 'Dear Mrs. Gupta', 'Dear Miss Shukla' etc. If the correspondent is a close friend of the letter writer, he can greet him or her by first name as in 'My dear Robin', 'Dear Gangadhar', 'My dear Asha' etc.

Subject

The subject line is placed two spaces below the salutation. It precisely points out the subject matter of the letter. It lets the reader understand immediately the central idea of the letter, or reveals quickly the reference contained in the letter. It briefly mentions the theme of the letter and saves the time of the reader just as the Attention line or Reference line does it. The subject line is indispensable in case of lengthy letters.

The Sales Manager,
Modern Textile Mills Ltd.,
M.G. Road,
Bombay-14.

Dear Sir,

Subject : Your Consignment No. 193810.
With reference to your above consignment of. . .

Some business organisations prefer to put the subject line between the inside address and the salutation.

The Purchase Officer,
Sohan Fabrics,
Rajendra Prasad Road,
Bombay-38.

Subject : Payment of Bill No.S/51 of 16th July 1989.

Dear Sir,

With reference to the above payment of bill. . .

Body of Letter

The body of the letter is the principal part of the letter which consists the message. Its purpose is to obtain a suitable response or to secure certain action from the reader. The main and supporting ideas of the message are organised and properly arranged in the body of the letter. The body of the letter is also called as the text of the letter and its nature in each letter differ according to the objectives in view of the letter writer.

The first paragraph is the introductory part of the message which sometimes opens with reference to earlier correspondence. It prepares the reader's mind to receive the message with interest. It's first attempt is to catch the reader's attention and create interest in him for the contents of the letter. The opening paragraph helps the reader to put his thoughts in proper channel to receive the message. The opening paragraph should be prepared according to the purpose of the letter. But in any case, every business letter must begin with positive and pleasant approach, politeness and gratitude.

The main message is provided in the second paragraph which is the heart of the letter. It contains the main and supporting ideas of the subject matter. It provides every relevant details and all the quarries in the reader's mind about the subject to which the letter refers are answered. The completeness, clarity, correctness and simple language of this paragraph helps the writer to achieve the purpose. The letter writer must indicate his expectations and intentions in the closing paragraph. He must clearly state the actions or response which he expects from the reader. While giving a finishing touch to the message, the writer has to express his hopes and wishes for the reader to respond in a particular manner to the message given earlier. It should be written precisely and care should be taken to stimulate the reader for further action.

Complimentary Closure

Complimentary closure is courteous and polite way of ending the letter. Just as the letter has a courteous beginning with salutation, it has a courteous ending with complimentary expression. It is like saying 'good bye', 'Good night' or 'Thank you' while parting after personal talks.

The complimentary close is typed two spaces below the last line of the closing paragraph. The complimentary close should be consistent with the salutation. The close which does not correspond or agree with the salutation is a wrong one. The complimentary closure which matches the salutation are given below:

Salutation		*Complimentary closure*
Sir,	)	Yours respectfully or
Madam,	)	Yours faithfully

Dear Sir)	Yours faithfully
Dear Sirs)	(used as standard closure
Dear Madam)	for business letters)
Mesdames)	
Dear Sir)	Yours truely
Dear Sirs)	(used as less formal than
Dear Madam)	Yours faithfully)
Mesdames)	
Dear Shri Patil)	Yours sincerely
Dear Smt. Kadam)	
Dear Mr. Kale)	
Dear Miss Shukla)	
My dear Kum Patel)	
My dear Mr. Joshi)	
Dear Customer)	Yours sincerely
Dear Subscriber)	
Dear Prakash)	Yours sincerely
Dear John)	or
My dear Sheela)	Yours ever
My dear Sheetal)	or
Dear Kusum)	Yours forever

The letter writer should note the point that he should capitalise only the first letter of the closure. He should also remember to put comma at the end of the closure. He should avoid the old fashioned phrases of letter ending with 'We are', 'I am', 'I remain', 'We remain' etc.

Signature and Designation

Signature is placed below the complimentary close indicating assent of the writer to the message of the letter. It is a signed name of the writer. In order to provide enough space for the signature, the name of the letter writer is written four spaces below the complimentary closure. It should be written in the hand of the person who sends the letter. The signature must be followed by the official designation of the writer. The signature gives affirmation to the writer's views and commitments in the letter, therefore the signed letter has a legal significance. The business letters should never be signed with the rubber stamp. The rubber stamp signature lacks the courtesy and personal touch of the original signature. As many signatures are illegible, the name of the signature should be typed below the manuscript signature.

For a company or a partnership firm, any one of the partners or the officer whom the firm delegates the authority of signing letters can sign the letter. Such a partner or an employee with special authority to sign has to put per. Pro. or p.p. before the name of the firm. His signature is put below the name of the firm.

(i) Yours faithfully,
M.R. Shah
Proprietor

(ii) Yours sincerely,
Tinu and Minu Co.,
S. Minu
Partner

(iii) Yours faithfully,
S.P. Pillai
Secretary

(iv) Yours faithfully,
Ruia and Co. Ltd.,
P.R. Patel
Managing Director

(v) Yours faithfully,
Per-Pro Victor
Tradelines Ltd.,
S.K. Desai
Personnel Manager

(vi) Yours truely,
On behalf of Associated
Agencies,
P. Vilas
Sales Executive

Enclosures and Postscript

Enclosures are additional papers and documents like price-list, invoice, catalogue, Bill, Draft, Cash Memo, Cheque, Railway Receipt etc., which are sent along with the letter. The letter writer draws the attention of the reader towards such annexures or accompanying papers by referring to them in the body of the letter. He should mention the enclosures in the letter after signature and designation of the writer. It should be placed two spaces below the last line of signature and designation, at the left side margin. The number of enclosures should be specified if there are more than one enclosures.

Encl : one
Or
Encls : Three
Or
Encl : Price-list
Or
Encls : (1) ---
(2) ---
(3) ---
(4) ---

Or
Enclosed : (1) ---
(2) ---
(3) ---
(4) ---

Postscript is an additional information written after the letter is completely typed. Postscript shows that the writer did not pre-plan the letter. Postscript is included in the letter only when it is absolutely essential. If necessary, the postscript should be placed two spaces below the close of the letter at the left hand margin.

FORMS OF LETTER LAYOUT

All the ten elements of a business letter are arranged in following forms:

1. Indented form
2. Full Block form
3. Block form
4. Semi-Block form
5. Hanging Indentation form

Indented Form

The indented form of letter writing is most conventional and perhaps the oldest one. The lines of inside name and address and all the first lines of each paragraph in the body of a letter are indented from three to seven spaces. The typists who prefer deeper indention can use as many as ten spaces for it, but seven spaces are sufficient for paragraph indention. Every line of the inside name and address is also indented four spaces to the right of the letter. The complimentary close in this form ordinarily begins like the first lines of each para, but the typist can begin it after leaving some more space also. Generally closed punctuation is used in this form. Though it requires more time to type with indented style and closed punctuation, the pleasing form compensates for the extra time and energy used by the typist.

Full Block Form

In complete block form all elements of letter begin from the left margin except the printed heading of the letter. The date line, the inside name and address, salutation, each paragraph in the body of the letter, the complimentary close the signature and the designation etc start from the left hand margin. This results in lopsided and imbalanced appearance of the letter. The letter appears heavy on the left side.

Though this form of layout is not as pleasant and popular as that of the conventional indented form, the full block style has now established itself as the recommended modern way of setting letters. As indention is not required for any part of the letter, this form of a letter saves time of the typist. Generally open punctuation is followed in this form. Only few essential punctuation marks are used except in the body of the letter where punctuation cannot be avoided without destroying meaning of the sentences. There can be complete absence of punctuation marks in the date line, the inside name and address, the salutation, the subject line and the complimentary closure. In full block form, the typist should leave generous margin. The letter writer must keep his paragraphs short so that too much reading material does not appear in it. It must not look heavy and hard to read.

Block Form

The block form is modern form of letter layout and it is widely used by business organisations. In it every line of inside name and address and each paragraph in the body of the letter begin from the left hand margin. The date line, complimentary close, signature and designation are written on the right side of the letter, but the signature and designation are blocked under the complimentary close. In order to show separation of paragraphs and division between different parts of letter double spacing is used. As most of the parts of letter and all the paragraphs are aligned with the left margin, indention does not take time of the typist except for the date line, complimentary close and signature. Generally, mixed punctuation is used in this form. Thus this form not only saved the time of the typist but also looks pleasant to the eyes of the receiver.

Semi-Block Form

Semi-block form is a combination of the block and indented forms. In this form of layout, all the parts of the letter except the paragraphs in the body are indented. The indented paragraphs make the letter easier to read and more balanced in appearance than the block and full-block forms. The inside name and address and the complimentary close are written in block form. The indented form is used in the body of the letter. Each paragraph in the body of the letter is indented seven spaces. The date line is placed below the heading at the right side of the letter. The inside name and address is placed against the left hand margin in block form. The complimentary close, the signature, the typed name and designation are placed at the left margin in block form. Generally open punctuation is used in all the parts of the letter except in the paragraphs of the body.

Hanging Indentation Form

The hanging indentation form is an eye-catching form and it differs in many respects from the layout forms discussed earlier. Though like a block form, the first line of each paragraph is aligned with the left margin. All the following lines in each paragraph are indented seven spaces. Thus it makes its appearance different, unusual and eye catching. Though it catches the attention of reader rather quickly, it may distract the readers attention from the message. The reader is likely to focus his attention on the unusual appearance of the form rather than on the message of the letter. The date line is placed under the heading at the right side of the letter. The inside name and address is written in block form. The complimentary close is indented. The signature, the typed name and designation of the writer are blocked under complimentary close. This form requires extra typing time because of its irregular placing of the different parts of letter. This form is not used for everyday business correspondence but it can be used for sales letters.

Indented Form :

Heading

____

____

____

Date : __________

Inside Address

____

____

____

Salutation

Body of the letter ____

____

______________________________.

Complimentary close

Signature

Full-Block Form :

Heading

____

____

____

Date : ________________

Inside Address

____

____

____

Salutation

Body of the letter ______________________________________

____

____

____

______________________________.

____

____

____

____

______________________________.

____

____

______________________________.

Complimentary close
Signature
Designation

Block Form :

Heading

____

____

____

Date : __________________

Inside Address

____

____

____

Salutation

Subject :

Body of the letter ____

____

____

____

____________.

____

____

____

____

____.

____

____

_______________________________.

Complimentary close
Signature
Designation

Semi-Block Form :

Heading

Date :

Inside Address

Salutation

Subject :

Body of the letter

Complimentary close
Signature
Designation

Hanging Indentation Form :

Heading

Date :

Inside Address

Salutation

Subject :

Body of the letter

Complimentary close
Signature
Designation

Exercises

1. What is the significance of letter-writing in modern business? What are the main purposes of the business correspondence?
2. What are the essentials of effective business correspondence? What should a businessman learn to write effective letters?
3. "All business letters are sales letters" Discuss.
4. What are the Six 'C's of effective business letter-writing?
5. "Business letters must be written in simple modern English to make them clear in meaning" — Discuss.
6. Why should a business letter writer write his letters from the reader's point of view?
7. Why should so much importance be given to courtesy in business correspondence?
8. Why should the letter writer avoid jargon and monotony in his letters?
9. Why is it necessary to plan a business letter?
10. Why should a business letter writer have an adequate knowledge of the subject and command of the language?
11. How does the success of a business letter depend on the effectiveness of its opening and closing paragraphs?
12. Write short notes on the following :

    (a) The Letter-head
    (b) The Date Line
    (c) The Inside Address
    (d) Salutation
    (e) The Body of a letter
    (f) Complimentary close
    (g) Signature and Designation
    (h) Enclosures
    (i) Postscript

13. What is meant by the 'lay-out' of a business letter?
14. What are the 'balanced' and 'unbalanced' layouts of business letters?
15. What are the forms of letter lay-outs? How do they serve different purpose?
16. Write short notes on the following:

(a) Block Form
(b) Semi-Block Form
(c) Full-Block From
(d) Indented Form
(e) Hanging Indented Form
(f) Per Pro. Signatures
(g) The Use of Reference Number.

13

ENQUIRIES AND REPLIES

The Inquiry letters are written with the writers own initiative or sometimes, in response to the appeals and offers made by the manufacturers, dealers and the sellers. The purpose of writing inquiry letters is to secure general information and estimates, information about the availability of specific goods, and to obtain the quotations, catalogues or price lists, samples and so on. The letter writer writes the inquiry letter to the individuals or the organisations and asks them to quote their rates and terms of transaction for supplying the required goods. In a routine of business transactions, inquiry is the first step through which the prospective buyers determine the specific goods required and also at what prices they are to be purchased. The buyer invites a number of quotations from several manufacturers and dealers to find out the cheapest and best source of supply of required goods. He spends several inquiry letters to different suppliers at the same time with the view to quickly obtain the information and to locate the right supplier with whom the best articles are available at the most competitive prices.

How to write Inquiry Letters?

1. The letter writer should clearly and precisely states his needs. He should give detailed specifications such as variety, trademark, style, size, shape, quality, brand, etc. of the goods he intends to buy.
2. He should be courteous, compact and definite. He should courteously request the seller to quote his prices and other terms of transactions.
3. He should give a rough estimate of the approximate or probable quantity of goods required.
4. He should ask the supplier to send the samples, because the samples are useful to the buyer to make selection of the

suitable articles.

5. He should indicate specific period of time by which the goods ought to be supplied.
6. He should request for descriptive literature which provide data regarding the utility, usage and specialities of the goods.
7. In case of complicated machines, he should request the manufacturer or the dealer for trial demonstration of how to operate the machine.
8. If necessary, he should ask for the guarantee of the goods and its normal expected life.
9. He should ask the supplier to state the credit and discount facilities offered by his company.
10. He should ask the supplier to state the terms of payment.
11. He should ask the supplier about the accessories and spares, if needed.
12. He should request the supplier to quote the lowest rates.

Specimen of Inquiry Letters :

REMI TRADERS
5, Main Road
Belgaum

Date : 7th July 1989

The Manager,
The Boswell Co. Ltd.,
5, G.P. Road,
London,
U.K.

Dear Sir,

We have read your advertisement in 'TIMES' dated 5th July 1989 regarding the new electronic typewriter. We have been importing the typewriters from West Germany, U.S., Japan etc. for last fifteen years, and we are happy to inform you that ours is an established trading company dealing with various types of typing, printing and duplicating machineries.

We should be grateful if you would kindly quote your lowest rates and full particulars of the various typewriters available with you. Send us a copy of your latest catalogue and let us know your terms and conditions for order of one hundred and fifty typewriters. You can expect our large orders provided your terms are competitive.

Awaiting to hear from you,

Yours faithfully,

—

Quotation Letters OR
Replies to the Inquiries

The quotation letters are the replies to the inquiries. The quotation letters are very important in the sales transactions. A reply to the inquiry letter is an opportunity for promoting the sales. As this reply is addressed to the prospective buyer in answer to his inquiry, it is necessary to give prompt attention to it. The Sales Manager must look into the inquiry letter for a particular company's problem of purchasing certain articles. In order to conveRt the 'inquiry' into 'order', the supplier must not lose time in sending complete reply.

A quotation letter is an offer by the seller to sell certain products or services with specific prices, terms and conditions. The suppliers usually use standard quotation form for quoting prices and all necessary details of the product or services. But such a printed quotation form should accompany with a courteous covering letter which shows personal interest and friendly attitude towards the party which sends an inquiry letter. A quotation letter specifically mentions the terms regarding packing the articles, modes of despatch or transportation, time of delivery, modes of payment, discounts and concessions offered etc. It also consists the details regarding the stock of goods available with the supplier. If the inquired goods are not available in the required quantity, the supplier requests the inquirer to wait for an anticipated period.

How to write Quotation Letter

1. The letter writer must promptly attend the letter of inquiry.

2. He must thank the inquirer at the beginning of the message.
3. He should give brief, clear and complete description of the goods available with him.
4. In case of machines and engines, he should offer trial demonstrations at a suitable place.
5. He should mention the quote of goods available with him.
6. He must send a price-list or catalogue with the letter, or he must mention the prices clearly in the letter itself.
7. He must mention the other incidental charges like those for package, freight, carriage insurance etc.
8. He must state whether the prices include the other incidental charges mentioned above.
9. He should mention the discount offered on the catalogue prices, if any.
10. He must mention the period particularly, if the cffer is open for a specific period.
11. He must specify the desired mode of payment.
12. He must mention the rate of cash discount for early payment, if he offers any.
13. If he offers credit facilities, he must clearly mention the terms of credit and the time of payment.
14. He must state the time, mode and place of delivery in case the order is received.
15. He must appeal the inquirer to place orders by emphasising the competitive prices and terms of transaction.

KOIMTUR SILK CO.
Ballarpur Road
Koimtur

21st July 1989

The Proprietor,
Sheetal Silk Emporium,
25, Main Road,
Kolhapur.

Dear Sir,

We thank you for your inquiry of 19th July, 1989 for assorted 'Flora' silk sarees. We appreciate the interest that you have shown in our products. You might, perhaps be knowing that ours is an established silk manufacturing unit with over fifty years of reputation. Recently we have introduced three new varieties of silk sarees namely 'Flora', 'Radha' and 'Ramayana' in rainbow colours and attractive designs.

All the three varieties which we have introduced in market from June 1989 consist small and medium size flowery designs. The designs on 'Ramayana' saree are mixed with matching colour stripes. 'Radha' and 'Ramayana' sarees are with border and pallu, but 'Flora' sarees are with and without border and pallu.

Since we earnestly desire to secure large orders, we have quoted very low prices and liberal terms regarding packing. The prices are C and F — Kolhapur. No packing charges will be levied on the order exceeding of Rs. 30,000. As there are indications of rise in silk prices, we shall be unable to repeat these prices and terms when our present stock is exhausted. We recommend you to place your order before 1st August 1989. Your order will receive our prompt attention.

Yours faithfully,

Encl : Catalogue.

Some Inquiries and Replies
An Enquiry

VINIT ENTERPRISES
10, Edwardo Road
Bombay-1

15th July 19 . . .

The Commercial Attache',
Japanese Embassy,
Delhi-5.

Dear Sir,

We are planning to add to our stock — standard electronic software and hardware of Japanese manufacture. We shall be glad if you send us a list of Japanese manufacturers who are likely to be able to supply us Printers, Integrated Circuits, Computer monitors, Keyboards, Floppy Disk Drive, Hard Disk Drive, Tape Drive etc. The specifications of the same are attached herewith.

Please let us know whether you will be able to supply information from your records. We hope we may hear from you very soon.

Yours faithfully,
S. Gopalan
General Manager
Vinit Enterprises

Reply :

JAPANESE EMBASSY
Delhi-5

18th July 19 . . .

M/s Vinit Enterprises,
10, Edwardo Road,
Bombay-1.

Dear Sirs,

Thank you for your enquiry letter of 15th July 19. . . . We are pleased to learn from your letter that you are interested in the electronic paraphernalia of Japanese manufacture. We are enclosing herewith the illustrated catalogues and price-lists of the material required by you. The price-lists and catalogues are obtained from different Japanese manufacturers. We have marked the items on the catalogues which match the specifications in your letter.

We shall be glad to send you any further information you may need.

Yours faithfully,
Joe Huan
'The Commercial Attache'
Japanese Embassy

An Enquiry :

BHARAT TRADING CO.
41, B. Tambe Road,
Pune-5.

25th July 19 . . .

Sales Manager,
Titan Quartz,
Sona Towers,
71, Miller Road,
Bombay-52.

Dear Sir,

We understand that TATA has introduced new types of world class Titan Quartz Watches. We shall appreciate detail information about each of the Titan Quartz Watches along with the illustrated catalogue and price-list. We also want to know about the guarantee for each of the quartz watches.

When replying please state the terms of payment and discounts you would allow for the order of larger quantities of individual items.

We hope that this enquiry of ours will receive your prompt and best attention.

Yours faithfully,
R. Somaiah
Proprietor
Bharat Trading Co.

Reply :

TITAL QUARTZ
(Corporate Office)
Sona Towers, 71, Miller Road,
Bangalore-560 052.

28th July 19 . . .

M/s Bharat Trading Co.,
41, B. Tambe Road,
Pune-5.

Dear Sir,

Thank you for you enquiry of 25th July 19 . . . , for Titan Quartz Watches. We are happy to learn about your interest in our world class quartz watches and enclose herewith our illustrate catalogue and price-list.

We have introduced an international collection of over 350 fine quartz watches pricing Rs. 380 onwards. With Titan Quartz the customer has the Tata assurance of many years of faultless performance. Every Titan Quartz watch is guaranteed for two years. Our after sales network offers service with speed and economy.

Any orders you may place with us will have our prompt and careful attention.

Yours faithfully,
S. Gopikrishnan
Sales Manager
Titan Quartz.

An Enquiry :

THE DAWN MILLS CO. LTD.
Ferguson Road
Lower Parel
Bombay-13

19th July 19 . . .

M/s Modi Mirrlees Blackstone Ltd.,
DDA Shopping Centre,
New Delhi-110065.

Dear Sirs,

We have read your advertisement in "Business India" of 25th June 19 . . . , regarding power generating sets. We shall be obliged if you will send us particulars of your power generating sets of different electrical and engine output.

We should like to know whether you can supply the power generating set of high fuel efficiency. We require the set which is suitable for continuous, base load, heavy duly operation.

We look forward to hearing from you within next few days.

Yours faithfully,
C. Parikh
General Manager
The Dawn Mills Co. Ltd.

Reply :

MODI MIRRLEES BLACKSTONE LTD.
DDA Shopping Centre
New Delhi

21st July 19 . . .

The General Manager,
The Dawn Mills Co. Ltd.,
Ferguson Road,
Lower Parel,
Bombay-13.

Dear Sir,

We are gratified to learn from your letter of 19th July 19 . . . , that you are interested in our power generating sets and have pleasure in sending you our illustrated catalogue describing the engine types with their engine output and electrical output.

Ours are the world's most reputed and most proven power generating sets. They are suitable for continuous, base load, heavy duty operations. Their unique features are high fuel efficiency, reliable operation and rugged design. We assure prompt after-sales service and ready availability of spares.

We hope you will take full advantage of our offer.

Yours faithfully,
M.G. Mahajan
Sales Manager
Modi Mirrlees Blackstone Ltd.

Exercises

(1) What points should a business letter writer keep in mind while writing a business Enquiry ?
(2) What are the essentials of drafting quotation letters ?
(3) Write a letter to M/s Saynak and Sons asking for a copy of latest catalogue of Titan Watches.
Write a reply to the above enquiry.
(4) Write an enquiry letter Sharada Electricals asking for an estimate for electrical fittings in your newly built lodging house.
Write a reply to the above enquiry.
(5) Draft a letter to Shalimar Paints asking them to submit quotation for the paints and varnishes.
Write a reply to the above enquiry.
(6) Write an enquiry letter to the dealer of electrical products asking him if he can supply the electrical products of Bajaj India Ltd.? Ask for the detailed catalogue and price-list.
Write a reply to the above enquiry.
(7) Janata Departmental Stores is holding its annual Diwali Sale. Write an enquiry letter asking them to send their catalogue and price-list.
Write a reply to the above enquiry.
(8) Messrs Mirchandani and Sons sell a large variety of cotton, woollen and nylon goods. Write them an enquiry letter asking for samples, prices and terms.
Write a reply to the above enquiry.
(9) Write an enquiry letter to the prospective supplier to send quotations for 'Raybon', 'Vinoo', 'Bravo' and 'Sheetal' sun-glasses.
Write a reply to the above enquiry.

14

ORDERS AND THEIR EXECUTION

The Buyer makes inquiries and receives quotations from different suppliers. After considering their competitive prices, qualities and other terms, he selects one of them which suits and fulfills his requirements. The quotations are 'offers' which provide all the essential information to the buyer and enable him to place the order for goods. They are the 'replies to the inquiries' which give the suppliers an opportunity to obtain orders from the prospective buyer. The order placed by the buyer is an acceptance of the offer made by the supplier through the quotation letter. The letter of order establishes legal relation between the buyer and the supplier.

Sometimes, the Purchase Manager appoints a purchase committee which scrutinises various quotations and the committee recommends the names of some supplier who quotes competitive prices and takes the decision about the final selection of the supplier and places orders with him, for machineries, equipments, spare parts, tools, raw material and other essential commodities and services which are required for the production. In some cases the suppliers send their sales representatives to the purchase committee for interviews and personal discussions in order to understand the needs, requirements and problem of the buyers. Such personal interviews and face-to-face discussions are effective in persuading the buyers to place the orders. But the suppliers must send the quotation letter before meeting the buyer personally for that purpose.

Before placing orders, the purchase manager or the purchase committee must know the following points:

1. The order letters have legal significance. It can be produced as legal evidence if the matters go to the court. Therefore, the letter writer must draft it carefully.
2. The letter writer must thank the supplier for his quotations, especially when the supplier offers special terms and

discounts.

3. He must give all the essential details of the goods to be supplied. He has to give the following specifications clearly and accurately.

    (i) Description of the articles, its exact trade name, quality, size, shape, colour, design, style, modes etc.
    (i) Prices (with reference to catalogue number)
    (iii) Discounts
    (iv) Alternative goods.

4. He must clearly mention the exact quantity desired for each item in words as well as in figures to avoid confusion.
5. The special instructions about the packing are important from the point of view of transportation and safety.
6. He must specify the mode of transport. He must mention whether the goods are to be dispatched by rail, road or water transport.
7. He must specify the time and place of delivery.
8. He must give special instructions about the insurance of goods, if needed.
9. He should specifically ask for after-sales services, if needed.
10. He should affirm in order letter the agreed terms of quotation relating to the manner of payment e.g. draft, cheque, Bill of Exchange, etc.

Order Forms

The correspondence concerning orders is largely routine and repetitive. The buyers do not correspond for placing orders in the manner they correspond for inquiries. Instead, they use printed order forms or order blanks. These standardised order form are printed with the columns or 'blanks' for filling necessary information. They consist all the necessary instructions and information which is to be given to the supplier. They are commonly used for repeated, regular and routine orders. As these forms are pre-prepared and pre-numbered, they are easy to refer in future. The important details put in its specific columns cannot be easily overlooked by the suppliers. Although they have number of advantages, they should not be sent in isolation. Such order form should be accompanied by a covering letter which indicates courtesy and friendly business approach.

REGENT AGENCIES
(Wholesale Cloth Merchants)
Ferguson Road
Bombay-12.

Date: 14th July 1989

The Dawn Fabrics
Lower Parel
Bombay-14.

Dear Sir,

Thank you for your quotation letter of 12th July 1989 and especially for sending us the patterns and samples of hosiery and other items manufactured in your company.

I am glad to inform you that our purchase committee has appreciated the quality of your suitings, shirtings, sarees and hosiery items and has directed me to place the order with you. I am pleased to place the order for following items which are selected from your catalogue on understanding that they will be supplied from the current stock and at catalogue prices.

Quantity	Items with Pattern No.	Price (net)
30 meters	Shirting - PN 27	Rs.36 per meter
30 meters	Shirting - PN 41	Rs.45 per meter
30 meters	Shirting - PN 48	Rs.28 per meter
30 meters	Shirting - PN 50	Rs.55 per meter
2 dozens	Sarees - PN 5	Rs.280 each
2 dozens	Sarees - PN 7	Rs.235 each
30 meters	Suiting - PN 11	Rs.110 per meter
30 meters	Suiting - PN 12	Rs.140 per meter

The goods ordered are urgently required by one of our regular and valuable customer, therefore, please despatch the consignment in time to reach us by 30th July 1989. We reserve the right to cancel the order and to refuse the delivery after this date.

Your faithfully,

Jose Daniel

Purchase Manager
Regent Agencies

Execution of Orders

When the supplier receives an order he must at once acknowledge it either by a short letter or by a printed postcard. A Printed acknowledgement or postcard may suit for the small routine orders, but the supplier can make use of an opportunity provided by every order to build an abiding, friendly and profitable relationship with the buyer by writing a special acknowledgement letter. In such acknowledgement letter he should state when the delivery may be expected and, if the goods ordered cannot be supplied, he should clearly explain why he cannot supply it. The acknowledgement of an order must have cheerful and pleasant approach. It must express gratitude and must appreciate the buyers interest in the goods ordered. The supplier can even mention the favourable aspects of the goods, competitive prices and other terms and services.

The supplier has to promptly despatch the goods as per the directions of the buyer. He must take quick steps to execute the order. The correspondence reaches the important stage of actual transaction when the supplier executes the order. The supplier must be careful and punctual in executing the order. If he sends the right goods of right quality at right time, he builds sound reputation and goodwill of his organisation. If he shows concern for the buyer's convenience, he certainly brings flow of further orders. If the goods are in ready stock, the instructions should be given to weight or measure the goods. It should be promptly and properly packed for safety and convenience of transportation. It should be despatched to the buyers address by specified mode of transport. Before despatching the goods, it is essential to verify the quality and quantity of goods and also the name and address of the buyer to whom it is to be despatched. Sometimes by sheer mistake or overlooking the goods are misplaced and the buyers receive the wrong goods, therefore verification of the goods and its buyers is essential before forwarding the consignment. The next step in the process of order fulfilment is to prepare the invoice which states the amount payable by the buyer and description of the goods in consignment.

Hints for Drafting

1. The supplier has to thank the party for his order.
2. He has to provide specifications regarding the despatch of goods ordered by the party and the date on which the consignment is despatched.
3. He has to attach a copy of invoice to the letter.
4. He has to mention the mode of despatch or transportation like post parcel, rail, road, ship, air etc.
5. He has to mention the enclosures of receipts such as lorry receipt, railway receipt, bill of loading etc. If they are not enclosed in the letter he should state whether they have been sent through bank or by V.P.P.
6. He may mention the superiority, popularity and quality of the goods. He may express his hope that the goods will fulfil the needs and requirements of the buyer.
7. He has to request for the payment as per the terms agreed between them through previous correspondence.
8. He should maintain cheerful, pleasant and personal tone throughout the letter and express his readiness to serve the buyer in all possible ways.

HINDAL COOKERS CO. LTD.
5, Dasara Road
Bombay-56

Date: 7th Oct 1989

M/s Sarda Brothers,
50, Mangal Mansion,
Vihar Road,
Kolhapur-10.

Dear Sirs,

Subject: Your Order No. AC 501 dated 27th Sept. 89

We are pleased to inform you that your above order for 154 assorted cookers is fully executed today. They are packed as per your instructions and despatched by our lorry. The consignment should reach you by tomorrow. The invoice and Delivery Notes will be handed over to you.

We hope you will find that the consignment supports our claim to sell the best cookers of their kind at the price and solicit further orders which will receive our most careful attention.

Yours faithfully,

Shree Gopalan

Sales Manager
Hindal Cookers Company Ltd.

Declining the Order

In certain situations a seller does not accept an order from the buyer. He declines the order because he does not find himself in a position to executes the order. His refusal of order is due to some unavoidable circumstances. The reasons for declining the order can be given as under:

1. The seller is not satisfied with the prices mentioned in the order, especially when the prices are less than quotations.

2. He is not satisfied with the ordered quantity, particularly when the ordered quantity is too small.
3. He has to execute a large number of orders on hand from the existing limited stock.
4. There is an acute shortage of the ordered goods in the market.
5. The goods are not available in the market.
6. He is not agreed with the buyer's terms and conditions.
7. He suspects the buyers creditability.
8. He learns about the sudden bankruptcy or the unsound financial position of the buyer.
9. The production unit faces the difficulties like strike of the employees, shortage of raw material etc.
10. The sale is through the authorised selling agency which is granted by the manufacturer to the dealer of that locality.

Hints for Drafting

1. He has to thank the buyer for his order.
2. He has to express regret for his inability to meet the buyer's needs.
3. He can propose an alternative product, if available.
4. He must politely state the reason for refusing the order.
5. He must politely draw the buyers attention to the quotation. He must convince the buyer that the quoted prices are the lowest and the further price reduction is not affordable to him.
6. He has to express his willingness to fulfil the order at the earlier quoted prices.
7. He has to express his hope for the opportunity to serve the buyer another time.

ORIENT ELECTRONICS
Nariman Road
Bangalore-7

Date: 10th Oct. 1989

M/s Vallabha Traders,
40, Station Road,
Pune-1.

Dear Sir,

Subject: Your Order No.VA15 dated 5th Oct. 1989.

We were very glad to receive your order of 5th Oct. 1989 for the supply of twelve television sets. We appreciate your interest in our world class products for which there is ever rising demand from the customers in this country and from abroad. We really wish we were in a position to accept your order. However, we cannot execute your order at the prices and discount desired by you.

In our letter of 1st Oct. 1989 we have offered you the lowest quotation for the quantity ordered by you. The quoted prices leave us with only the smallest margin. In fact the prices are lower than those of our competitors for the sets of similar quality. If you give further thought to this matter and agree with the quoted prices, we shall be pleased to promptly execute the order.

We shall always be very happy to hear from you and to offer you our services for the future orders from you.

Yours faithfully,

V. Parthasarathy

Sales Manager
Orient Electronics

Some Specimens of Orders and Replies

Order :

KOLHAPUR MILK PROJECT
17, M.I.D.C., Kolhapur

17th March 19 . . .

M/s Elgi Equipments Ltd.,
Indian House,
Trichy Road,
Coimbatore-641 018.

Dear Sirs,

We are thankful for your quotation of 14th March 19 . . . forwarding details of your range of compressed air appliances. We find both quality and prices satisfactory and are pleased to place an order for your Elgi Screw Compressor-ES55.

You can draw on us a Bill of Exchange for one month and forward it with the R/R through Syndicate Bank, Laxmipuri, Branch, Kolhapur. We note that you can supply the compressor from stock, and, look forward to delivery within the next few days.

Yours faithfully,

Govindrao Patil

Director
Kolhapur Milk Project

Reply :

M/S ELGI EQUIPMENTS LTD.
India House
Trichy Road
Coimbatore-641 018

20th March 19 . . .

The Director,
Kolhapur Milk Project,
17, M.I.D.C.,
Kolhapur.

Dear Sir,

We acknowledge with thanks your order of 17th March 19 . . . for 'Elgi Screw Compressor-ES55. Our truck will deliver the compressor at Kolhapur Milk Project, Kolhapur by the evening of 25th March 19. . . . You will be handed over with the relevant documents as the Invoice and Delivery Notes. As required we have drawn upon you at 40 days.

We hope you will be well pleased with the compressor and that we can establish a pleasant and lasting business connection with you.

Yours faithfully,

V.V. Thomas
Sales Executive
Elgi Equipments Ltd.,

Order :

NORTHSTAR ELECTRICALS
14, Bhuleshwar Road
Nasik-1

19th Aug. 19 . . .

M/s Sylvania Electricals Ltd.,
5, Prasad Mansion,
Henry James Road,
Bombay-5.

Dear Sirs,

We are in receipt of your catalogue and price-list of 14th Aug. 19 . . . , for the various electrical items manufactured by you. We note with pleasure your kind gesture to allow us a discount of 5 per cent on our orders.

Please supply the following merchandise at the rates and terms specified in your catalogue.

Particulars	Quantity	Unit Prices
1. Sylvania Bulbs 100 W	50 Boxes	Rs. 110
2. Sylvania Bulbs 40 W	100 Boxes	Rs. 90
3. Electric Heater 500 W	20 Sets	Rs. 28
4. Electric Heater 100 W	20 Sets	Rs. 35
5. Sylvania Tubes	10 Boxes	Rs. 950

Kindly pack the articles in plywood cases and mark them as N.E.N. while booking the parcel. Please send the articles by passenger train, carriage forward to Nasik Station. We reserve the right to cancel the order and reject the consignment if the delivery is not made on or before 30th Aug. 19. . . .

We shall be grateful for prompt delivery as the goods are needed urgently.

Yours faithfully,

S.Patwa
Proprietor
Northstar Electricals

Reply :

M/S SYLVANIA ELECTRICALS LTD.
5, Prasad Mansion
Henry James Road
Bombay-5

23rd Aug. 19 . . .

M/s Northstar Electricals,
14, Bhuleshwar Road,
Nasik-1.

Dear Sirs,

We were very pleased to receive your order of 19th Aug. 19 . . . for various electrical items manufactured by us. We welcome you as our one of the most valued customers. The consignment is despatched today by passenger train, carriage forward to Nasik Station.

We hope the consignment will reach you in good time. We have confidence that our handling of your first order will lead to further business between us.

Your faithfully,

G.G. Manik

Sales Manager
M/s Sylvania Electricals Ltd.
Bombay-5

Order

FERGUSON COLLEGE OF ARTS AND COMMERCE
Lincoln Road
Calcutta-5

25th Jan. 19

M/s Trinity Book Stores,
M.G.Road,
Delhi-5.

Dear Sirs,

We thank you for your letter of 21st Jan. 19 . . . enclosing the publisher's catalogues. We would be glad if you accept our order for the following books on the usual discount terms of 20% off the catalogue prices.

Title	Author	Copies	Catalogue price
1. Messages	LM Parkar	10	Rs. 215
2. Conference Leadership	PS Bolinger	10	Rs. 85
3. Personnel Management	Mamoria	15	Rs. 165
4. Business and Society	K. Davis	15	Rs. 200
5. Tempest	Shakespeare	100	Rs. 55

We Shall be grateful for prompt delivery as the books are needed urgently.

Yours faithfully,

William Collins
Librarian
Ferguson College

Reply :

TRINITY BOOK STORES
M.G.Road, Delhi-5

28th Jan 19 . . .

The Librarian,
Fergusion College of Art and Commerce,
Lincoln Road,
Calcutta-5.

Dear Sir,

We thank you for your order of 25th Jan. 19. . . . We are pleased to inform you that the books included in your order have been sent to you today by post.

We have been very happy to serve you and look forward to receiving your further orders.

Your faithfully,

N.Swamy

Proprietor
M/s Trinity Book Stores

Order :

TRIBHUVAN MEDICALS
10, R.N. Bhave Road
Bombay-17

15th May 19 . . .

M/s Modern Medical Stores,
40, Rajaram Road,
Thane-7.

Dear Sirs,

Thank you for your letter of 10th May 19 . . . and the detailed catalogue and price-lists of the medical products of different pharmaceutical companies. We enclose herewith our official order for sixteen of the items.

All these items are urgently required by our customers. We therefore hope you will send them immediately. We reserve the right to cancel the order and refuse the delivery if the consignment does not reach us on or before 25th May 19. . . .

Yours faithfully,

S. Tribhuvan

Proprietor
Tribhuvan Medicals
Bombay-17

Reply

MODERN MEDICAL STORES
40, Rajaram Road
Thane-7

19th Aug 19 . . .

Mr. S.P. Tribhuvan,
Proprietor,
Tribhuvan Medicals,
10, R.N. Bhave Road,
Bombay-17.

Dear Sir,

We were glad to learn from your letter of 15th May 19 . . . that you have placed a large order for a number of items included in our quotation. Except Zandu Chyavanprash, all the ordered items are in stock.

Considering the matter of urgency for the delivery of all the item stated in your letter, we have substituted the 14th item with Baidya Chyavanprash. It is identical with Zandu Chyavanprash in quality, taste and market demand. If you do not accept this, please return it at our expense.

We trust the goods will reach you safely and in good time and that you will be pleased with them.

Yours faithfully,

S.K. Patil
Proprietor
Modern Medical Stores, Thane-7.

Order :

KASTURI TAILORS
87, Shahu Road
Kolhapur-2

12th May 19 . . .

M/s Vrindavan Trading Co.,
5, Kanchan Marg,
Parle (West),
Bombay-7.

Dear Sirs,

I have pleasure in placing an order with you for two "AK-5' Ringer Sewing Machines. The order is placed strictly on the condition that the delivery is to be made on or before 20th May 19. . . .

Please send the machines by S.T. Parcel, carriage forward to Kolhapur Central Bus Stand from where the consignment will be collected.

Yours faithfully,

Vinod Shah

Proprietor
Kasturi Tailors
Kolhapur-2.

Reply :

VRINDAVAN TRADING CO.
5, Kanchan Marg,
Parle (West),
Bombay-7

15th May 19 . . .

Mr. Vinod Shah, Proprietor,
Kasturi Tailors,
87,Shahu Road,
Kolhapur-2.

Dear Sir,

Thank you for your letter of 12th May 19. . . . Placing an order for two 'AK-5' Ringer Sewing Machines. But we regret to inform you that we can no longer supply these machines.

In recent years the demand for Ringer Sewing Machines has fallen to such an extent that we have ceased to stock them in our shop. In their place we can offer you new Royal Sewing Machines. The large number of repeat orders received from the tailors is an evidence of its popularity.

The illustrated catalogue of Royal Sewing Machines is attached herewith. If you place an order for these machines, we could meet it within three days.

Yours faithfully,

S.Kumar
Proprietor
Vrindavan Trading Co.
Bombay-7.

Order :

TANDAN TRADERS
28, Netaji Subhash Road
Bangalore-8

14th Aug. 19 . . .

M/s Vinayak Trading Co.,
51, Line Bazar Road,
Calcutta-10.

Dear Sirs,

While thanking you for your prompt reply of 10th May 19 . . . . We are glad to place an order for 1100 packs of Brooke Bond Red Label Tea, each containing 500gms of tea.

We note that you can supply the tea from stock and look forward to delivery within fifteen days. Our usual terms of payment are one month from date of invoice and we hope they will be satisfactory to you.

Yours faithfully,

Ramesh Tandan

Proprietor
Tandan Traders

Reply :

VINAYAK TRADING CO.
51, Line Bazar
Calcutta-10

17th Aug 19 . . .

Mr. Ramesh Tandan,
Proprietor,
Tandan Traders,
28, Netaji Subhash Road,
Bangalore-8.

Dear Sir,

We thank you for your order No.53 dated 14th Aug. 19 . . . for 1100 packs of Brooke Bond Red Label Tea. But we regret to inform you that we do not have the stock of this tea in the size required by you.

At present we have a stock of 500 packs of Brooke Bond Red Label Tea, each containing 500 gms. We expect further deliveries within a week, and will notify you immediately after our stocks come in.

Your faithfully,

P. Mehta

Manager
M/s Vinayak Trading Co.
Calcutta.

Exercises

1. What points should be included in an order letter?
2. Place an order for 500 Beeja bulbs of 40 W and 50 Surya Tubes for your retail electricals shop, and reserve the right to reject the consignment if it is delayed.

   Send an acknowledgement letter to the customer who has ordered the above goods.
3. Place an order with a wholesale garment supplier for 300 T-Shirts and 100 Jean Pants in assorted sizes and colours. Ask the seller to give you a concession or discount.

   Write a suitable reply to the above customer explaining him your inability to execute the order due to an unexpected labour problem.
4. Place an order for 10 gross parker pens and 5 gross sharp pens with Messrs Poonawala Traders. Ask for a discount. Write a suitable reply to the above order and inform the customer that you do not have the Parker and Sharp pens in stock, but can supply the substitutes.
5. Place an order with Usha Sewing Machines for six sewing machines. Inform the supplier that the machines are urgently needed by some of your valuable customers. Specify the mode of transport and mode of payment.

   Draft an acknowledgement letter to the above order, and assure the party that you are executing the order promptly.
6. Messrs Gokul Lodging, Poona, place an order for 100 steel cots, 50 tables and 100 chairs with Laxmi Furnitures, Bombay.

   They request the supplier to hold the goods at their disposal until they make an arrangement for transport.

   Write a tactful reply to the above customer who has placed a first order with you, but has made no mention of payment.
7. Place an order for 5 steel shelves with Modern Steel Fabricators, Bombay.

   You had sent a special low price quotation to the above customer for acceptance within one month. The customer's order comes two months after the expiry of the firm offer.

   The prices of the steel have already risen. Write a reply to the customer persuading him to confirm the order at the raised prices.

15

CREDIT AND STATUS ENQUIRIES

Meaning of Credit

The word 'credit' is derived from the latin word 'credo' meaning 'I believe' and 'credere' meaning 'to trust'. The goods are sold for cash and sometimes on credit. It is a facility provided by the supplier to enable the buyer to buy the goods without cash payment. The supplier who extends the credit believes in his buyer's dependability. He collects the credit information of his customer and on the basis of this information he trusts that the customer will pay the bill when it is due. He allows the buyer to take possession of the goods and to pay for them later.

The supplier can expand his business by extending credit to the individual customers or organisations. But for the buyers, to expect credit facility, have to show their ability and reliability for making payments within a given period of time.

Advantages

A great deal of trading involves credit and it plays vital role in the growth of any business. The credit sales is useful both to the buyers and the suppliers. It enables the suppliers to keep the old buyers and to attract the new buyers. It enables the buyers who run retail shops and to hold stocks without making cash payment. They make payment for the stock out of the proceeds of their later sales. In business, the buyers are not always in the position to buy on full cash payment. In such cases, credit facility helps them to run their business with less capital. The insufficient capital or even the lack of it does not become hinderance in conducting buyer's business. The credit facility increases his working capital as he holds the stocks and makes further payments in instalments from the proceeds of his later sales. As for the daily customers, credit facility enables them to buy and use the goods before they save the amount of money needed for it. The credit customers tend to buy in the shop where the account is kept, hence the seller gets guaranteed market and regular sales.

Disadvantages

The risk of bad debts is the main disadvantage of credit. In some cases the supplier extends the credit facility to a person who does not remain steady and trustworthy. A buyer may enjoy the credit facility but may not make payments within a prescribed limit of time. The buyer may show honesty and integrity till he gets the credit facility, but later he may not show his sense of obligation. The buyer who does not have enough capital for his business turnover, can hardly be expected to make payments in prescribed period. If he proves unsuccessful in his business, there is a risk of bad debt. If, due to unfavourable circumstances, he fails to make progress and loses ground, there is a risk of bad debt. Sometimes, he may not get the expected opportunities to expand his business. In such cases, the stock held by him may suffer from the lack of demand from the parties.

The supplier who extends credit facility to his customers has to involve himself in the extra work of maintaining records of the goods sold on credit and later, he has to write series of collection letters to the customers who do not make regular payments. Writing collection letters takes extra expenditure, time and energy of the supplier. Credit has the disadvantages for the buyers also. The buyer is inclined to buy at the shop where his credit account is kept. He does not feel free to buy anywhere else like the cash customers. He has to pay more for the goods bought on credit when the supplier raises the prices to cover his extra expenses.

Sources of Information

1. Personal interviews with the customer.
2. The salesman's report and office records about the customers creditability.
3. Customer's present employer.
4. Customer's previous employer.
5. The financial statements of the customer.
6. The bank with which the customer is associated.

7. The traders with whom the customer had business ties in past.
8. Chambers of commerce.
9. Trade associations.
10. Inquiry Agencies.

Essential Information About the Customer

1. *Character:* The information regarding the customer's character include details about his honesty, fairness, punctuality, reliability and trustworthiness.
2. *Business aptitude:* This includes information about how well the customer attends his business and builds his business relations.
3. *Eligibility and capabilities:* It includes information about the qualifications, training, knowledge, experience, resourcefulness and physical fitness required to carry the duties and responsibilities of a particular business.
4. *Business location:* This includes information about the suitability of the customer's business location.
5. *Business progress:* This includes information about the kind of progress being made by the customer.
6. *Business capital:* This includes information about the reserves, assets and liabilities.
7. *Business competition:* This includes information about the rivals and competitors of the customer.
8. *Business setbacks and achievements:* This includes information about the customer's difficult financial circumstances in past, its outcomes and his remarkable achievements.

Hints for Drafting Credit Inquiries

(i) The supplier has to thank the buyer for placing order.

(ii) He has to express his pleasure at the request made by the party for credit facility.

(iii) He has to explain the need of producing credit information.

(iv) He has to assure the customer that all the information about him and his organisation will be kept confidential.

(v) He has to request the customer to provide the names and addresses of the referees like the credit-applicant's banker and the associated traders who can give information about his credit worthiness.

Hints for Drafting Status Inquiries

(i) The supplier has to make an humble request to the referees to provide necessary information about the status and credit worthiness of the customer.

(ii) He has to mention the complete name and address of the customer or the organisation.

(iii) He has to mention the amount of credit and the period for which it is asked by the customer.

(iv) He has to inform the customer's banker or the trade referee that the customer had asked him through previous correspondence to refer to them.

(v) He has to ask the referee to provide information about the customer's character, business capacities and resourcefulness, his financial position, his business activities in past, his present status in a particular business line, his knowledge and experience etc.

(vi) He has to request the referees to give their advice or suggestions about extending credit to the customer.

(vii) He has to request the referees to suggest the maximum amount and period of credit that may be extended to the customer.

(viii) He has to assure the referees that all the information provided by them will be considered strictly confidential.

(ix) He has to enclose a self-addressed envelope with the letter.

(x) Such letters should be always courteous, compact, confident and definite.

Letters of credit and status inquiry — Making Credit Inquiry:

NOVELTY TRADING CORPORATION
147, LINE BAZAR ROAD
Bombay-35

Date: 4th Oct. 1989

M/s Lucky General Stores,
N.M. Joshi Road,
Kolhapur-1.

Dear Sirs,

We are thankful for your order of 1st Oct. 1989 for five dozens of 'safari' suitcases of assorted sizes and colours. We appreciate your interest in our products. Our business relations with you over last one year has been satisfactory and, we are glad to inform you that your request for open account facilities is under our consideration.

As you wish us to extend you the open account facility, it will be very kind of you to furnish us with your bank reference and two trade references which would enable us to settle the credit of your firm. We do not have any doubt about the credit standing of your firm but it is a regular practice of our firm to ask for the trade and bank references before opening the credit account.

In order to avoid delay in your shipment, please write to us by return mail. Your order will be executed promptly after the completion of routine credit inquiries with your referees. We hope that the opening of this account will strengthen our business relations.

Yours faithfully,
Brijmohan Sinha

Sales Manager
Novelty Trading Corporation.

Furnishing References :

M/S LUCKY GENERAL STORES
N.M. Joshi Road
Kolhapur-1

Date : 6th Oct. 1989

The Sales Manager,
Novelty Trading Corporation,
147, Line Bazar Road,
Bombay-35.

Dear Sir,

Thank you for your letter of 4th Oct. 1989. According to your general policy requirements we are giving below our three credit references :

(i) M/s Jamunalal Bhattacharya and Company,
51, Bindu Road, Kolhapur-5
(ii) M/s Bombay Bag House,
D.N. Ranade Road, Pune-2
(iii) The Branch Manager,
Veerashaiv Bank, Laxmi Road, Kolhapur-1

We have an open account with M/s Jamunalal Bhattacharya and M/s Bharat Bag House. They have been our regular suppliers for more than last three years. Veerashaiv Bank, Laxmipuri Branch, Kolhapur-1 is our banker with whom we are having credit limits since 1979.

Please write to us if you require any additional information. As we have to add to our stock for the Deepavali season, we request you to complete your credit formalities within ten days and proceed to supply the goods by 20th of this month.

Yours faithfully,
Bansi Lal
Proprietor
Lucky General Stores

Making Status Inquiry :

M/S NOVELTY TRADING CORPORATION
147, Line Bazar Road
Bombay-35

Date : 7th Oct. 1989

M/s Bharat Bag House,
D.N. Ranade Road,
Pune-2.

Dear Sirs,

We have received order from M/s Lucky General Stores, N.M. Joshi Road, Kolhapur-1 for the supply of five dozens of 'safari' suitcases valued at Rs. 14000. They wish to open an account with us for the period of two months and have given us your name as credit reference.

We shall appreciate an early reply from you. Please let us know your views on the credit limits that can be allowed to the above party.

All the information provided by you will be treated as strictly confidential.

Yours faithfully,
Brijmohan Sinha
Sales Manager
Novelty Trading Corporation

Reply to Status Inquiry :

M/S BOMBAY BAGS HOUSE
D.N. Ranade Road
Pune-2

Date : 9th Oct. 1989

The Sales Manager,
M/s Novelty Trading Corporation,
147, Line Bazar Road,
Bombay-35.

Dear Sir,

In reply to your letter of 7th Oct. 1989, we are glad to inform you that M/s Lucky General Stores, N.M. Joshi Road, Kolhapur-1 is a sound business party on our accounts for the last three years. Their record of payment has been satisfactory during this period. They enjoy respect and confidence in the local market.

Their purchase average in the peak season is over Rs. 25,000 a month and about Rs. 15,000 during the other period. We have granted them credits for large amounts and have found that they clear their dues regularly.

We consider M/s Lucky General Stores worthwhile for the credit limit you have mentioned. Though this information is given according to our best knowledge and belief, it does not commit us to any responsibility.

Yours faithfully,
Vinod Panchal
Proprietor
Bombay Bags House

Letter of Credit and Status Inquiry — B

Asking for References :

OGALE GLASS MANUFACTURING CO. LTD.
Karve Road, Oglewadi
Poona-77

18th April 19 . . .

M/s Classic General Stores,
65, Jamadar Lane,
Belgaum-13.

Dear Sirs,

We are thankful for your order of 15th April 19 . . . for 40 dozen cups, 40 dozen saucers, 40 dozen tumblers and 40 dozen plates. We appreciate your interest in our products, and we are glad to know that you wish to have business dealing with us.

According to the standing policy of our company, we require trade and bank references that support your business and financial standing. We would request you to send the names of your bankers and two trade referees. It will enable us to execute your order on credit basis.

On completing our routine credit inquiries with your referees, we shall execute your order immediately.

Yours faithfully,
A.S. Vaze
Sales Manager
Ogale Glass Mfg. Co. Ltd., Oglewadi

Reply Furnishing Referenes :

CLASSIC GENERAL STORES
65, Jamadar Lane
Belgaum-13

21st April 19 . . .

The Sales Manager,
Ogle Glass Manufacturing Co.Ltd.,
Karve Road, Oglewadi,
Pune-77.

Dear Sir,

We are in receipt of your letter of 18th April 19 . . . and accordingly we are giving below our credit references :

(1) Canara Bank
Tilakwadi Branch
Belgaum-7

(2) Mr. Manik Mehta
Proprietor
Anupam Departmental Stores,
37, Tilakwadi,
Belgaum-7

(3) M/s Vikas General Stores,
37, Shahapur Road,
Belgaum.

We hope that these references will be found satisfactory to you and we request you to complete the credit formalities within a week. We look forward to your prompt execution of our order which will pave way to a mutually profitable business relationship.

Yours faithfully,
S.V. Shastri
M/s Classic General Stores,
Belgaum-13.

Status Inquiry Letter (Trade References)

M/S OGLE GLASS MANUFACTURING CO. LTD.
Karve Road, Oglewadi
Poona-77

23rd April 19 . . .

Mr. Manik Mehta
Proprietor
Anupam Departmental Stores,
37, Tilakwadi,
Belgaum-7.

Dear Sir,

We have received an order from M/s Classic General Stores, 65, Jamadar Lane, Belgaum-13, for glassware amounting to Rs. 45000. They have given us your name as a reference.

M/s Classic General Stores have asked for the credit facility for a period of two months. As we did not have the pleasure of dealing with them in the past, we want to know about their credit-worthiness. We shall be grateful if you will give us information relating to their business standing and financial status. As we understand that you have been dealing with them for many years, we request you to let us know, in particular, whether you consider it would be reasonable to grant them credit for the amount and period mentioned above.

Any information that you give us will, of course, be treated as strictly confidential.

Yours faithfully,
A.S. Vaze
Sales Manager
M/s Ogle Glass Mfg. Co. Ltd.,
Oglewadi.

A Favourable Reply :

M/S ANUPAM DEPARTMENTAL STORES
37, Tilakwadi
Belgaum-7

26th April 19 . . .

The Sales Manager,
Ogle Glass Mfg. Co. Ltd.,
Karve Road,
Oglewadi,
Poona-77.

Dear Sir,

We have received your inquiry of 23rd April 19 . . . and are glad to inform you that the firm in question enjoys respect and unquestionable confidence in the local market. It is a sound business party known to us for the last fifteen years. From our dealing with them, we have always found them prompt in the settlement of their account. They have built up a flourishing business and are rated high in the local business circles as trustworthy and competent.

We consider them worthwhile for the credit limit under your contemplation. This opinion is given to you without obligation on our part and it does not commit us to any responsibility. But we fully believe that you will find our information borne out by facts.

Yours faithfully,
Manik Mehta
Proprietor
Anupam Departmental Stores, Belgaum-7

Status Inquiry Letter (Bank References)

M/S OGLE GLASS MANUFACTURING CO. LTD.
Karve Road, Oglewadi
Poona-77

23rd April 19 . . .

The Branch Manager,
Canara Bank,
Oglewadi Branch,
Poona-77.

Dear Sir,

We have been asked by M/s Classic General Stores, 65, Jamadar lane, Belgaum-13 to supply goods to the tune of Rs. 45000 against their first order on open-account terms. But, as it is first time we are dealing with them, we should like to get some information about their financial and credit standing.

The bank reference they give us is that of 'Canara Bank' Tilakwadi Branch, Belgaum-7. Any information you will be giving us will be regarded as absolutely confidential.

Yours faithfully,
A.S. Vaze
Sales Manager
Ogle Glass Mfg. Co. Ltd., Oglewadi

A Favourable Reply :

CANARA BANK
Oglewadi Branch
Poona-77

30th April 19 . . .

The Sales Manager,
Ogle Glass Manufacturing Co. Ltd.,
Karve Road, Oglewadi,
Poona-77.

Dear Sir,

We are pleased to state that the information received about the creditworthiness of M/s Classic General Stores, 65, Jamadar Lane, Belgaum-13 is favourable. The firm was founded fifteen years ago and it enjoys a good reputation. A credit of Rs. 45000 for two months can be considered as reasonable and safe.

This information is strictly confidential and is given without any financial responsibility on our part.

Yours faithfully,
R.G. Dave
Branch Manager
Canara Bank
Oglewadi.

Letter Granting Credit :

OGLE GLASS MANUFACTURING CO. LTD.
Karve Road, Oglewadi
Poona-77

30th April 19 . . .

M/s Classic General Stores,
65, Jamadar Lane,
Belgaum-13.

Dear Sirs,

Thank you for your letter 21st April 19. . . . We have completed our inquiries relating your firm and are pleased to inform you that we have decided to open Charge Account in your name with a credit limit of Rs. 45000 for a period of two months. M/s Anupam Departmental Stores, 37, Tilakwadi, Belgaum-7 has informed us that you have been prompt in setting their accounts.

We are executing your order of 15th April 19 . . . and you will receive the consignment by 5th August 19 . . . along with the related invoice. We hope you will be well pleased with the goods and that we can establish a pleasant and lasting business connection with you.

Yours faithfully,
A.S. Vaze
Sales Manager
Ogale Glass Mfg. Co. Ltd.,
Oglewadi.

Letter Refusing Credit :

OGLE GLASS MANUFACTURING CO. LTD.
Karve Road, Oglewadi
Poona-77

30th April 19 . . .

M/s. Classic General Stores,
65, Jamadar Lane,
Belgaum-13.

Dear Sirs,

We have carefully considered your request of 15th April 19 . . . for credit facilities. We are satisfied to learn about your interest in our product. The credit references you had mentioned all speak favourable of you. But, we regret our inability to execute your order on credit basis.

Firstly, you are still expanding your business and are yet not well-established. Secondly, we feel that the location of your stores is not favourable enough to provide a good market. In such a case, our company cannot grant you the credit facilities.

We shall be glad, however, if you place a smaller order with us on a cash basis at a special discount of 8.5% of net invoice value. We hope that you will accept this offer and give us the opportunity of proving our best services to you.

Yours faithfully,
A.S. Vaze
Sales Manager
Ogle Glass Mfg. Co. Ltd., Oglewadi

Letters of Credits and Status Inquiry — C

Asking for References :

SYLVANIA ELECTRICALS LTD.
5, Prasad Mansion
Henry James Road
Bombay-5

21st Aug. 19 . . .

M/s Northstar Electricals,
14, Bhuleshwar Road,
Nasik-1.

Dear Sirs,

It was a pleasure to receive your order dated 19th Aug. 19 . . . for various electricals items manufactured by us. We appreciate your interest in our products.

According to the standing policy of our company, we ask customers for trade references while opening new accounts with us. The trade references are required to support the business and financial standing of the customer. Perhaps therefore you will be good enough to send the names and addresses of two other suppliers with whom you have dealings. If will enable us to execute your order on credit basis.

On completing our routine credit inquiries with your references, we shall execute your order immediately.

Yours faithfully,
G.G. Manik
Sales Manger
M/s Sylvania Electricals Ltd.,
Bombay-5

Reply Furnishing References :

NORTH ELECTRICALS
14, Bhuleshwar Road
Nasik-1

24th Aug. 19 . . .

The Sales Manager,
Sylvania Electricals Ltd.,
5, Prasad Mansion,
Henry James Road,
Bombay-5.

Dear Sir,

Thank you for your letter of 21st Aug. 19. . . . We quite understand the need for trade references and accordingly we are giving the names and addresses of our banker and two trade references with whom we have had business dealings for many years.

(1) M/s Vidyut Bhandar,
38, Sadashiv Road,
Pune-10.
(2) Purohit Electricals
23, Bazar Road,
Thane-13.
(3) The Manager,
State Bank of India,
Shaniwar Peth Branch,
Nasik-1.

We hope that these references will be found satisfactory to you and note that we may expect delivery of the goods, by the first week of the September. We look forward to receiving the consignment in good time. Your prompt handling of this first order will lead to further business between us and it will mark the beginning of a happy working relationship.

Yours faithfully,
S. Patwa
Proprietor
M/s Northstar Electricals, Nasik-1.

Status Inquiry Letter (Trade References):

SYLVANIA ELECTRICALS LTD.
5, Prasad Mansion
Henry James Road
Bombay-5

26th Aug. 19 . . .

M/s Vidyut Bhandar,
38, Sadashiv Road,
Pune-10.

Dear Sirs,

We have received an order from M/s Northstar Electricals for various electrical items manufactured by us. They have given us your name as a credit reference.

M/s Northstar Electricals have asked for the credit facility for a period of three months. As we did not have the pleasure of dealing with them in the past, we want to know about their creditworthiness. We shall be grateful if you will give us information relating to their business standing and financial status. As we understand that you have been dealing with them for many years, we request you to let us know in particular, whether you consider it would be reasonable to grant them credit for the amount of Rs. 16,000.

Any information that you give us will, of course, be treated as strictly confidential.

Yours faithfully,
G.G. Manik
Sales Manager
M/s Sylvania Electricals Ltd.
Bombay-5.

A Favourable Reply :

VIDYUT BHANDAR
38, Sadashiv Road
Pune-10

29th Aug. 19 . . .

The Sales Manager,
Sylvania Electricals Ltd.,
5, Prasad Mansion,
Henry James Road,
Bombay-5.

Dear Sir,

We have received your inquiry of 26th Aug. 19 . . . and are pleased to state that the firm referred to in your letter is a small but well-known and highly respectable firm. The proprietors of the firm enjoy respect and unquestionable confidence in the local market. It is a sound business party known to us for the last fifteen years. From our dealing with them for over ten years, we have always found them prompt in the settlement of their account. They have built up a flourishing business and are rated high in the local business circles as trustworthy and competent.

The credit we have allowed the firm has at times been well above the Rs. 16,000 you mention. We consider the firm worthwhile for the credit limit under your contemplation. This opinion is given to you without any obligation on our part and it does not commit us to any responsibility. But, we fully believe that you will find our information borne out by facts.

Yours faithfully,
S. Meghanathan
Proprietor
Vidyut Bhandar
Pune-10.

Status Inquiry Letter (Bank Reference) :

SYLVANIA ELECTRICALS LTD.
5, Prasad Mansion,
Henry James Road,
Bombay-5

26th Aug. 19 . . .

The Branch Manager,
Canara Bank,
Parel Branch,
Bombay-5.

Dear Sir,

We have today received an order for Rs. 16,000 worth, of goods from M/s Northstar Electricals, 14, Bhuleshwar Road, Nasik-1. They have asked for the credit facility for the period of three months. But, as it is the first time we are dealing with them, we should like to get some information about their financial and credit standing before dealing with their order.

The only bank reference they give us is that of the "State Bank of India, Shaniwar Peth Branch, Nasik-1". We shall be grateful for the information you can obtain for us. Any information you will be giving us will be regarded as absolutely confidential.

Yours faithfully,
G.G. Manik
Sales Manager
Sylvania Electricals Ltd.,
Bombay-5.

A Favourable Reply :

CANARA BANK
Parel Branch
Bombay-5

29th Aug. 19 . . .

The Sales Manager,
Sylvania Electricals Ltd.
Henry James Road,
Bombay-5.

Dear Sir,

We have received information about the creditworthiness of M/s Northstar Electricals, Nasik-1 from their banker "State Bank of India, Shaniwar Peth Branch, Nasik-1". We are glad to inform you that the firm you mention is a private company and was founded fifteen years ago. It enjoys a good reputation. A credit of Rs. 16,000 for three months can be considered as reasonable and safe.

This information is strictly confidential and is given without any financial responsibility on our part.

Yours faithfully,
C. Parikh
Branch Manager,
Canara Bank
Bombay-5.

Unfavourable Reply :

CANARA BANK
Parel Branch
Bombay-5

29th Aug. 19 . . .

The Sales Manager,
Sylvania Electricals Ltd.
Henry James Road,
Bombay-5

Dear Sir,

We have now received the information about the credit-worthiness of M/s Northstar Electricals, Nasik-1, from their banker, 'State Bank of India, Shaniwar Peth Branch, Nasik-1'. This is a private firm and it is operating on a very small scales. We regret to inform you that we cannot give you the assurance you seek in regard to this.

More detailed information we have received suggests that it is better to have cash transactions only. Please note that the information is given in strict confidence and we accept no responsibility in the matter.

Yours faithfully,
C. Parikh
Branch Manager,
Canara Bank
Bombay-5.

Granting Credit :

SYLVANIA ELECTRICALS LTD.
5, Prasad Mansion
Henry James Road
Bombay-5

5th Sept. 19 . . .

M/s Northstar Electricals,
14, Bhuleshwar Road,
Nasik-1.

Dear Sirs,

We have pleasure to inform you that we have decided to extend credit facilities to you for the period of three months at 5% from 10th Sept. 19. . . . We feel that the credit facilities extended to you may help you in speeding up your business.

We are executing your order of 19th Aug. 19 . . . and you will receive the consignment by 10th Sept. along with the related invoice. We hope our business relation will develop into a prosperous one.

Yours faithfully,
G.G. Manik
Sylvania Electricals Ltd.
Bombay-5.

Exercises

(1) What is meant by 'trade reference' and 'bank reference' ? What role does credit enquiry play in granting credit ?

(2) Write a reply to the customer's letter of an order for 40 steel chairs to be supplied on the credit of two months. In a reply ask the customer to furnish credit information.

(3) You have received a large order for goods worth Rs. 35,000 from Messrs Ranjit and Sons. They have asked for the credit facility for two months. Write a tactful reply requesting them to give the names of two trade references.

(4) Messrs Ratnamala Wastra Bhandar have received an order for 1000 sets of customs jewellery in assorted colours and designs from Messrs Deepali Cloth Stores. Messrs Deepali Cloth Stores have asked for credit terms and have given two trade references. Write the credit enquiry letters from Messrs Ratnamala Wastra Bhandra to those two trade references asking them to give information about the creditability of Messrs Deepali Cloth Stores.

(5) You have received a credit inquiry letter from Messrs Patel and Sons, Bombay, regarding the business and financial status of Messrs Vijaya General Stores, Thane. You had been the supplier of goods to Messrs Vijaya General Stores in the past. Write a suitable reply to the enquiry.

(6) Messrs Handa and Bros. have given your name as a credit reference. They have requested Messrs Navjot Trading Co. for credit of Rs. 80,000 for thirty days. Write a reply to Messrs Navjyot Trading Co. who have enquired about the status of Messrs Handa and Bros.

(7) The replies from the trade references show that Messrs Raguttam and Sons do not have large working capital. Their credit is known to be Rs. 10,000 though they have requested you for a credit of Rs. 25,000. Draft a suitable reply to Messrs Raguttam and Sons.

(8) Messrs Shah and Sons have placed an order with you for the goods worth Rs. 20,000. The enquiries show that their financial position is satisfactory. Inform the customer that his request for credit has been approved and the consignment has already been sent to him.

16

COMPLAINTS AND ADJUSTMENTS

Complaint Letters

Even in well managed business houses, people are subjected to imperfections, errors and even to blunders of serious kind. The supplier accepts the order and starts making necessary arrangements for sending the goods. There are a number of people involved in this process and sometimes someone of them commits mistakes quite unknowingly. When the buyer discovers any mistake or discrepancy, he brings it to the notice of the supplier by writing a complaint letter. It is written with the hope that the supplier might settle the matter without any further conflict between them. The mistakes made by the supplier may cause inconvenience and even financial loss for the buyer.

Many buyers discover genuine mistakes soon after receiving the consignment. Such mistakes must be immediately brought to the notice of the supplier. But, he should do so without displaying his anger and sarcasm. He should not feel that the mistake of the supplier gives him an opportunity to be disgruntled and sarcastic. His anger and sarcasm can only snap the good and friendly business relations between them. Like all other business letters, complaints are also to be drafted with special care and tact. Instead of entering into unnecessary disputes, he should follow courteousness, clarity, art of persuasion and an inoffensive style of language in his complaint letter.

There are many occasions for writing a claim or complaint letter. Some of them are as follows:

1. The goods supplied are of unsatisfactory and inferior quality.
2. The wrong goods are supplied.
3. The goods are in defective packing.
4. The goods are delivered in damaged condition.
5. Delay in the execution of the order.

6. Variance in the ordered quantity of goods.
7. The excessive prices of the goods are charged.
8. Variance in the agreed terms and conditions of transaction.

Making a Complaint

1. It should be made to the person who is directly responsible for sorting out the buyer's problem.
2. It should be made immediately after discovering the mistake. The wrongs cannot be easily righted if the complaints are delayed. The delayed complaint not only weakens the position of the buyer but also puts the supplier in an awkward position because it becomes more difficult for him to find out why and how the mistake was committed.
3. It should begin with the expression of regret over the need to make complaint.
4. It should be fair, courteous, temperate and polite. It should not express anger, threates and lack of patience. The letter writer should try to avoid rudeness because it will hurt the feelings of the supplier from whom he has to expect help, adjustment and compensation.
5. It should not be apologetic.
6. The statement of the mistake must be clear, specific, factual and firm.
7. The date of the order, the date and time of delivery, the quotation, the goods ordered and the goods complained about should be clearly mentioned in the letter.
8. The buyer has to assume that the supplier will put the matters right.
9. He has to explain the nature and extent of inconvenience or damage caused by the mistake.
10. He has to make a polite inquiry about what the supplier proposes to do about the complaint.
11. He has to make firm request to the supplier to attend the matter promptly.
12. He should give concrete suggestions to the supplier as to how he should put the matter right.
13. The letter should be complete in the sense that it should provide all the necessary details which the supplier might require to make adjustment.
14. The buyer should acknowledge his own mistake if his complaint is proved to be unjustified.

VIJAY CLOTH STORES
61, Station Road
Hubli-12

Date: Oct. 7, 1989

The Sales Manager,
Mayur Trading Co.,
Backbay Industrial Estate,
Bombay-5.

Dear Sir,

Subject: Your consignment No.PM51 dated 3rd Oct. 1989.

Thank you for the despatch of five dozen Mayur Sarees sent to us by you as per our order No.V55 dated 30th Sept. 1989. On going through the consignment, our foreman has found that the quality of the sarees is much poorer than the sarees which were supplied previously.

The sarees certainly do not match the samples you sent us. It confirms the fact that there must be some mistake in making up the order. We are returning one of these sarees together with a sample from a previous order so that you may compare them and realise the fact.

As these sarees are not of the ordered quality, we have no choice but to ask you to take them back and replace them with the sarees of ordered quality. Please let us know what you propose to do in this matter as soon as possible.

Yours faithfully,
Mukund Desai
Proprietor
Vijay Cloth Stores

BHARAT ELECTRONICS
Bhausinghji Road
Kolhapur-10

Date: 5th Oct. 1989

The Sales Manager,
Modern Radio Pvt. Ltd.,
Chandni Chowk,
Bombay-7.

Dear Sir,

Subject: Your consignment No.MR118 dated 3rd Oct. 1989.

While thanking you for your promptness in delivering the consignment of fifteen 'Baron A' and ten 'Knight 001' transistor sets as per our order No. BE52 dated 1st Oct. 1989, we regret to inform you that two sets of 'Baron A' and three sets of 'Knight 001' are badly scratched and damaged. The sets in such damaged condition are unfit for sale.

When we unpacked the consignment and discovered the damaged sets, we immediately called an officer of the carriers to inspect the damaged sets. On a careful examination it was found that the cases used for packing were not sufficiently strong and safe to protect the sets in transit.

We are forced to return these damaged sets. We shall be grateful if you will replace all the five sets and if you would make sure that they arrive safely.

Yours faithfully,
Mukesh Babu
Proprietor
Bharat Electronics

BHUDEVI TRADERS
12, Shivaji Market
Pune-10

Date: 28th Oct. 1989

M/s Manilal Mehta and Sons,
102, Shahu Road,
Gadhinglaj,
Kolhapur-5

Dear Sirs,

Subject: Your consignment No.MM158 dated 26th Oct. 1989.

We thank you for the prompt delivery of the Royal Batteries ordered on 24th Oct. 1989. We had placed the order for one hundred 'Royal Batteries' but only seventy batteries were delivered by your carrier. Neither he could explain the shortage nor you have sent any prior explanation for it.

We still need the ordered quantity because they are to be supplied to one of our valuable regular customers. We shall be grateful if you will arrange the prompt delivery of the remaining thirty batteries.

Yours faithfully,
Champaben Shah
Proprietor
Bhudevi Traders

Adjustment Letter

A complaint letter must be welcomed by the supplier even though he can't really enjoy it. It may express anger or dissatisfaction of the buyer for the inconveniences caused to him due to the supplier's mistakes. But, the supplier should be glad to receive the opportunity provided by the complaint letter to realise his mistake and to correct it. The adjustment letter is a reply to the complaint letter. In order to safeguard the business relations, business interests, goodwill and reputation of his organisation, the supplier must handle this correspondence tactfully, carefully and delicately. He has to find out when and why the customers have the causes to complain. He has to thank the customers for making complaints because they could have even abandoned him and placed the orders with the other suppliers. Therefore, the complaint must be treated as an opportunity to save a customer, to explain the matters, to preserve the customer's goodwill and to put the things right. He has to answer the complaints promptly, specifically and satisfactorily so that the customer realises his sincerity and willingness to serve. His promptness in reply should not be due to his hasty decisions which are taken without carefully going into the details of the matters. The decision regarding the customer's claim must be taken only after sound thinking and investigation. If this requires more time, the supplier should at least send an immediate acknowledgement of the complaint.

Making Adjustments

1. A complaint must be answered as promptly as possible. If full reply requires more time because of investigation and collection of information from various sources, the supplier must immediately acknowledge the complaint. Delay in dealing with the complaints give better chances to incur additional annoyance of the customer. When the matter requires investigation, the supplier should inform the customer that the claim would be considered and the full reply would be sent as early as possible.
2. The complaint is to be regarded as an information of the event which had caused some damage, loss or trouble to the buyer.
3. It is not necessary to assume that the customer is always right, but there is no harm in assuming that he 'may be' right.
4. It should aim at keeping the customer and his goodwill.

5. It should make it known to the customer that the correspondent is trying to help him.
6. It should not display any argumentative sarcastic and critical attitude.
7. The justified complaint must be admitted readily and the supplier must express his regret for any trouble caused to the party.
8. In case of justified complaint, the supplier should explain the reason why the things went wrong in executing the order.
9. The tone of the adjustment letters should be always conciliatory and courteous.
10. The supplier must assure the customer to improve the production policies and services of his organisation if the genuine defects are found in it.
11. If the complaint is unjustified and unreasonable, it should be brought to the notice of the customer in polite manner.
12. A sarcastic and abusive complaint should not be answered in the same style, but on the other hand, it should be replied, with more sympathy and courtesy. No attempt should be made to rebuff the customer.
13. The supplier has to assure the customer that the similar mistakes will not recure in future.
14. The supplier must accept the responsibility of the mistake even though it is committed by any one of his staff. He must accept the blame readily and should not excuse himself by blaming his subordinates.

MAYUR TRADING CO.
Backbay Industrial Estate,
Bombay-5

Date: 10th Oct. 1989

M/s Vijaya Cloth Stores,
61, Station Road,
Hubli-12.

Dear Sir,

Subject: Our consignment PM 51 dated 3rd Oct. 1989.

Your complaint letter of 7th Oct. 1989 about the mistake in our consignment has caused us a good deal of concern and regret. We are thankful to you for bringing the matter to our notice.

We shall be grateful to you if you return the consignment to us. We shall gladly replace it with the ordered goods. We are sorry for the inconvenience caused to you. We assure you that such mistake will never occur again.

Yours faithfully,
C.S. Patel
Sales Manager
Mayur Trading Co.

MODERN RADIO PVT. LTD.
Chandani Chowk,
Bombay-7

Date: 7th Oct. 1989

M/s Bharat Electronics,
Bhausinghji Road,
Kolhapur-10

Dear Sir,

Subject: Our consignment No.MR,118 dated 3rd Oct. 1989.

We thank you for your letter of 5th Oct. 1989 from which we learn that two sets of 'Baron A' and three sets of 'Knight 001' are badly scratched and damaged when they reached you. We have already sent the replacement this morning by parcel post.

In order to avoid such inconveniences, we have decided to use sufficiently strong and safe cases for packing. According to packing consultants, these new cases will surely protect the sets in transit. We ensure you that you will have no cause for complaint against us in future.

Yours, faithfully,
Subodh Joshi
Sales Manager
Modern Radio Pvt. Ltd.

Specimens of Complaints and Replies

Complaint for Delay

KOLHAPUR MILK PROJECT
17, M.I.D.C., Kolhapur

30th March 19 . . .

M/s Elgi Equipments Ltd.,
India House, Trichy Road,
Coimbatore 641018.

Dear Sirs,

We placed an order for Elgi Screw Compressor ES55 on 17th March 19 . . . stressing the importance of delivery by 25th March at the latest.

We regret to inform you that the inordinate delay on your part is causing considerable inconvenience to our Milk Processing Division. the delay in delivery has brought the work of this division to standstill, and it may well spoil the prospects of our project.

As per your letter of acceptance any further delay gives us a right to sue you for damages. However, in view of the cordial relations between us, we are prepared to wait till 8th April 19. . . . We assume you will be taking up the matter with the carrier at your end.

Yours faithfully,
Govindrao Patil
Director
Kolhapur Milk Project

Reply :

ELGI EQUIPMENTS LTD.,
India House, Trichy Road,
Coimbatore 641018.

Date: 1st April 19 . . .

The Director,
Kolhapur Milk Project,
17, M.I.D.C., Kolhapur.

Dear Sir,

We have your letter of 30th March 19 . . . and regret that you should have cause to complaint about delay in the delivery of Elgi Screw Compressor ES55.

We are second to none in keeping up the promised schedules of delivery. But, the production at our factory stood suspended in last week due to sudden breakdown of our machinery. Although we made every effort to get the machines in working order, the work could not resumed till 28th March 19. . . .

While appreciating the patience you have shown in extending the date of delivery to 8th April 19 . . . , we assure you that we are doing all we can to speed up delivery. We offer our apologies for the inconvenience you have suffered.

Yours faithfully,
V.V. Thomas
Sales Executive
Elgi Equipments Ltd.,
Coimbatore 641018.

Complaint for Delay

NORTHSTAR ELECTRICALS
14, Bhuvaneshwar Road
Nasik-1

5th Sept. 19 . . .

M/s Sylvania Electricals Ltd.,
5, Prasad Mansion,
Henry James Road,
Bombay-5.

Dear Sirs,

It is regretable that goods ordered by us on 19th Aug. 19 . . . have not yet been delivered till this day.

Our order was placed with you on the understanding that the goods will reach us before 30th Aug. 19. . . . We have received no acknowledgement of the order, nor have the goods been delivered. The delay has created an odd situation for us. We are daily turning back our scores of valuable customers. In view of this pressing urgency we request you to inform, by return post, the exact date when delivery could be made.

We shall be glad if you will look into matter at once and let us know the reason for the delay. Unless the goods are received within five days, we may have to withdraw our order.

Yours faithfully,
S. Patwa
Proprietor
Northstar Electricals, Nasik-1.

Reply :

SYLVANIA ELECTRICALS LTD.
5, Prasad Mansion,
Henry James Road,
Bombay-5.

8th Sept. 19 . . .

M/s Northstar Electricals,
14, Bhuvaneshwar Road,
Nasik-1.

Dear Sirs,

We are very surprised and concerned to learn from your letter of 5th Sept. 19 . . . that the goods we sent to your order of 19th August 19 . . . did not reach your until 5th Sept. 19. . . .

As all the items in your order were in stock, we passed it to our warehouse the next day. Our despatch manager confirms that the goods were collected by Sahyadri Transport on 21st Aug. 19 . . . , for delivery to you, carriage paid. We have already taken the matter up with the transport authorities.

We assure you we are doing all we can to speed up delivery and apologise for the inconvenience the delay is causing you.

Yours faithfully,
G.G. Manik
Sales Manager,
M/s Sylvania Electricals Ltd.,
Bombay-5.

Complaint for Damaged Goods

NORTHSTAR ELECTRICALS
14, Bhuvaneshwar Road
Nasik-1.

11th Sept. 19 . . .

M/s Sylvania Electricals Ltd.,
8, Prasad Mansion,
Henry James Road,
Bombay-5.

Dear Sirs,

While thanking you for your consignment of Sylvania bulbs, Tubes and Heaters against our order of 19th Aug. 19 . . . , we are sorry to report that three boxes of Tubes are badly damaged when delivered on 10th Sept. 19. . . .

On a careful examination it was found that the tubes were not carefully packed in the boxes. With this letter we are sending the labels from the boxes of the damaged tubes and shall be glad if you will replace all the three boxes of the damaged tubes.

Yours faithfully,
S. Patwa
Northstar Electricals
Nasik-1.

Encl: 3 Labels

Reply :

SYLVANIA ELECTRICALS LTD.
5, Prasad Mansion
Henry James Road
Bombay-5

14th Sept. 19 . . .

M/s Northstar Electricals,
14, Bhuvaneshwar Road,
Nasik-1.

Dear Sirs,

We note with regret the contents of your letter of 11th Sept. 19 . . . and feel sorry to learn that 3 boxes of Sylvania tubes in our consignment were received in a damaged conditions.

Our enquiries with the warehouse manager revealed that all the possible care was taken while packing the tubes in the boxes. It seems that the damage to those boxes must have been caused by rough handling in transit. The consignment of bulbs and tubes require delicate handling in carriage. We are taking up the matter with the authorities of transport.

Please send the boxes of damaged tubes to us at our cost. We will be able to replace them next week.

Yours faithfully,
G.G. Manik
Masale Manager
M/s Sylvania Electricals Ltd.,
Bombay-5.

Complaint for Damaged Goods

FERGUSON COLLEGE OF ARTS AND COMMERCE
Lincoln Road, Calcutta-5

2nd Jan. 19 . . .

M/s Trinity Book Sellers,
M.G. Road,
Delhi-5.

Dear Sirs,

Thank you very much for the despatch of 150 books for which we had placed with you an order in our letter dated 25th Jan. 19. . . .

But, on opening the package, it is found that two copies of 'Personnel Management' and four copies of 'Tempest' are damaged. These books are so badly damaged that they are of no use to us.

We request you, therefore, to replace them immediately or send us credit note for the amount of six books. We shall return the damaged copies on hearing from you.

Yours faithfully,
William Collins
Librarian
Ferguson College.

Reply :

TRINITY BOOK STORES
M.G. Road
Delhi-5

5th Jan. 19 . . .

The Librarian,
Ferguson College of Arts and Commerce,
Lincoln Road,
Calcutta-5.

Dear Sir,

We are sorry to learn from your letter of 2nd Jan 19 . . . that some of the books supplied to you were damaged when they reached you.

We regret that you should have a cause to complain about the damaged books. We have already sent the replacement by parcel post this morning. We hope the steps we are taking for improving the packing will ensure the safe arrival of all your orders in future.

Yours faithfully,
N. Swamy
Proprietor
M/s Trinity Book Stores.

Complaint for Wrong Goods

TRIBHUVAN MEDICALS
10, R.N. Bhave Road
Bombay-17

23rd May 19 . . .

M/s Modern Medical Stores,
40, Rajaram Road,
Thane-7.

Dear Sirs,

We ordered two boxes of 'Candid D--sting Powder' of Glenmark by our order of 15th May 19. . . . To our surprise, however, it was found that the parcel contained three boxes of 'Shower to Shower' prickly heat powder' of Johnson and Johnson.

We regret that we cannot keep 'Shower to Shower' Prickly Heat Powder' as we have an adequate stock already. We are therefore returning them by parcel post for replacement.

We shall be glad if you look into the matter as one of the urgency and let us know when the replacement may be expected.

Yours faithfully,
S. Tribhuvan
Proprietor
Tribhuvan Medicals, Bombay-17.

Reply :

MODERN MEDICAL STORES
40, Rajaram Road
Thane-7

25th May 19 . . .

M/s Tribhuvan Medicals,
10, R.N. Bhave Road,
Bombay-17.

Dear Sirs,

We hasten to reply to your letter of the 23rd May 19 . . . and express our regret that any mistake should have occurred in dealing with your order of 15th May 19. . . .

It was due to an oversight that the stores clerk supplied to our packing department the powder boxes of the specifications and sizes mentioned in the order by M/s Rafan Medical Stores, Gandhinagar. We apologise for the inconvenience this mistake has caused to you.

We are sending you today a fresh consignment of 'Candid Dusting Power' by parcel post. We assure you that there will not be such a lapse in future.

Yours faithfully,
S.K. Patil
Proprietor
Modern Medical Stores, Thane-7.

Complaints for Defective Quality

KASTURI TAILORS
87, Shahu Road
Kolhapur-2

19th May 19 . . .

M/s Vrindavan Trading Co.
5, Kanchan Marg,
Parle (West)
Bombay-7.

Dear Sirs,

We have received the consignment of sewing machines despatched by you on 18th May 19 . . . against our order of 12th May 19. . . . When we came to examine the machines, we found that one of them is having glaring defects in it. The machine having defective quality is 'RP2R' Royal Sewing Machine. The defects are inexplicable in comparison with the other model 'RP5R'.

'RP2R' model of your sewing machine is quite unsuitable to our needs and we have no choice but to ask you to take it back and replace it by the model 'RP5R' Royal Sewing Machine. If this is not possible, then we are afraid we shall have to ask you to cancel our order.

May we expect your reply by return of post?

Yours faithfully,
Vinod Shah
Proprietor
Kasturi Tailors
Kolhapur-2.

Reply :

VRINDAVAN TRADING CO
5, Kanchan Marg
Parle (West)
Bombay-7

22nd May 19 . . .

M/s Kasturi Tailors,
87, Shahu Road,
Kolhapur-2.

Dear Sirs,

We note with regret the complaint contained in your letter of 19th May 19 . . . that you are not satisfied with the quality of the 'RP2R' Royal Sewing Machine supplied to your order of 12th May 19. . . . Considering your adverse opinion about the operational aspect of the machine, we have instructed our technical representative, Mr. N.R. Premdasa to contact you immediately to examine the machine.

It is disappointing that 'RP2R' model having good reports from the scores of the tailors was found unsuitable by you. We shall supply the 'RP5R' model within a week if the defective 'RP2R' machine could not be repaired to your satisfaction.

We hope this will now settle the matter to your complete satisfaction.

Yours faithfully,
S. Kumar
Proprietor
Vrindavan Trading Co.,
Bombay-7.

Complaint Concerning Quantity

TANDAN TRADERS
28, Netaji Subhash Road
Bangalore-8

24th Aug. 19 . . .

M/s Vinayak Trading Co.
51, Line Bazar Road,
Calcutta-10.

Dear Sirs,

We thank you for your promptness in delivering the tea we ordered on 14th Aug. 19. . . . The consignment was received by us on 23rd Aug. 19. . . . We regret to inform you that the number of the packs delivered by your carrier this morning was, however, 500 whereas our order was for 1100 packs. He was unable to explain the shortage, nor have we received any explanation from you.

As your consignment cannot cover our needs at present, we request you to send the full quantity ordered and shall be glad if you will arrange to deliver the remaining 600 packs as soon as possible.

We look forward to hearing that the goods will be sent straight away.

Yours faithfully,
Ramesh Tandan
Proprietor
Tandan Traders,
Bangalore-8.

Reply :

VINAYAK TRADING CO.
51, Line Bazar Road
Calcutta-10

28th Aug. 19 . . .

M/s Tandan Traders,
28, Netaji Subhash Road,
Bangalore-8.

Dear Sirs,

We are much obliged to you for your letter of 24th Aug. 19 . . . and have noted with regret that you should have been put to such inconvenience.

We are sorry to inform you that we do not have the stock of Brooke Bond Red Label Tea in the size required by you. We expect further deliveries within a week. We shall despatch the remaining 600 packs to you immediately after receiving our deliveries.

We apologise once more for any inconvenience we might have caused you.

Yours faithfully,
P. Mehta
Manager
M/s Vinayak Trading Co.
Calcutta.

Exercises

1. You had placed an order for variety of silk sarees with Messrs Mehta and Sons, Bombay. The sarees were required to meet the demands of the customers during Diwali season. Unfortunately, you have received the consignment after the date of delivery which had been adequately stressed in the order. Write a complaint letter to the supplier for the delay.
2. You had placed an order for ten barrels of refined edible oil with Messrs Navnath Oil Mills, Hyderabad. After receiving the consignment, you found that three barrels contained the un-refined oil. Draft a letter of complaint and suggest a mode of adjustment.
3. You have received electric goods from Messrs Hirachand and Sons, Ahmednagar in damaged condition. Write a complaint letter to the supplier suggesting how you would like the matter to be adjusted.
4. As a retail merchant write a complaint letter to the manufacturer of plastic water tanks who has sent you fifteen tanks, of which two tanks have been found leaking. Explain how your customers were annoyed at the defective water tanks.
5. Write a letter to Messrs Motibhai Shah and Sons, the suppliers of stationary goods, threatening them to cancel a contract for supplying the goods of inferior quality.
6. Write a letter of complaint to Messrs Jamunalal Sethi and Sons, the suppliers of paints and hardware, informing them that the consignment of paints received from them does not match the samples shown before placing the order with them.
7. Messrs Maruti Kirana Merchants had ordered 70 bags of rice and 50 bags of wheat from Messrs Motwani Bros. Write a letter of complaint for the shortage in weight of 40 rice bags and 10 wheat bags. Give full details of the shortage and claim compensation.
8. Some office furniture which was ordered from Messrs Chandagiram Furnitures, has arrived in a damaged condition. Write a letter of complaint to the supplier asking them for an inspection of the goods damaged in transit and requesting adjustment.
9. Why should a businessman welcome complaints instead of resenting them.

10. 'Complaint are blessings to the businessman' – Discuss.
11. How does a letter of 'complaint' usually contain 'claim'?
12. Explain the importance of courtesy in handling business complaints.
13. What are the essentials of effective complaint letters?
14. Write a tactful letter to your customer who has complained that the electrical goods that you sent him were received in a damaged condition.
15. Messrs S.G. Bata and Sons, Poona, complaint that the silk sarees received from you were required to meet the customer's demand during Diwali season, and, they have received the consignment after the date of delivery. Write a tactful reply to Messrs S.B. Bata and Sons explaining the reasons for delay.
16. Messrs Porwal Saree Emporium complaint that silk sarees received from Madhavi Silks Ltd., are of inferior quality. They have returned the consignment at the suppliers cost. They have asked for the replacement of goods within seven days. As a supplier, write a suitable reply to the complaint.
17. How should a businessman give reply to the letters of complaint?
18. What is the purpose of a letter of adjustment? What should be the tone of an adjustment letter?

17

COLLECTION LETTERS

The supplier has to shoulder a delicate responsibility of collecting the dues and retaining the customers. He requires insight, tact, good judgement and understanding of the customer and his business. There can be various causes behind the failure of the customer to keep up to the schedule of payment and any of them is sufficient to irritate and annoy the supplier. It is always easy for him to grant the credit account facilities to the customers but it is difficult to collect the bad debts and the amounts due on the accounts. Apart from maintaining accounts of credit, preparing periodical statements and collecting the dues promptly, the supplier has to write a series of collection letters to the customers. It is natural that he might get annoyed on the customers who delay in making payments but he should not allow his annoyance to find expression in the collection letters. Majority of the customers clear their accounts according to the agreed terms but there are always some customers who just overlook to pay the dues. Some customers are unable to pay off their dues in time because of the unfavourable circumstances or slack in their business. Yet, the supplier cannot survive in his business if his credit sales are unduly delayed or result in bad debts. He has to persuade the customer to make at least the part payments in easy instalments. If he has to realise the profit and facilitate his business, he must promptly collect the dues locked in the credit accounts.

How to write an Effective Collection Letter

1. Before drafting collection letter, the supplier must try to understand the peculiar nature of the customer and his present business condition. In case of the honest and prompt paying customers, a statement of account is sufficient and there is no need to make hasty suggestion for prompt payment. Some customers are honest but miserly and

slow-paying. They do not have any intention of deceiving the suppliers. The supplier has to handle them with skill and tact. They must be dealt with polite, firm and non-offensive approach. In case of the customers who are dishonest, reckless, negligent and fraudulent, the supplier has to deal with all firmness. They are to be informed that their delinquent account will be entrusted to the solicitor for legal action. The last category of the customers consist of those who are unable to pay because of financial difficulties and unfavourable circumstances. These customers must be considered with sympathetic approach. They should be helped with some kind of compromise arrangement.

2. The supplier has to refer to the previous correspondence regarding the terms of credit agreement, statement of account, reminders etc.
3. The tone of all the collection letters should be cheerful, positive and firm.
4. He must assume that the customer will clear his account. He must sound optimistic in his letter.
5. He should make use of the "You" attitude to persuade the customer that it is to his own advantage to clear the account. The supplier has to make an appeal to the customer's honour, pride, fairness and good reputation. A request should be made to the customer to shield his credit by prompt payment.
6. Through collection letter the supplier should not ask for customer's favour. He should not sound apologetic in requesting payment from his customer.
7. An informal, courteous and friendly approach impells the customer to send favourable reply to the letter. The language used should not be offensive. It should neither be blunt nor unduly soft.
8. The figures and facts about the overdue accounts should be stated clearly.
9. The supplier should always express his confidence in the customer's integrity.
10. He has to request the customer to explain the delay in remittance.
11. He should suggest definite and immediate action for the customer.
12. It should not be drafted on a post card.

13. It should not be too brief.
14. There should be an interval of a week or two between two collection letters.
15. The supplier should remember that threates, ruthless approach and inconsiderate policy usually results in losing the customer.
16. When a threat of legal action is made, it must be carried out.

Procedure of Collection Letter

The routine and well-established procedure of collection has following stages:

1. Sending Statement of Account.
2. Reminder.
3. Stronger Reminder.
4. Inquiry and Discussion.
5. Appeal, Urgency and Demand.
6. Legal Action.

Sending Statement of Account

Statement of Account is a copy of the customer's credit account which shows the balance to be paid by the customer before a given date. The collections correspondence starts from the first stage of sending the statement of account to the customer. To send this statement is supposed to be a duty of the supplier. It is periodically sent to the customer to show the amount due to be paid by him. It reminds the buyer that he owns a particular amount which ought to be paid at a given date. It does not consist any request for payment. It simply tells the buyer that his account is due. It helps both the parties to verify correctness in their accounts.

Reminder

If the supplier does not receive any reply to the statement of account or if the statement does not bring the payment, he has to assume that the customer has failed to respond because of oversight. He needs the reminder in almost the same terms stating that the amount due is unpaid. The correspondent should not presume that the customer had deliberately neglected the statement of account. In this letter he has to express his opinion that the customer might have perhaps, overlooked the previous letter. He has to enclose the statement of account with the reminder. A request should be made for prompt payment.

Stronger Reminder

If the supplier does not get any response to the reminder he has to send a stronger reminder in which he asks the customer to pay off his dues without further delay. He refers to amount due and also to the reminder already sent. The customer is asked to pay immediately and sense of disappointment is expressed over his failure to pay according to schedule. He should neither use threatening words nor express his doubts about the customer's intensions.

Inquiry and Discussion

When any of the reminders do not bring expected response from the customer, the supplier should assume that the customer may be facing certain difficulties in business. He has to ask the customer why the payment is withheld. He should invite the customer for free and frank discussion, which may enable them to find certain solution to the problem. He should not give up the hope of collecting the amount due from the delinquent customer. He should try to find out the reasons for the delay of payment.

Appeal, Urgency and Demand

If the customer replies to the inquiry and gives reasons for withholding payment or expresses his desire to pay, the supplier will have to respond accordingly. But, if the customer does not reply the inquiry and if he neglect the offers of assistance, the supplier may deal with his customer in a different manner. As it becomes almost certain that the customer does not want to make payment, the supplier should adopt a stern attitude. For a poor risk he may write a strongly worded letter but, in case of good risk he should make appeal to the customer's self-interest in business. He should set a deadline for receiving payment and should demand that the payment should be made by a certain date. He should warn the customer about the unpleasant consequence which may follow if the amount due is not remitted before the given date.

Legal Action

The supplier should tell the customer that he was regretfully compelled to entrust the matter in solicitor's hand for legal action. Now, the supplier is certain that the customer who has never responded to any letter is certainly willing to avoid payment. He is not concerned about retaining the customer but about collecting the money and the only course left for him is to take legal action. Even in this letter he may give a definite time to the customer to clear his dues or to reply before that and to avoid unpleasant litigation.

Collection Letters-A

Reminder-1:

KASTURI TRADERS
18, Dhawal Building
Shahu Road,
Kolhapur

30th July 19 . . .

M/s Vrindawan Stores,
5, Kanchan Marg,
Nipani, Dist. Belgaum.

Dear Sir,

Your attention is called to our Account No.B-15 dated 5th June 19 . . . of Rs. 8000 which has not yet been settled. Perhaps it has escaped your notice. A cheque for this will oblige.

We are enclosing the statement of account for your ready reference. We look forward to an early settlement and to receiving your next order.

Yours faithfully,

R.K.Bahu
Proprietor
Kasturi Traders

Encl: Statement of Account

Reminder-2

10th Aug 19 . . .

Dear Sirs,

May we refer again to our letter of 30th July and our June Statement of Account indicating the payment of the balance of Rs. 8000 due to us from you? We now ask you to be good enough to send us your cheque within the next few days.

Yours faithfully,

——

Reminder-3

25th Aug. 19 . . .

Dear Sirs,

We are sorry that our letters dated 30th July and 10th Aug. requesting you for the settlement of our account of Rs. 8000 have remained unnoticed. No doubt there is some special reason for the delay in payment and we should welcome an explanation and also your remittance by return of post.

Yours faithfully,

——

Reminder-4

10th Sept. 19 . . .

Dear Sirs,

We very much regret that we have not received any reply to our three previous requests of 30th July, 10th Aug and 25th Aug. for payment of the sum of Rs. 8000 still owing on your account.

We cannot keep this account open still longer and we call upon you to favour us with your cheque for the overdue payment without further delay.

Yours faithfully

——

Reminder-5

20th Sept. 19 . . .

Dear Sirs,

It is very difficult to understand why we have not received any reply to our four previous letters of 30th July, 10th Aug, 25th Aug. and 10th Sept. about the sum of Rs. 8000 overdue on our June statement of account.

Though we are most anxious to avoid doing anything from which your credit and reputation might suffer, we are forced to inform you that unless we receive your cheque in full settlement by 30th Sept. 19 . . . we shall be compelled, much against our will, to take legal steps to obtain payment.

Yours faithfully

——

Final Collection Letter

30th Sept. 19 . .

Dear Sirs,

We are both surprised and disappointed for not having received any answer from you to our letter of 20th Sept. 19 . . . regarding the long overdue payment of Rs.8000 on your account.

Although our relations in the past have always been good, we cannot allow the amount to remain unpaid indefinitely. We regret to inform you that we are now reluctantly compelled to place the matter in the hands of our solicitors.

Yours faithfully,

——

Collection Letters-B

Reminder-1

ANANT GLASSWARE MANUFACTURERS
Babasaheb Bhosale Path,
Ratnagiri-55.

4th Feb. 19 . . .

M/s Janseva Cutlery Mart,
7, Jagajitsing Rathod Marg,
Pune-50.

Dear Sirs,

We are enclosing a Statement of Account for the glassware supplied to you on 29th Nov. 19. . . . You will find from the statement that a sum of Rs. 6085 is already a month overdue.

We wonder whether there is any special reason why we have not received the payment of the above account. We look forward to an early settlement.

Yours faithfully,

——

Encl: Statement of Account.

Reminder-2

20th Feb. 19 . . .

Dear Sirs,

Our letter of 4th February 19 . . . for a settlement of account of Rs. 6085 remains unreplied. Please give your attention to our dues and send us your cheque within the next few days.

Yours faithfully,

——

Reminder-3

1st March 19 . . .

Dear Sirs,

Our letters of 4th Feb, and 20th Feb. calling attention to your unsettled account of Rs.6085 have still remained unanswered. No doubt there is some special reason for the delay in payment. Therefore, we would welcome an explanation for the delay of payment.

We are enclosing a duplicate of the Statement of Accounts for your ready reference. Can we hope to receive your remittance by return of post?

Yours faithfully,

——

Encl: Duplicate of the Statement of Account.

Reminder-4

10th March 19 . . .

Dear Sirs,

It is hard to believe that our three reminders of 4th Feb., 20th Feb. and 1st March addressed to you to settle your overdue balance of Rs. 6085 have remained unanswered till today.

We cannot keep this account open still longer and once again stress the need for its prompt clearance. We call upon you to favour us with your cheque for the overdue payment without further delay. A self-addressed envelope is enclosed to bring your cheque promptly.

Yours faithfully,

——

Reminder-5

21 March 19 . . .

Dear Sirs,

It is very difficult to understand why we have not received any reply to our four previous letters of 4th Feb, 20th Feb, 1st March and 10th March. You still own us Rs.6085.

Knowing you as our regular and responsible customer, we are most anxious to avoid doing anything from which your credit and reputation might suffer. We should appreciate if you let us know your problems so that we may find some suitable way of straightening the account and reducing the burden of indebtedness. If we do not receive explanation for delay or your cheque in full settlement by 30th March 19 . . . , we shall be compelled, much against our will, to take legal steps to obtain payment.

Yours faithfully,

——

Final Collection Letter

31st March 19 . . .

Dear Sirs,

We are both surprised and disappointed for not having received any word from you in answer to our letter of 21st March regarding non-payment of Rs.6085 on your account.

Although our relations in the past have always been good, we cannot allow the amount to remain unpaid indefinitely. We regret to inform you that we are now reluctantly compelled to place the matter in the hands of our solicitors.

Yours faithfully,

——

Exercises

1. What are the objectives of collection series?
2. Why should a collection letter have firm tone and courteous language?
3. Discuss some of the appeals that could be made in the collection series?
4. How can a businessman keep his customer and collect the account through collection letters?
5. Write a letter to Messrs Janata General Stores, and remind them that they have not replied to your previous reminders. Bring it to their notice that they own you Rs. 7000 and this amount has been left unpaid for three months. Offer to take instalment payments in case the customer is in financial difficulties.
6. Messrs G.D.Patel and Sons have not settled their account although several remainders have been sent. Write them a letter and ask for the reason why they have not yet paid the bill of Rs. 7000. Enquire whether they have any complaint against your goods and services.
7. Messrs J.J. Tata and Sons have not replied to any of your reminders, offers and requests. They own you an amount of Rs. 25,000 which was to be paid nine months ago. Inform Messrs. J.J. Tata and Sons that unless the account is settled within fifteen days, you will place the matter in the hands of solicitors.

18

CIRCULAR LETTERS

When a businessman has to communicate a formal message to a number of customers, shareholders, suppliers, business friends, employees etc., he sends it through circular letters. It conveys message about certain fundamental changes in the structure and policy of the business organisation. It circulates the same message to all the receivers. Its subject-matter is of common interest to all the customers and other business associates. It is cyclostyled or printed on large scale because the same message is transmitted to several receivers. Therefore, it must be drafted carefully and appropriately. It must have attractive style, effective language, appropriate meaningful and catchy words, suitable tone and 'you' attitude.

The circular letters are advantageous especially because it saves time and money. A large number of circular letters can be despatched in a day. The cyclostyled, printed or duplicated circular letters are comparatively less expensive. The correspondent finds easy and simultaneous access to different people living at different places. As they contain common message, they can be made comprehensive enough for communicating the business policy of the correspondent and for other important information regarding the decisions taken by the management and changes made in the structure of the firm.

Occasions that need Circular Letters

Change in address

When the firm has to shift to a new location, the circular letters are sent to the customers which point out the reasons behind shifting to a new place. The new address is to be given at the beginning of the body of the letter. The convenience and advantages of the new place should be mentioned. The customers should be assured that they will be given better services and an appeal should be made to them to continue their patronage.

Opening of new departments, shops, branches and expansion of premises

Circular letter which announces the opening of new shops, departments, branches or expansion of premises, describes the growth of that firm's business. It highlights the firm's need to open the new branches and expand the premises so as to extend more facilities to the customers. The letter should give stress not only on the development of business but should also explain how it could develop with the goodwill and patronage of the customers. It gives address of the new branch, the date of commencement, particulars of the goods and services and sometimes, the particulars of the manager of the new branch.

Introducing a new product

It describes a new product with full details and creates interest in the reader with some appealing statements. It is a kind of sales letter which stresses the qualities of new product which suit the requirements of the customers. It briefly outlines the company's progress and regular improvements. It describes how the company feels concerned about the customer's convenience. After describing the features and utility of new products, it solicites trial order from the customer.

Announcing rise or reduction in prices

Circular letters can be used to announce rise in the price. While announcing rise in the prices of the goods and services, the supplier should explain the circumstances which might have compelled him to increase the prices. While announcing reduction or clearance sale, the writer has to mention the reason for holding reduction or clearance sales sessions. He should mention the occasion for which the reduction sale is arranged. He has to specify the extent or percentage of reduction in the rates of the commodities. He should give the opening date and the period of reduction sale. He should clearly state that the qualities and varieties of goods to be sold at the reduction sale sessions are in no way inferior. If the goods are shop-spoiled or slightly damaged, he should not hesitate to mention it. He should invite the customer to pay visit to the store well in time.

Announcing the agency obtained

While announcing the agency obtained, the writer should give the details of the agency. He should mention the merits of the products, their utility, quality, durability, popularity, excellence of the services and fairness of prices. He has to refer to the arrangements made for the delivery of the goods. He has to mention the area of agency operation. He can offer special discounts if it is permitted under the agency contract. He can notify that the customer should not place his order directly with the manufacturer, but should send them to the agent only.

Announcing retirement or death of partner

While announcing retirement of a partner, the writer should express his regret over the loss of services of the retiring partner. If he is retiring due to his old age or ill-health, the cause should be clearly stated. The customer should be assured that the business will be conducted on the same lines as before and the standard of services will be continued as before. While announcing death of a partner, he should express his regret and acknowledge the services rendered by the deceased. If the decision is taken to change the name of the firm, the new name should be mentioned. The customer should be informed that the change in the constitution of the firm does not change its business policy with the customers. If a new partner is taken in place of the deceased, his name, experience and capabilities should be mentioned. At the end of the letter, the writer should solicit the customer's patronage.

NAYANA ELECTRONICS
5, Vidyanagar
Vinayak Road
Bombay-58

Date : 28th July 19 . . .

____
____
____

Dear Sir/Madam,

We are pleased to inform you that we are opening a new branch of wholesale electronics stores on 5th Aug 19. . . . The name and address of the new branch is given below:

NAYANTARA ELECTRICS
7, Vijaya Bazar
Ferguson Road
Lower Parel
Bombay-13

At this new branch all our well-known goods and services will be available. As this place is spacious, we are able to receiver our customers more conveniently at the counter. We have also arranged customer's waiting room and show room at this branch. Our branch manager Mr. S.K. Desai and his assistants eagerly await your visit. They will be very happy to receive you at the counter.

Yours faithfully,
M.K. Desai
Manager
Nayana Electronics

BHARAT EMPORIUM
87, Nariman Road
Ahmedabad-12

12th Nov. 19 . . .

____
____
______

Dear Sir/Sirs,

We are pleased to inform you that we have been entrusted with the sole Distributing Agency of 'Mafatlal Fabrics' and 'Bombay Textiles' in Ahmedabad, Baroda, Jaipur and Bikaner market. The sarees of 'Bombay Textiles' as well as the suitings and shirtings of 'Mafatlal Fabrics' are world famous and they hardly need any introduction. There is a steadily increasing demand for the textile products of these manufacturers in the market. As we keep ready stock on a large scale, we shall be able to execute your orders promptly.

We have enclosed a catalogue and price-list with the letter which will help you to make selection. All prices are subject to 8% trade discount. As we are the sole distributing agency of the manufacturers, you will get trade discount facility from us only. We look forward to receive your order and serve you to the best of our ability.

Yours faithfully,
Hari Prasad
Manager
Bharat Emporium

PATEL, PRASAD AND CO.
Babubhai Bhulabhai Road
Bombay-15

Date : 5th Dec. 19 . . .

____
____
____
____

Dear Sir/Madam,

We regret to inform you that Mr. J.N. Patel, an active and valued partner of this firm is retiring due to old age. Mr. Patel had been working with us for last twenty three years and he is quite familiar to our customers. His pleasant, courteous and friendly nature had made him popular. But, in recent past, his family doctor has asked him to take complete rest due to his ill-health. However, he will be associated with our firm in an advisory capacity.

Though Mr. Patel has retired, the firm will continue to do business under the same old name. Mr. Prasad will sign as the Managing Partner. We request you to extend your usual patronage to us.

Yours faithfully,
P.L. Prasad
Managing Partner
Patel, Prasad and Co.

Exercises

1. What is a circular letter ? Mention some of the reasons on which circular letters are sent out.
2. Janata Bazar opens a new branch at Kagal. Draft a circular announcing the opening of a new branch.
3. Messrs Janata General Stores have decided to shift their main sales depot from Kagal to Kapshi. Draft a circular letter announcing shifting of the location.
4. Krishna Food Products Ltd. have expanded and renovated their existing structure. Draft a circular letter announcing this renovation and expansion.
5. Messrs Ghatge, Patil and Company announce the retirement of their founder partner Mr. J.R. Ghatge. Draft a circular letter announcing retirement of this old partner.
6. Messrs Bharat Enterprises announce the death of a partner, Mr. J.M. Pateil — who was one of the founder partners of the firm. Draft a circular letter announcing death of this partner.
7. A change is proposed in Messrs Dalmia, Oberoi Company. They want to convert their concern into a private company. Draft a circular letter announcing this conversion.
8. Messrs S.J. Mirje and Sons have received an agency of Godrej Products. They propose to open their new sales depot at Kolhapur. Write a circular letter announcing the agency and opening of the new sales depot.
9. Godrej Soaps Pvt Ltd. have terminated the services of Mr. R.S. Vasudevan who was their representative at Sangli. Draft a circular letter to the customers of Godrej Soaps Pvt. Ltd. that Mr. Vasudevan is no longer in their employment.
10. Mr. J.K. D'Souza has purchased a firm — Navbharat Enterprises at Bombay. He decides to run the firm as 'Monica Enterprises'. Draft a circular letter announcing the purchase of the firm and the change in its name. Mr. J.K. D'Souza does not intend to change the policies of the firm.

19

AGENCY LETTERS

A large business house has often its own purchase and sales departments, but a large number of small business houses conduct their trade through the system of agency. A person or a firm which acts for another is an agent, and a person or a firm which appoints agent is called as the principal of that agent. The smaller firms buy or sell through commission agents, brokers, commercial travellers and other types of agent. Appointment of agents is always preferable to opening the branches. Generally, agents handle the products of several manufacturers but when a manufacturer opens a branch he sells the products of his own firm only. Therefore a small manufacturer finds agency system more economical than opening of the branches.

The agents sell the products of the manufacturers for a commission. A commission is paid to the agent for taking possession of goods, for handling it and for negotiating it's sale. The rate of commission depends upon the sales potentials, area covered and other facilities offered by the agent such as show-rooms, advertising, trained and experienced sales representatives, guarantee of regular payment etc. The commission agent is paid extra commission when he is authorised to sell on credit and bears the risk of bad debts. The brokers do not take possession of goods like the commission agents. They simply bring the buyers and sellers together for commission. Brokerage means the commission or the charges made by a broker. Usually, the brokers buy and sell the business shares and bonds for others. The commercial travellers are representatives of the principal. They get special allowances in addition to salary for making sales contracts and for securing orders from the parties. They collect information about the needs, requirements and attitudes of the customers and also about the trends in the market.

Generally, the agency contracts are given for a fixed period which can be renewed at the end of each contract period. The confirmation of agency depends on the sales potentialities, turnover during the last contract period, regularity of payment etc. The terms and conditions of renewed contract may remain the same as before or they may be modified. Generally the agents have to strictly adhere to the prices of the goods and other conditions in the contract. They submit periodical accounts and reports to the principal.

Offers of Agencies and the Agent's Reply

While offering agency to some person or firm, the principal refers to the market waiting to be developed. He explains the merits of his goods, describes the qualities, varieties, brand names, popularity and reasonable prices. In order to persuade the agent to accept the agency, he has to concentrate the correspondent's attention on the special merits of his goods. He has to convince the agent that the goods are bound to sell because of the potential market for his goods of exceptional quality and reasonable rates. He has to mention the percentage of commission, area of operation and other terms and conditions of agency.

While replying to the letter of offer, the agent should thank the principal for the offer of agency. If he agrees with the terms of the agency and accepts the offer, he has to communicate his decision promptly. If he cannot accept the offer, he should express his inability in courteous manner.

Application for an Agency and the Manufacturer's Reply

The applicant who is willing to obtain an agency, has to write to the manufacturer in persuasive language. He has to mention his wide experience in that line of business, his well-established position, his knowledge of the market and the facilities of advertising, showroom etc. which he can provide. While drafting the letter, he should make a reference to the advertisement of the manufacturer. If his application is based on the information provided by any other source, he should refer to that source. If he writes on his own initiative, he should begin with introducing himself as an agent. He should express his sincere desire to offer his services and to work as an agent to promote the sale of the products in a specified area.

In the following paragraph, the applicant has to give his particulars which include information about his business contacts, business experience, financial capability, knowledge of the market, his arrangements for show-rooms, window display, godown etc. In the closing paragraph, he can ask the manufacturer to specify the terms and conditions of agency. The applicant can also mention the Trade References and Bank References.

To this application for agency, the manufacturer must reply with thanks. He should appreciate the correspondent's interest in the agency. If he is satisfied with the particulars furnished by the applicant and if he is prepared to grant agency, he should promptly inform the applicant about it. If he is not prepared to grant the agency, he should courteously reply with reason for his inability in granting the agency.

The letters announcing cancellation of agency by the principal and the letters of announcement regarding obtaining agency are the circular letters.

FLOXE INDIA LTD.
Bansari Road
Thane-12

19th Nov. 19 . . .

M/s Oriental Associations,
Mangalwar Market,
Bombay-5.

Dear Sirs,

Mr. S.J. Richards, the Sales Manager of Bombay Pharmaceuticals has recommended you as a reliable and progressive firm of agents. We need a firm with experience of the pharmaceuticals, trade and good business connections with the leading buyers in the area of Bombay, Poona, Kolhapur and Ratnagiri. We prefer the firm with centrally placed offices, showrooms and godowns in the above mentioned cities. We have been informed that you have the kind of experience and the facilities we need.

There is a steady and promising market for our pharmaceutical products in different parts of our country and there is no doubt that a really active agent like you can bring about big increase in our sales. If you are interested in handling this agency, we should be pleased to make you this offer.

We earnestly hope that this agency would prove mutually beneficial. As we wish to reach a quick decision, we look forward to hearing from you very soon.

Yours faithfully,
P. Alexander
Floxe India Ltd.

M/S ORIENTAL ASSOCIATIONS
Mangalwar market
Bombay-5

25th Nov. 19 . . .

The Sales Manager,
Floxe India Limited,
Bansari Road,
Thane-12.

Dear Sir,

Thank you for your letter of 19th Nov 19 . . . , offering us an agency for your pharmaceutical products in the area of Bombay, Poona, Kolhapur and Ratnagiri. We are sure that we shall be able to develop good demand for your goods with our well established business relations. We are aware of the popularity of your products in other districts of Maharashtra. With our contacts, goodwill and efforts we shall successfully introduce your goods in these markets.

Before meeting with you to discuss the details, it is right to inform you that we consider minimum commission rate of 8% on net invoice values. A lower rate of commission will not be considered. Secondly, we require the agency contract for the minimum period of five years to compensate for the hard work in the initial stages. We would also like to know about the arrangements for publicity.

We hope that you would agree with our basic terms. Your offer will be accepted with pleasure if the stated terms are agreed by you.

Yours faithfully,
Manuel D'Souza
Manager
for Oriental Associations

M/S PALMER AGENCIES
5, Blue Haven
Ashwinikumar Road
Allahabad-2

7th Nov. 19 . . .

The Sales Manager,
Floxe India Ltd.,
Bansari Road,
Thane-12

Dear Sir,

We understand from Messrs Davies Associations that you have a plan to appoint a sole agent for the States of Uttar Pradesh and Rajasthan. There are good market potentialities for your products in these states. We have pleasure to offer our services as sole Agents for your products in these states.

We have been in the trade of wholesale distribution of pharmaceuticals for the last twenty years and we have well-established business contacts in the entire area of Uttar Pradesh and Rajasthan. We have rendered satisfactory services to the native as well as foreign manufacturers and have promoted the sale of their products in these states. We have wholesale units situated at strategic places in the cities of Uttar Pradesh and Rajasthan. Our travelling salesman have rich experience and wide knowledge of the customers and the market. They shall have no difficulty in successfully introducing your products in the market.

We hope you will see worthwhile opportunity in our proposal and let us know your terms and conditions for the agency. The following are the trade and bank referees for our credit, reputation and financial status.

1. The General Manager,
   Glasgo India Ltd.,
   M. Karve Road,
   Allahabad-1.

2. The Branch Manager,
   Syndicate Bank,
   M.G. Road,
   New Delhi-5.

We shall be glad to hear from you soon.

Yours faithfully,
C. Abraham (Manager)
for M/s Palmer Agencies.

Exercises

1. What are the essentials of drafting effective agency letters?
2. Why does a letter requesting for an agency appear partly like a job application and partly like a sales letter?
3. Messrs Ajanta Pharmaceuticals have offered you a sole agency for the sale of their products in the States of Maharashtra and Gujarat. Draft a letter to your prospective principal, accepting the offer. Request the principal to increase the percentage of commission and duration of contract.
4. Messrs Motilal and Bros., Kolhapur apply to the Dawn Mills Co. Ltd., Bombay for their agency. They state that they have very good business contacts in Kolhapur district. They ask for a commission of twelve percent. Draft the letter.
5. Messrs. Dawn Textiles, Bombay write a letter to Messrs Victoria Traders, Bangalore, offering them an agency for the sale of their textile products in south Karnataka. Draft this letter of granting an agency.
6. Messrs Dawn Fabrics, Bombay want the agents for the sale of their products in Gujarat state. Draft a persuasive letter to the prospective principal offering your services as a sole agent.
7. Write a letter to Messrs Burfi Radio Ltd., Thane, informing them that you do not wish to continue their agency after the expiry of the period of present contract.
8. You have received an application for an agency in Poona. There is already a sole agent covering the area of Poona district and there is no need of another agent. Write a tactful letter to the applicant giving the reason for refusal.
9. The sales of Messrs R.G. Kale and Sons, Nagpur, the sole agent of Rainbow Plastics Pvt Ltd., have declined. Write a letter to the agent requesting him to find out and explain the causes of the decline. Ask the agent to make efforts to improve the sales activities.
10. Draft the agent's reply to the above letter from the principal, explaining the cause of the decline in sales. Request the principal to co-operate in improving the business.

20

SALES LETTERS

The sales letters are written to selected class of customers to sell particular kinds of goods and services.

The selected class of customers may belong to the specific religious group, age group, financial group, social group or professional group. A general advertisement or publicity may face competition from other advertisements in the same newspaper and periodical, but the sales letter is free from such competition. A general advertisement does not appeal to all the readers but the sales letters are written to those customers who are likely to respond to the sales appeal. The sales letter writer always keeps in his view the needs and requirements of the receiver but the general advertisements do not consider the needs and requirements of each and every reader.

A sales letter is written with the purpose of persuading and convincing the prospective buyer to buy a particular product or service from the manufacturer or the dealer. It aims at promoting the sale of what it tries to sell. In order to introduce new goods in the market and to promote its sales, the writer makes the article seem attractive and necessary to the prospective customer. By describing the special features, merits and uses of the products and services, it educates the customers and helps him to select the right type of product or service. It stresses those features of the product or services which are superior to others of its kind and stresses them from the customer's point of view.

To create and maintain goodwill among the customers, the sales letter writer tries to make his letter as personal as he can. He knows that the customers are primarily interested in themselves. He knows that his letters can be effective only when they are written from the reader's point of view. He knows that the readers accept the message with pleasure and respond to it promptly, when it is drafted with "You" attitude. If the sales letter writer does not know these basics of sales letter, he cannot serve his purpose through them. A general advertisement in newspaper or magazine may sound impersonal but a sales letter must sound personal. Each sales letter must be addressed to a particular person by name if the name of the addressee is known to the sender.

The sales letter must make strong appeal to the buying motive of the customer at the very beginning of it. If it fails to attract the reader's attention, it may find its way into dust-bin. To attract attention and to arouse interest, the writer has to use good stationary, attractive letter-head, smart printing and a good envelop. It will give the sales letter an appearance of a well-dressed salesman. The opening paragraph which introduces the subject to the reader, must appeal to his buying motive with some striking statement. It must push him into the message with curiosity and interest.

Having aroused the reader's interest and curiosity, it has to refer to the merits or the 'selling points' of the product which creates a desire in him to buy the product. If it is written to a person who knows very little about the product or the service offered, it must describe and explain the product or the service in such a way that it must appeal the reader's concern for himself. It should give full description of the product and should explain how it is useful to the reader. But, the claims made in favour of the product should not sound superficial. The sales letter should persuade the reader with the factual evidences that support the claims made in favour of the product. The false and exaggerated claims can spoil the good name of the business house.

Having proved the worth of the product or service through factual information the sales letter has indirectly created confidence in the customer. The proof and promise about the worth of the product or service goes hand-in-hand with an appeal to the customer's basic human desires. When the sales letter is successful in creating desire for the product or service, it comes to the final stage of effective close which motivates the reader to follow a course of action. To secure prompt action from the reader, it offers premiums, discounts, samples, trials, reply cards or envelops, special services etc.

HIS DESIGNS CLOTH EMPORIUM
7, West Coast Market
Worli, Bombay-13

10th Dec. 19 . . .

Mr. R.P. Rao,
19, Habib Building,
Lower Parel,
Bombay-13.

Dear Mr. Rao,

Here is a splendid opportunity for you to buy HIS DESIGNS Shirts and Pants at exclusive prices.

Every man dreams to look handsome and elegant on some special occasion. Our 'HIS DESIGNS' shirts and pants are made for those special occasions to make your dreams come true. 'HIS DESIGNS' shirts and pants are made of fine material and expert tailoring. As you are one of our regular customers, we would like to tell you about our completely new velvet textured terene safari shirts and pants. At their amazingly low prices, they are really a splendid value for your money.

The stock of velvet textured terene safari shirts and pants at exclusive prices is limited. We are offering them only to our regular customers. We are giving a special discount of fifteen percent for you until 25th December. So don't delay, place your order today.

Yours faithfully,
M.V. Patil
Sales Manager
His Design Cloth Emporium

Specimens of Sales Letters

Sales Letter No.1

PHOTOPHONE INDUSTRIES INDIA LTD.
7, Saki Vihar Road
Bombay-400 072

7th Dec. 19 . . .

Miss Rekha Shah,
Maharaja Mansion,
35, R.M. Roy Road,
Bombay-37.

Dear Madam,

We bring for you India's most favourite Hot Shot cameras made by PHOTOPHONE. We put a smile behind the camera with an easy breezy range in the 110 and 35 mm formats. This is the widest range you could get — 10 clever little cameras. Choose just what you want — a built-in-flash — a tele lens — automatic features. All the PHOTOPHONE HOT SHOT cameras have an exclusive Universal Focus System.

We also bring you the Minolta-Photophone with micro processor control ! With Hot Shot cameras instructions can be compressed into the single line — just aim — and shoot ! This is fun on a strap. Hot shot goes out with the family everywhere — to picnics, parties, weddings — and of course, on holidays ! Photophone bring you Konica — India's best-selling film and those unbeatable Konica prints too.

With Konica film, a thing of beauty can really be a joy forever. You can capture anything you want. You can bring home a rainbow. You can immortalise a smile. You can take life's memorable moments — and make them everlasting. If you have any questions on photography or on any of our products, please write to us.

Yours faithfully,
C.J. Abraham
Sales Manager
Photophone Industries India Ltd.

Sales Letter No. 2

BRITISH HEALTH PRODUCTS (INDIA) LTD.
15, Floor, Chiranjiv Tower
43, Nehru Place
New Delhi-110 019

14th July 19 . . .

Dear Mr. Joshi,

Does a short run leave you exhausted? Do you have the energy to play with the kids after the day's work? No? Then you are in poor health, and it may be weight related.

The good news is you can do something about it with a little help from British Health Products. British Health will offer, not miracle cures' or instant solutions, but products that are scientific, simple, proven and most of all, safe. These will be nutritional and dietary supplementation plans to help you attain the right weight through weight loss or gain, as necessary. These will also be a plan to help you maintain your weight.

British Health will also introduce other products for people whose busy lives leave them with very little time to look after their health. These will be a range of products designed specifically for quick energy, for digestive disorders, for feminine problems and others. The British Health range will also include everyday foods formulated in a nutritionally correct manner. All made in association with Booker of the UK. Booker is the market leader in health foods and nutritional supplements. British Health products brings you the best-selling healthcare products modified to suit Indian climates, culture and food habits.

For any information on these products and how to obtain them by V.P.P., just fill and send the postcard attached herewith.

Yours faithfully,
Rajeshwar Murthy
Sales Manager
British Health Products

Sales Letter No.3

LOHIA MACHINES LIMITED
7, Nariman Point
Bombay

11th Dec. 19 . . .

Mr. J.R. Patel,
27 Kazi Bazar Road,
Kurla, Bombay-32.

Dear Sir,

Are you in search of a scooter that's built with your safety in minds? Then, buy LML Vespa which is built safer by design.

Think of yourself on a scooter, with your wife and a little one. There is a speeding traffic to be careful of, potholes to be avoided, and, you are trying your best to ride safely. What you need then, is a scooter that thinks like you do, and responds as you would like it to. You need LML Vespa, a scooter that's built with your safety in mind.

Each of our scooters, built around an unique aerodynamic chassis, is designed to be better balanced than most other scooters. You have to brake suddenly at some critical moments. It is the double action suspension and unique movable front brake back plate of the LML Vespa that together ensure that you stop safely, without skidding.

LML Vespa is powered to steer you through risky situations. It recognises how important it is to have the pick-up that's sometimes necessity to get you out of dangerous traffic situations. It offers greater power than any other scooter in its category. We have provided built-in indicators on both the front and rear of our scooters. When you are riding on LML Vespa at night there's a 12V magneto making sure that neither your headlight nor tail-light dim when you are slowing down, or while idling.

We should be pleased to welcome you to our showroom at any time to give you a demonstration.

Yours faithfully,
Manoj Prabhakar
Marketing Manager
Lohia Machines Ltd.

Sales Letter No. 4

EAGLE FLASKS INDUSTRIES LTD.
Eagle Estate
Talegaon-410 507
Pune (Maharashtra)

7th Dec. 19 . . .

Mrs. Kanchan Sudhakar,
35, Rajaram Road,
Pune 17.

Dear Madam,

Are you waiting to purchase an excellent set of flasks, mugs and bowls? We would like to inform you that every Eagle product is an expression of your good taste.

Eagle products like Vacuumware, Thermoware, Crockery and Lighters etc. are exquisitely beautiful, impeccably designed, each crafted to be a work of art that reflects your goods taste. Presented in a vast variety of designs and capacities, and a stunning array of coordinated graphics and colours, they make gifts that are valued. That are a pleasure to give and a delight to receive. Yes, as gifts Eagle Products make so much more sense.

There is a staggering range to choose from — stand alones and sets — at prices to suit every budget with attractive terms for bulk buyers. . . . . So gift on Eagle, today. Even if it is to yourself.

Yours faithfully,
Ramakant Naidu
Sales Representative
Eagle Flasks Industries Ltd.

Sales Letter No. 5

EMAMI PRODUCT LTD.
Ring Road
Madras

7th Dec. 19 . . .

Dear Miss Geeta Rao,

Do you want to look so fair, and fabulous?

You can certainly look fair and fabulous by using Emami Naturally Fair Fairness Cream. Believe us, it is the most effective fairness cream you can find. It is so effective because it's the only one that works in two ways. It prevents darkening from the sun and, at the same time, it treats skin conditions that cause darkening. It effectively treats the skin conditions such as dehydration, under-nourishment, acne, pimples and even everyday wear and tear.

Only Emami Naturally Fair has a unique natural sunscreen that guards against the sun's ultra-violet rays, preventing further darkening. It has a unique combination of pure natural ingredients that work deep from within to treat the problems skin. It nourishes the sub-layers of the skin.

Its natural ingredients are : Milk, for nourishment and a fair, creamy complexion; coconut water, to wash away suntan and make your skin supple; Cucumber, to tighten skin and prevent wrinkles and lines; and special Ayurvedic Herbs that tighten the skin naturally and cure skin ailments. Unlike some fairness creams, Emami Naturally Fair does not bleach your skin. It makes you fair naturally. Believe us, within a week's time your skin will look fairer, healthier and more supple. We are sending our sales girl for home delivery.

Yours faithfully,
R.K. Chaman
Sales Manager
Emami Products Ltd.

Sales Letter No. 6

BOMBAY OIL INDUSTRIES LTD.
Dadabhai Neoroji Road
Bombay-51

8th Jan. 19 . . .

Mrs. Radha Prasad,
17, Vikram Nagar,
Dadar Bombay-12.

Dear Madam,

Is your cooking oil giving you taste at the cost of your health? The sooner you realise it, the better.

You must know that cholesterol, a constituent of the edible oils, is dangerous for human heart. Many diseases related to heart are caused by cholesterol. You may be getting high cholesterol with the good taste of your cooking oil. You may be getting even high saturated fats and digestion problems too !

You can switch to 'Sweekar Refined Sunflower Oil', the oil that gives you both good taste and good health. 'Sweekar' is made from fresh, nutritious sunflower seeds. It enhances the natural taste in your food. It gives you good health, because it is light and has low saturated fats. It controls and reduces cholesterol too !

Switch to Sweekar and bring home good taste, good health and good cheer.

Yours faithfully,
Sheetal Guha
Sales Manager
Bombay Oil Industries Ltd.

Sales Letter No. 7

TITAN QUARTZ INDIA LTD.
5, Azad Road
Thane-2

27th March 19 . . .

Mr. K.C. Pant,
25, Gulab Mansion,
Gulmohur Lane,
Thane-5.

Dear Sir,

Do you want to take centre stage? Put an Aqura on your wrist, and get ready to get noticed.

Aqura from Titan is the new range in Titan's international collection of fine quartz watches : contemporary, bold, distinctive. The looks range from the vibrantly colourful and sportilly luminous to those with neo-classical flair. Rugged and water resistant, an Aqura is ready to go anywhere.

With over one hundred designs to choose from, you'll find it easy to pick at least one that's right for you. And Aqura's price tag is as surprising as it looks, from Rs. 370 to Rs. 450. Aqura comes with the Tata assurance of reliability and a 2 year guarantee. Wear one. You'll get used to the attention.

Yours faithfully,
G.R. Chaturvedi
Sales Representative
Titan Quartz Pvt Ltd.

Sales Letter No. 8

BAJAJ AUTO LTD.
93, L.B.S. Marg
Mulund (West)
Bombay-49

19th July 19 . . .

Mr. Sanjay Vichare,
41, Vinayak Chawl,
Bombay-26.

Dear Sir,

Do you want to ride the most stylish and futuristic bike on the road? Bajaj High Technology assures it with their 'Kawasaki RTZ KB100'. The RTZ is a stunning looker and it has breath-taking style.

Kawasaki RTZ has vibrant metallic colours, gleaming chrome, flowing decals and beautiful body lines. It has double rear-view mirrors and an extra heavy chrome trim. RTZ is simply the best looking bike in the country. But there is a lot more to the RTZ than style. A unique tachometer (no other bike has it) controls your revs. for economical cruising or moving away swiftly at the traffic lights. A resonator gives you a sensitive throttle response without sacrificing fuel-economy. A long travel ceriani, front fork suspension, adjustable rear shockers, powerful 12 V electricals and a variety of useful gadgets, all add up to make the RTZ the most futuristic bike on the road.

But there is more to the RTZ than its futuristic features. The new Delta engine with 10-5 BHP of responsive power, the double cradle chassis, longest wheel base, low center of gravity for superb road handling unmatched by any other 100 cc bike, and the most competitive price in the country.

You have to ride a bike before you choose it. Test ride the RTZ at your nearest Bajaj dealer today. Our unique network will give this dream bike the finest after-sales service available in the country.

Yours faithfully,
Vijay Malhotra
Sales Executive
Bajaj Auto Ltd.

Sales Letter No. 9

VENUS WATER HEATERS
S-2, Green Park Extension
New Delhi-110 016

17th May 19 . . .

Mr. Rajeshwar Mehta,
26, Ramlingam Lane,
Delhi-110 010.

Dear Sir,

If you look up to the leader in quality, you'll find nothing else but VENUS WATER HEATERS. When you buy it, you don't pay more, you buy value for money. You will value quality when you see it in VENUS water heaters.

The exclusive safety features like fusible plug, pressure release and vacuum release value are quality add-ons at no extra cost. Every VENUS water heater is built for trouble-free, long-haul service. The cartridge type element never comes into contact with water. So, no shock. You can choose from a quality range of 10, 15, 25, 35, 50, 70 and 100 litres capacity in vertical, horizontal and dwarf models.

In a rare call for service, you need not run after the dealer. Just one call is enough. VENUS may be the only water heater which bears ISI mark in 10 of its models. We offer you a special offer of 10% discount. This special offer is open only up to 30th May 19. . . .

Yours faithfully,
C.V. Rajan
Sales Manager
Venus Water Heaters

N.B. These sales letters are prepared with the help of the descriptive features of various products that appeared in newsmagazines and newspapers.

TABE TREATMENTS CLINICS
Gowalia Park
Bombay-400 036

Tel 521836 30th Nov. 19 . . .

Mrs. Kanan Sen,
Saolia Park,
Pitroda Road,
Bombay 4000 026.

Dear Mrs. Kanan,

Does crippling pain in the joints make your life a misery? . . . . Yes. We know how it makes you feel like !

Everyday movements such as walking, climbing, sitting down or standing up can be exenuciating. And your movements get restricted and your life seems to be all tied up in knots.

So if crippling pain in the joints is your sufferance in life, do not despair. Tabe treatment clinics may be able to help you. We have been able to help a number of people already.

Remember Tabe Treatment Clinics does not sell drugs over the counter. With Tabe treatment there is no drug to be swallowed. The treatment does not involve any kind of surgery. Just an external application of a modern Ayurvedic treatment for crippling pain in the joints or arthritis.

Get in touch with Tabe Treatment Clinic today. We may be able to help you too. For appointments call 52 18 36 from 9.00 a.m. to 7.00 p.m. Also open on Sundays.

Yours faithfully,
George D'mello
Secretary
Tabe Treatment Clinics

Exercises

1. How should a business letter-writer design the structure of his sales letters?
2. What are the functions of a sales letter?
3. What are the methods of drafting an effective sales letter?
4. What are the different 'appeals' made in the sales letters in order to hook the customers to buy the goods or services?
5. Draft sales letters to promote the sales of the following :

   (a) Paras Refrigerator
   (b) A book on 'Child Psychology'.
   (c) Pictoria Colour TV
   (d) Rupali Office Files
   (e) Silkoo Shampoo
   (f) An Ayurvedic Tonic
   (g) Ratnakar Food Products
   (h) Ratna Mango Jam
   (i) Tony Sun-glasses
   (j) Caruti Mini Car
   (k) An Oxenfold Universal Dictionary of English
   (l) Seema Sewing Machines
   (m) Mona Washing Mashing Machines
   (n) Tickkoo Automatic Camera
   (o) Super Fan

6. You have started manufacturing unit of 'Sarita Washing Machines' in collaboration with a Japanese Company. As a manufacturer of these machines write a sales letter to the wholesaler in Bombay and offer attractive terms.
7. Draft a sales letter to promote the sales of an Instamatic Camera in which photos develop themselves in few minutes.
8. You have opened a Five Star Hotel at Simla. Draft a sales letter to be sent to the families of high income group.
9. Draft a sales letter to promote the sales of Dictaphones, highlighting their features and expert after sales services.
10. Draft a sales letter to promote the sales of Usha Multipurpose Mixer and Grinder.

21

REPORTS AND OTHER WRITTEN COMMUNICATIONS

Meaning and Significance

C.A. Brown defines report as a communication from someone who has to inform to someone who wants to use that information. It describes the events or individuals to someone who requires it. The business reports are written by the individuals or by the committees as a part of their regular duties. Many of them are objective, factual and impartial in nature and they do not require interpretations or comments. But, some reports can be prepared only after careful investigation, experiments, research, surveys and logical thinking. Such reports often end with expert advice, suggestions and recommendations. In general, a business report presents an account of something, finds solution to some problem and submits information in organised form to the authorised person. It describes the sources of information and also the procedure and significance of data collection. After analysing the collected data, it reaches certain conclusions and if required, it includes suggestions and recommendations.

The complexity of modern business set up is growing rapidly due to continuous flow of scientific and technological innovations, increasing professionalism, departmentalisation in industries, specialisation of knowledge and skills, government policies of intra-national and international trade and commerce and number of such other factors. The managements of small as well as large business houses and multinational corporations are involved in numerous and wide spread activities. A large number of important decisions regarding these activities are taken on the basis of information, analysis, interpretation, recommendations and suggestions made in the reports. Whenever the management comes across a problem and feels necessity of analysing the situation, they appoint an individual or a committee or a panel to present the findings and to make the recommendations.

The report helps the management for evaluation, assessment and appraisal of the employees and their organisational activities. It forms a basis for their future planning and development. It helps the executives to secure efficient control over the situations and to improve the organisational structure. The large industries which employ thousands of workers in their various departments have to rely on reports furnished by different departmental heads and committees to bring coordination among them. A critical evaluation of their performance is essential for the progress, growth and expansion of the organisation. It depends on the detail and accurate reports which provide analysis and interpretations of the facts regarding the processes of purchase, production and sales. The progress reports of these processes are compared with those of other similar organisations.

Structure of Reports

Organisation of Reports

Though there is no hard and fast rules regarding the format of a report, it is essential to present all the facts in logical sequence. The constituent parts of the reports are organised in different manners to suit their purpose and contents. Sometimes the authority for whom the report is to be written prescribes a particular form for the report, but when there is no statutory obligation that report should be in a particular form, the report writer should organise his report in a systematic manner to meet its purpose.

A report can be organised in three ways:

1. Letter form
2. Letter-text combination form
3. Memorandum form

Letter Form

The brief and informal reports are usually written in letter form. It is written in first person "I" or "We". It consists of the following parts:

(i) Heading or Title
(ii) Date line
(iii) Inside Address
(iv) Salutation
(v) Body of the report

  (a) Introduction
  (b) Findings
  (c) Conclusions
  (d) Recommendations

(vi) Complimentary close
(vii) Signature and designation.

Letter-text combination form

The letter-text combination form is suitable for the lengthy and complex reports. Though it is normally divided in three parts, each of the three parts are further sub-divided into smaller units.

I. Introductory Material

  (a) Letter of transmittal
  (b) Title page,
  (c) Preface,
  (d) Acknowledgements,
  (e) Contents,
  (f) List of illustrations,
  (g) Summary or Synopsis

II. Body of the Report

  (a) Introduction

    (i) Definition of problem
    (ii) Methodology

  (b) Findings
  (c) Conclusions
  (d) Recommendations

III. Supplementary Material

(a) Appendix
(b) List of References
(c) Bibliography
(d) Glossary
(e) Index
(f) Signature and designation

Memorandum form

The memorandum form is the simplest way of report organisation. In it the report writer does not follow the formalities of the letter-form. The printed memorandum report forms of various types are used in the business houses which ensures uniformity, clarity and simplicity in the presentation of the reported information. The memorandum form can be divided in the following parts:

(a) Title
(b) Name of the report-writer
(c) Date line
(d) Actual text of report under various headings and sub-headings
(e) Conclusions.

Constituent Parts of the Reports

Title/Title Page

It gives the title or the heading of the report. It also contains the name of the author, name of the authority to whom the report is submitted, the number of the report and the date of submission.

Letter of Transmittal

The letter of transmittal is also called as 'forwarding', 'introductory' or 'covering' letter. It is a routine letter for the transmittal of the report from the writer to the recipient. It simply serves as a permanent written record of the transmission of report to its primary recipient. It also contains the date of submission, the name and designation of the writer and the name of the authority. Sometimes it invites the readers comments on the report.

Preface

Preface is the author's explanatory remarks about the report. It introduces the report and offers it to the readers. It may contain almost all the information of the covering letter.

Acknowledgements

In acknowledgements the author's mentions the names of the individuals and the organisations that have helped him in report writing. If the report includes published material, he gives the list of sources.

Contents Page

Contents page is essential for the lengthy reports. It gives the titles, sub-titles and page numbers of each chapter. It not only helps the reader to locate a particular chapter but also gives him an overall view of the report at a glance.

List of Illustrations

If the report consists of a large number of pictures, diagrams, tables and other figures, a list of illustrations is given after the contents page. It gives the titles and page numbers all the illustrations.

Summary/Synopsis

The summary of the report is also called as the 'synopsis' and the 'abstract' of the report. It gives substance of the report in brief. It describes the methodology, findings, conclusions and the recommendations in nutshell. The summary or synopsis is unnecessary for a short report of three-four pages but it is extremely useful to the reader if the report is lengthy.

Introduction

The introduction includes a brief historical background of the subject, scope of study, methods of data collection, definition of problem and definitions of special terms and concepts.

Findings

Findings is the main part of the report and it is also called as the text proper. All the facts are presented in chronological or logical sequence. The writer analyses the facts and passes comments on them. It may include diagram, charts, graphs, tables, pictures and other essential figures.

Conclusions

The report writer analyses the data and draws conclusions on the basis of his 'findings'. The conclusions are supported by the findings and their explanations and analysis. The report writer may derive a number of conclusions based on the analysis of different facts. They should be grouped suitably and should be presented in the descending order so that the important conclusions are mentioned in the beginning.

Recommendations

Recommendations logically follow the conclusions of the findings. But, all the reports do not include the recommendations or suggestions. In some reports the conclusions and the recommendations are combined. This combination may suit the short reports up to five-six pages, but for lengthy reports the recommendations should be written separately to suggest the future course of action. The recommendations in committee report are put in the form of resolutions.

Appendix

The appendix contains diagrams, charts, maps, pictures, statistical data and other material which supports the main body of the report. The details which are separated from the body of the report are included in the appendix. The reader can understand the contents of the reports without it but if he desires to go through the details of the related evidences, supporting material and documents, he can find them in the appendix.

List of References

The list of references helps the reader to locate a piece of information in the original source. Some reports are based on exclusive research. It is a customary that the writer of such a report should give the list of published or unpublished works referred by him in his report. If this list is lengthy, it should be arranged in alphabetical order and should be given at the end of the report. If the number of references is small, they can be mentioned in the footnotes.

Bibliography

Bibliography is a list of published and unpublished works to which the report writer is indebted for certain ideas. It may also contain names of works for further study. The list of works in bibliography is arranged in alphabetical order. Bibliography of the works to be consulted is often prepared before writing the report.

Glossary

The technical or jargon words are usually explained in the footnotes. If the number of such words is large, a list of those words is prepared in an alphabetical order. This list is called as glossary. If the reader's field of expertise is different from the subject dealt in the report and if the technical words used in the report are likely to be unknown tc him, the glossary becomes on essential part of the report.

Index

In case of lengthy reports, an index is helpful to the reader to locate easily and quickly any topic or sub-topic of the contents. Index is included in the report if the table of contents cannot help the reader to point out all the aspects of the contents. It is always needed in bulky reports. The entries in the index are made in alphabetical order and page numbers are mentioned before each entry.

Signature

A report is signed by a person who submits it to the authority. If it is prepared by a committee, the chairman of the committee signs it. Sometimes all the members of the committee are required to sign it. The members who disagree with certain matters in the report usually sign it with a note of dissent. Signature of the other members indicate their assent to the subject matter of the report.

Types of Business Reports

Though most of the business reports are presented in written form, some of them are presented orally also. The oral reports might save the reporter's time but they cannot be preserved for future references unless they are tape recorded and secondly, they are likely to be less accurate then the written reports. Thirdly, the oral reports are less formal than the written reports but their informal situations. The formal written reports are either informational or interpretative. The informational reports present the facts and data collected by the reporter in a systematic manner, whereas the interpretive reports include both the facts and their interpretation. We may clarify these business reports into the following three broad categories:

A. On the basis of the nature or methodology of report.

(i) The Periodic or Routine reports
(ii) The Progress Reports
(iii) The Examination Reports
(iv) The Statistical Reports
(v) The Recommendation Reports

B. On the basis of the number of persons entrusted to draft the reports.

(vi) Reports by Individuals
(vii) Reports by committees and sub-committees.

C. On the basis of legal formalities.

(viii) Formal Reports.
(ix) Information Reports.

Periodic or Routine Reports

The periodic reports record the routine business activities. These reports are submitted annually, quarterly, monthly, weekly or at any other prescribed intervals in the routine of business. Usually these reports are informational. They present the collected data and the facts without evaluating them. They do not include any suggestions, opinions and recommendations of the report writer. The reports of companies to the shareholders, Administrative reports of the Government departments, Municipalities, Universities, Trade Associations etc. are some examples of periodic reports.

These reports provide a brief summary of the important events, the account of production and turnover, the financial statements, important changes in the managerial set up and an account of company's achievements during the given period etc.

Progress Reports

The progress reports describe the progress made by the organisation in a particular period. It gives an account of the work in chronological order. It covers the details of the work already done, work in progress and the work yet to be completed. It refers to past achievements and future prospects. It also gives an account of the special problems and obstructions that might have come in the way of work in progress. The progress reports include the reports concerning the construction works of factory buildings, dams, water supply schemes etc.

Examination Reports

The examination reports are interpretative in the sense that they are compiled only after thorough investigation and study of the given subject. The report writer goes through various sources of information. He conducts surveys, circulates questionnaires, studies the relevant literature and old files, analyses the collected data and finally arrives to some conclusions. Such reports often end with useful suggestions or recommendations. The reports concerned with the problems of increasing cost of production, decline of sales etc. and the reports regarding the inventions and technological innovations are some of the examples of examination reports. These reports cover the details regarding its aims and objectives, methodology, findings conclusions and finally and with recommendations, if asked.

Statistical Reports

These reports are made up of statistical details including financial data, tabular columns of figures, mathematical charts etc. The statistical data are also used in other kinds of reports as supporting evidences to various statements, but the statistical reports mainly consist of the statistical data. The reports submitted by the costing departments in business houses are the examples of statistical reports.

Recommendation Reports

The recommendation report is a kind of examination report because its main purpose is to analyse, interpret and evaluate the facts. But, it specifically differs from the examination reports due to the fact that it invariably ends with some suggestions or recommendations. The report writer analysis and interprets the data in such a way that it naturally leads to some recommendations. The tone of such a report is always argumentative and persuasive.

The recommendation reports are useful to the business houses in policy-making and in making important decisions regarding setting up of a new business unit, expanding the business, opening a new branch etc. These reports include the information regarding the objectives and scope of the report, methods of data collection, analysis and interpretation of data, conclusions and recommendations with some programme of action.

Reports by Individuals

The reports submitted by the individuals are related to their own work and to the work of their departments. The reports submitted by the Departmental Heads, Company Secretary, Auditor, Cost Accountant, Solicitor etc. are the reports by individuals. The executive head of the sales department produces his report on the marketing strategies of the company rivals or on the causes of declining sales. The executive of production department submits report on the performance of his department. While drafting the report, the individual should make systematic arrangement of all the items to be embodied in the report.

Reports by Committees or Sub-Committees

Some business reports are concerned with more than one department or individual and some subjects are too important and expansive to be entrusted to one person for its research findings and recommendations. Such a subject matter requires careful and complete investigation by the committees and sub-committees in which a number of people are involved in the process of report writing. There is a cautious deliberation over all the issues of the subject-matter. The views and opinions of all the committee members are given serious consideration before they arrive to certain conclusions. It is usually written with impersonal and formal style.

These reports should invariably mention the objectives of the investigation, methods of data collection, explanation or interpretation of collected data, details of evidences gathered, the conclusions of the deliberations and recommendations or suggestions given by the committee or the sub-committee. They should also mention the names of a person or body to whom the report is addressed. Such a report is usually signed by all the members or by the chairman of the committee.

Formal Reports

The formal reports are prepared and presented according to some established statutes or procedures. The formal reports are classified under two heads: (a) Statutory Reports, (b) Non-Statutory Reports. The statutory reports are prepared and presented according to laws. The non-statutory reports are not required under laws but they are required to be submitted by the individuals or the committees to their respective managements in order to help later to take important decisions and to frame the business policies. The reports which Directors and the Secretary of the company submit to the shareholders and the Auditor's reports are some of the examples of statutory reports.

The non-statutory reports are not required to be prepared and presented under laws, but they are required to be submitted by the individuals or the committees to their respective managements in order to help the later to take the important decisions and to frame their business policies. Some of these reports are the part of the routine business procedures but some of them are required to be produced only on the special occasions when the management executives have to use them in making estimates, controlling the operational functions and taking the policy decisions. The reports of Finance Committee, Arbitration Committee, Ad-hoc Committee etc. are some of the examples of non-statutory reports.

Informal Reports

Informal report is a person to person informal communication. It neither abides any formal procedure of communication nor any statutory obligation. It can be written like a personal letter to someone who does not bring any statutory or formal obligation on the writer. Its purpose is to fulfil the informal requirements. It can be written in a formal of short letter or memorandum.

Press Reports

The press reports are the reports of the events and activities published in the newspapers and periodicals so that the news reach to the large number of people simultaneously. A reader may not be interested in all the events and activities described in the newspapers and periodicals but he may come across certain topics of his interest. Some of the news definitely create curiosity and interest in every reader. As the social animals we are always curious to know about what goes on around ourselves. The press reports not only satisfy our curiosity but they also educate us in our daily walks of life by supplying us the news along with expert opinions, editorials and special articles.

Essential Aspects of a Good Press Report

1. *News Value*

The news value of a press report depend on the number of people being affected by the event or activity described in it. The Prime Minister's visit to a foreign country has more news value than a factory workers visit to his native place. A fathers money order to his son is not a news but the government's relief fund to the draught affected people makes a news. A marriage invitation letter from one's friend does not have a news value but the American's President's invitation to the Indian Prime Minister to visit his country has the news value.

2. *Clarity and Completeness*

Accuracy, Clarity and completeness: The press report should be accurate, clear and complete. If the headline of reports arouses curiosity, it should be clear and complete and accurate to satisfy that curiosity. The reported news should give accurate facts, figures and statements. It should be simple and clear enough so that the readers may readily understand it. It should never be biased, slanted or distorted. It should not mislead the readers. It should be complete in the sense that it should be able to satisfy all the querries of the readers.

3. *Attractive and Lucid Style*

The language of the press reports should be attractive, simple, lucid and catchy. Not only the language but the script also, should make a 'news sense'. If the readers find the news difficult to understand due to its style, it wont tempt the readers to read further.

4. *Feedback*

The news should be capable of receiving feedback from the readers. It should initiate the public to think over the events and activities described in it. It should mobilise the public views and opinions on the current topics of the public interest.

5. *Conciseness*

The press reporter should always remember that the readers time is precious and they should not feel that they are wasting their valuable time in reading the unnecessarily lengthy news. He should avoid the needless words and irrelevant details of information. But his brevity and conciseness should not be at the cost of the completeness and clarity.

6. *Reported Speech*

The press reports should be drafted in indirect speech and in past tense.

Organisation of Press Report

1. *Headline*

The headline of the press report is also called as the caption. It is a short title or heading of the news article. It is usually printed with a photograph or illustration.

It should be bold, catchy and attractive so that it may immediately attract the attention of the reader and tempt him to go through the news. It should suggest the central idea or the theme of the report. The reporter usually tries to make caption sensational and catchy but in this effort it is likely to mislead the readers. For faithful representation the press report headline should be accurate but mildly sensational.

2. *Place and Date of Reporting*

The place and date of reporting are usually mentioned either at the right or at the right hand corner of the report below the headline.

3. *Lead*

The lead of a press report means the first one or two paragraphs of the report. It is like synopsis or the summary of a long report. It gives the general sense or the main points of the news. The readers who do not have enough time to go through the whole report, can get the gist of the news in the lead. It should be presented in such a way that the reader will be induced to go through the whole body of the report.

4. *Body*

The lead is followed by the body of the report which consist of all the main and supporting points of the news. It gives all the details of certain occasions, activities, events, discussions, public speeches, etc. It should be written in simple and lucid style. The language used in the body should be invariably the every day spoken language of the readers. The paragraphs in the body must not be heavy and bulky. Each paragraph should be kept short and should cover one significant aspect of the news. The important point should be given at the beginning in the form of introduction. The important points must be followed by the supporting details and ideas. The least important details should be given at the end of the last paragraph. The reporter should provide the sub-headings to the paragraphs, if necessary.

5. *Conclusion*

The concluding paragraphs of the press report should give the gist of the report in such a way that it leaves final impression on the readers mind and mobilises his views and opinions of the topic.

Specimens of Business Reports

A Report on Safety and Cleanliness in J.J. Hospital, Bangalore.

Mr. R.R. Robinson,
Chairman,
Investigation Committee
J.J. Hospital,
Bangalore-5

12th April 19 . . .

Dr. S.P. Mathews,
Chairman,
J.J. Hospital,
Bangalore-5.

Sir,

Subject: A report on safety and cleanliness in J.J. Hospital, Bangalore

Ref.: The investigations were carried out in accordance with the instructions contained in the resolution of the Board of Directors meeting of 17th March 19. . . . The Board appointed a sub-committee of three directors to report on the safety and cleanliness in the hospital before 14th April 19. . . .

We, the members of the sub-committee inspected the safety measures and cleanliness maintained in the hospital. We held three meetings in the office of the hospital. We have had discussions with the patients in different wards, medical officers, pathologists, surgeons, pharmacists, laboratory assistants, visiting doctors, nurses, clerks, peons and the sweepers.

The objectives of investigations:

1. To find out the safety measures regarding fire and water.
2. To find out how the pathological samples are disposed.
3. To find out the problems and troubles arising from the poor electrical connections, fittings and irregular power supply.
4. To find out how the volatile substances are stored and handled.

5. To see the cleanliness of the laboratory, blood bank, and toilets.
6. To find out the safety and purity of the medicines, food and drinking water supplied to the patients.
7. To make suggestions regarding the safety measures and cleanliness in the hospital.

The *Findings* of investigation are as follows:

1. Safety measures regarding fire and water are inadequate. There is not even a single fire extinguisher in the laboratory. Water supplied by the Municipal Water Supply Department is sometimes polluted and unhygienic.
2. There is no separate water connection or water storage in the laboratory. Water supply in the laboratory is inadequate.
3. The irregular supply of electricity affect the operations in the operation theatre. It also affects the hospital works in laboratory, intensive care units, general wards and in blood bank. There is an immediate need of a power generator.
4. There is a free access to volatile substances. This is Dangerous.
5. The staff of the sweepers who look after the cleanliness and disinfection in the hospital, is inadequate.
6. The supply of disinfecting material is inadequate.
7. There is no proper disposal for the infected pathological samples.
8. There is no proper sanitation and cleanliness in the toilets provided for the patients.

Recommendations: In view of the information provided above, our committee unanimously recommends:

1. A separate overhead water storage is to be provided for the laboratory and blood bank.
2. A separate fire extinguisher is to be provided to the laboratory.
3. A power-generator of required capacity is to be provided to the hospital.
4. The number of the lower staff workers is to be increased.

5. The charge of the volatile substances is to be given to the responsible persons.
6. Adequate quantity and variety of disinfecting material is to be provided to the laboratory, blood bank and different wards of the hospital.
7. Proper ways of disposing infected samples are to be introduced and the employees doing this work are to be trained.

Yours faithfully,
R.R. Robinson
Chairman
Investigation Committee

Committee Report on starting a Milk Processing Plant at Gadhinglaj.

Mr. S.G. Kapase,
Chairman,
Dairy Report Committee
Warana Dudh Sangh Ltd,
Warananagar.

25th Aug. 19 . . .

The Chairman,
Board of Directors,
Warana Dudh Sangh Ltd.,
Warananagar.

Dear Sir,

Subject: Committee Report on starting a Milk Processing Plant at Gadhinglaj.

Ref.: Your Order No. WAR-7B-86 dated 19th July 19. . .

With reference to your above mentioned order, we are submitting a report on starting a new Milk Processing Plant of Warana Dudh Sangh Ltd., at Gadhinglaj, Dist. Kolhapur.

We, the committee members, have visited three tehsils – Gadhinglaj, Chandgad and Ajara during the first two weeks of August 19. . . . These three tehsils form the southern part of Kolhapur district. We discussed the proposed project with the general public, especially with the farmers who run a number or co-operative milk dairies in these tehsils. The project was discussed with the elected representatives of Panchayat Samities and also with the MLAs of these tehsils. After due deliberation with the concerned people, we come to unanimous opinion that Gadhinglaj would be an ideal location for the proposed Milk Processing Unit because of the following reasons:

1. The city is rapidly developing in agriculture, industry and education.
2. There are numerous large and small-size milk dairies.

3. It is a trading educational and industrial centre for the people of Chandgad and Ajara tehsils.
4. There is no other milk processing centre in this area.
5. The milk production of this area is high as compared to the milk production of other tehsils in Kolhapur district.
6. All the villages in these tehsils are linked to Gadhinglaj by roads. This facilitates milk collection in little time.
7. Water, electricity, skilled workers and transport facilities are easily available.

The open plots around Gadhinglaj range in size from 1000 sq. mts. to 1,00,000 sq. mts. After inspecting these plots of lands, we commend a vacant plot of 70,000 sq. mts. on Gadhinglaj-Sankeshwar Road. The plot is 2 km away from the town and it is available for Rs. 5,00,000 only. On verification we find it to be the most reasonable market price. As compared to the prices prevailing in Kolhapur city and Warana, it is very low. The plot is sufficient to accommodate the milk processing plant and the staff quarters. Being adjacent to other industrial estates, the plot has an easy access to electricity and water supply.

The town of Gadhinglaj has five junior and two senior colleges. It has one technical institute and two colleges of education. The skilled and unskilled workers are easily available here. The wage-rate at Gadhinglaj is lower than that prevailing at Kolhapur and Warana. The place has easy access to transport facilities.

It has prosperous financial and commercial establishments, a Civil Hospital, and more than fifteen banks to serve the Industrial Estate at Gadhinglaj.

We have been informed from the reliable sources that Gokul Dudh Sangh had also sent a survey committee for the similar project in this area. The survey committee of Gokul Dudh Sangh had been visiting these tehsils during the last week of February 19. . . .

In view of the information given above, we recommend that the proposal be finalised immediately and Warana Dudh Sangh should start the Milk Processing Plant at Gadhinglaj in the nearest future.

For and on behalf of the Committee
S.G. Kapase
Chairman
Dairy Report Committee

Report on boat-engines used by the fisherman in Sindhudurg district.

Mr. D.N. Palkiwala,
Sales Manager
Kirloskar and Company
Kirloskarwadi,
Pune-38

5th Aug. 19 . . .

The Managing Director,
Kirloskar and Company,
Kirloskarwadi,
Pune-38.

Dear Sir,

Subject: Report on boat-engines used by the fishermen in Sindhudurg district.

Ref.: Your letter No. KC-SJ-187 dated 4th July 19. . . .

In accordance with your instructions contained in your letter mentioned above, a survey was conducted among the fishermen in Sindhudurg district. The coastal towns and villages selected for this purpose were Chinder, Walawal, Porle, Rajiwada, Bhatye, Malwan, and Vengulla. The questionnaires used for the survey were supplied to the fishermen in the above villages.

The objectives of this report are as follows:

1. To study the reasons behind popularity of the boat-engines manufactured by the rival companies like Yamaha, Ruston, Ashok Leyland etc.
2. To study the problems and difficulties of the fishermen regarding purchasing, handling and performance of our boat-engines.
3. To study the market demand of our boat-engines and their spare parts.
4. To find out the causes responsible for the steady fall in the sales of our boat-engines.

5. To give useful suggestions to remedy the situation.

Findings: A careful examination of the various aspects of problem and the information obtained through interviews and questionnaires reveal the following details.

1. Popularity of the boat-engines introduced by other companies such as *Yamaha, Ruston, Ashok Leyland*:

   (a) The first reason behind the popularity of boat engines introduced by the companies mentioned above is that the fishermen in selected coastal towns and villages get attracted towards those engines because of their better performance, and lower fuel consumption. The second important factor is that the light weight of the engines. The weight of boat engines is an important factor for the fishermen because it affects the load capacity of the small boats. The running capacity of a small fishing boat depends on its own weight as well as on the weight of the engine. Yamaha engines are more light in weight as compared to those of ours. A fisherman can carry it easily on his shoulder from his hut to the his boat on the shore. Fishermen find Kirloskar engines very heavy in their weight. Secondly, Yamaha engines require less fuel as compared to the fuel requirement of our engines.

   (b) The middle and higher class fishermen having medium and large size fishing boats prefer *Ruston* and *Leyland* engines for heavy duty performance. Their interest in buying *Ruston* is mainly due to the reason that these machines have water cooling system, whereas our engines have air cooling system. Water cooling system effectively controls the excessive heat generated by the engine. The air cooling system of our engines which is not so effective in heat-controlling affects the fishing operations at long distances, especially in hot seasons.

   (c) Due to availability of the spare parts whenever necessary and due to their lower prices, the *Ashok Leyland* engines are more popular among the fishermen in Sindhudurg district. *Ruston* and *Leyland* offer guarantee of their products for a longer period.

2. Demotivating factors in buying and handling our engines and spare parts are as follows:

   (a) Our engines consume more fuel.
   (b) Spare parts of our engines are not readily available.
   (c) Our engines become much hot after a particular period.
   (d) Starting trouble: Our engines do not start readily and easily. They require more efforts in starting.
   (e) Bank Loan: While buying our engines on loan basis, the fishermen face problems in obtaining loan from the banks.

Conclusions: Fishermen in Sindhudurg district are attracted towards the engines introduced by *Yamaha, Ruston* and *Leyland* because of their clear advantages over our engines. Their easily obtainable loan-schemes, effective after-sale service net work and, lastly, the long term guarantee period of their engines and spare parts are some of the factors which have played an important role in enhancing popularity of their products in Sindhudurg district.

Recommendations: We can create interest among the fishermen in Sindhudurg to buy our engines and spare parts if:

1. We offer them better and prompt after sale service.
2. We make them available the spare parts whenever necessary at reasonable rates.
3. We improve the models of our engines by employing latest modern technology which will remove all the disadvantages and enhance the heavy duty performance of our engines.
4. We reduce fuel consumption rate of our engines.
5. We provide sufficient quota of our engines and spare parts to the corresponding dealers of our company.
6. We increase the number of our corresponding dealers.
7. We provide the fishermen of Sindhudurg some loan-scheme to enable them to buy our engines promptly on loan basis.

Yours faithfully,
Harsha Babu
Sales Manager
Kirloskar and Company

BANK OF INDIA
Rajarampuri Branch
Rajarampuri, Kolhapur

10th Jan. 19. . .

General Manager,
Bank of India,
Head Office,
Bombay-14.

Dear Sir,

Subject: Report on the installation of computer in the Bank
Ref.: Your Order No.BOI-74-175 dated 5th Dec. 19. . .

With reference to your order mentioned above I am submitting herewith a brief report on installation of computer in our branch at Rajarampuri, Kolhapur.

The objectives of this study report are as follows:

1. To study the advantages of computer in the bank.
2. To study the financial requirements for the installation of computer.
3. To find the possibility of diverting some staff members of Rajarampuri Branch to the extension-counter at Shivaji University.

Findings: A thorough inspection of the present position of Rajarampuri Branch and its customers was made during last three weeks for the purpose of presenting this report. This branch was established in 1975. During last two years I have found that the area covered by this branch is getting well-developed, and due to speedily increase in the number of shops, hospitals, dispensaries, appartments, industries, hostels, lodgings and educational institutions, our customers increased rapidly. In 1981, there were 5,000 depositors and now there are 24,000 depositors in this branch. Nowadays, we are finding it difficult to give the quick and satisfactory service to our customers due to such an increase in their number. For withdrawal of cash, the customer has to wait, at least, for twenty minutes. They are taking away their deposits from our bank as they prefer to open their accounts in other rival banks. Some of our rival banks in this area like Ratnakar Bank, Bank of Maharashtra, Canara Bank have already installed computer and they are giving quick services to the customers.

It is obvious that time is very important in this competitive world; and, to save time in bank procedures, there is no alternative other than computers. It gives rapid calculations and results in almost a fraction of seconds. The prices of computers are falling down and we can buy two computers in the investment of one lakh and forty thousand. There is no need to recruit the trained computer operators. We can give training to our employees and they will easily operate the computers after the completion of their training programme. After installing computers in Rajarampuri Branch, we can transfer half of its staff to our new extension-counter at Shivaji University. So, there is no need to employ new staff at the extension counter.

Exercises

1. What is a 'report'? What are the essential elements of a business report?
2. What is the significance of 'report writing' in business communication?
3. What are the ways in which business reports are classified?
4. What are the characteristics of a good business report?
5. What is the difference between special and routine business reports? What are essential elements of a special business report?
6. Distinguish between statutory and non-statutory reports.
7. Show the difference between a report written by an individual and a report written by a committee.
8. What are the ways in which a report can be organised? How can a report writer follow the arrangement of a business letter to write a business report? How can he present report in a memorandum form?
9. Which form should be adopted for a long business report?
10. What is a press report? What are the features of a good press report? How should a press report be organised?

BIBLIOGRAPHY

Adair, John, 1979 : *Training for Communication*, **In:** Pal, R. &. Korlahalli, J.S., *Essentials of Business Communication*, New Delhi: Sultan Chand & Sons.

Adelstein, M.E., 1971 : *Contemporary Business Writing*, New York: Random House.

Anastasi, T.E. (Jr.) 1974 : *Desk Guide to Communication*, Addison Wesley Publishing Co.

Atthreya, N.H., 1979 : *Effective Report Writing*, **In:** Pal, R. and Korlahalli, J.S., *Essentials of Business Communication*, New Delhi: Sultan Chand and Sons.

Bergin, F.J., 1979 : *Practical Communications*, **In:** Pal, R. and Korlahalli, J.S., *Essentials of Business Communication*, New Delhi : Sultan Chand & Sons.

Breth, Robert D., 1969 : *Dynamic Management Communication*, Addison-Wesley.

Brooks, C. and Warren, R.P., 1961 : *Modern Rhetoric*, New York: Harcourt Brace.

Brown, Leyland, 1973 : *Effective Business Report Writing*, New York: Prentice-Hall Publishing Co.

Cartier, F.A. and K.A. Harwood, 1953 : *Definition of Communication*, *The Journal of Communication*, November, **In:** Doctor, R. and A. Doctor, 1977 : *Principles and Practice of Business Communication*, Bombay: Sheth Publishers.

Chase, Stuart, 1954 : *Power of Words*, New York: Harcourt Brace.

Chappell, R.T. and Read, W.L., 1979 : *A Textbook of Business Communication*, **In:** Pal, R. and Korlahalli, J.S., *Essentials of Business Communication*, New Delhi: Sultan Chand & Sons.

Clark, L.R., K. Zimmer, J. Tinervia, 1988 : *Business English and Communication*, New York: McGraw-Hill International.

Davar, R.S., 1979 : *The Management Process*, **In:** Pal, R. and Korlahalli, J.S., *Essentials of Business Communication*, New Delhi: Sultan Chand & Sons.

Davis, Keith and J.W. Newstrom, 1989 : *Human Relations at Work*, New York: McGraw-Hill Book Co.

Doctor, R. and A. Doctor, 1977 : *Principles and Practice of Business Communication*, Sheth Publishers, Bombay.

Fry, Roland, 1979 : *Manual of Commercial Correspondence*, **In:** Pal, R. and J.S. Korlahalli, *Essentials of Business Communication*, New Delhi: Sultan Chand and Sons.

Gartside, L., 1981 : *Model Business Letters*, London: Pitman.

Hays, R., 1965 : *Principles of Technical Writing*, Addison-Wesley Himstreet, Porter and Maxwell : *Business English in Communication*, **In:** Pal, R. and J.S. Korlahalli, 1979 : *Essentials of Business Communication*, Sultan Chand and Sons.

Hicks, H.G. and C.R. Gullet, 1974 : *Modern Business Management*, New York: McGraw-Hill Book Co.

Howell, W.S. and E.G. Borman, 1971 : *Presentational Speaking for Business and the Professions*, New York: Harper and Row.

Lee, Irving J., 1952 : *How to Talk with People*, New York: Harper and Brothers.

Lesikar, R.V. and Pettit, J.D., 1989 : *Business Communication*, All India Traveller Booksellers.

Little, Peter, 1977 : *Communication in Business*, **In:** Doctor, R. and A. Doctor, *Principles and Practice of Business Communication*, Bombay: Sheth Publishers.

Mortenson, C.D. (ed.), 1973 : *Basic Readings in Communication Theory*, New York: Harper and Brothers.

Murphy and Peck, 1979 : *Effective Business Communication*, **In:** Pal, R. and Korlahalli, J.S., *Essentials of Business Communication*, New Delhi: Sultan Chand and Sons.

Myers, G.E. and M.T. Myers, 1975 : *Communicating When We Speak*, New York: McGraw-Hill Book Co.

Nadeau, R.E., 1972 : *A Modern Rhetoric of Speech Communication*, Addison-Wesley.

Newman, W. and Summer, C., 1977 : *Process of Management*, **In:** Doctor, R. and A. Doctor, *Principles and Practice of Business Communication*, Bombay: Sheth Publishers.

Rai, U. and S.M. Rai, 1989 : *Business Communication*, Bombay: Himalaya Publishing Company.

Ramesh, M.S. and Pattanshetti, C.C., 1986 : *Effective Business English and Correspondence*, New York: R. Chand and Co.

Sharma, R.C. and K. Mohan, 1986 : *Business Correspondence and Report Writing*, New Delhi: Tata McGraw-Hill Publishing Co.

Scott, William, 1977 : *Organisation Theory*, **In:** Doctor, R. and A. Doctor, *Principles and Practice of Business Communication*, Bombay: Sheth Publishers.

Smart, W.K. and D.R. Lang, 1979 : *Smart's Handbook of Effective Writing*, Jaico Publishing House.

Terry, G.R., 1977 : *Principles of Management*, **In:** Doctor, R. and A. Doctor, *Principles and Practice of Business Communication*, Bombay: Sheth Publishers.

Thomas, D.A. and Fryar, M., 1988 : *Business Communication Today*, National Textbook Company.

Tripathi, P.C. and Reddy, P.N., 1991 : *Principles of Management*, New Delhi: Tata McGraw-Hill Publishing Co.

Vogel, R.A. and W.D. Brooks, 1977 : *Business Communication*, Cummings Publishing Co., USA.

Wofford, J., E. Gerloff and R. Cummins, 1977 : *Organisational Communication*, Tokyo: McGraw-Hill Kogakusha.

Wolf, M.P., D.F. Keyser and R.R. Aurner, 1979 : *Effective Communication in Business*, South Western Publishing Co.

Zelko, H.P., 1957 : *Successful Conference and Discussion Techniques*, New York: McGraw-Hill Book Co.

INDEX